Final Exam

Script · **Peter David**
Pencils · **Pop Mhan**

Inks · **Norman Lee**
Colors · **Dan Jackson**
Letters · **Michael David Thomas**
Cover · **Pop Mhan & Dan Jackson**

ROCKET

Publisher · **Mike Richardson**

Editor · **Dave Land**

Assistant Editor · **Katie Moody**

Collection Designer · **David Nestelle**

SPYBOY: FINAL EXAM

This book collects issues 1 through 4 of the Dark Horse comic-book series SpyBoy: Final Exam

Dark Horse Books
A division of Dark Horse Comics, Inc.
10956 SE Main Street
Milwaukie, OR 97222

www.darkhorse.com

To find a comics shop in your area, call the Comic Shop Locator Service toll-free at (888) 266-4226

First edition: March 2005
ISBN: 1-59307-017-9

10 9 8 7 6 5 4 3 2 1
Printed in China

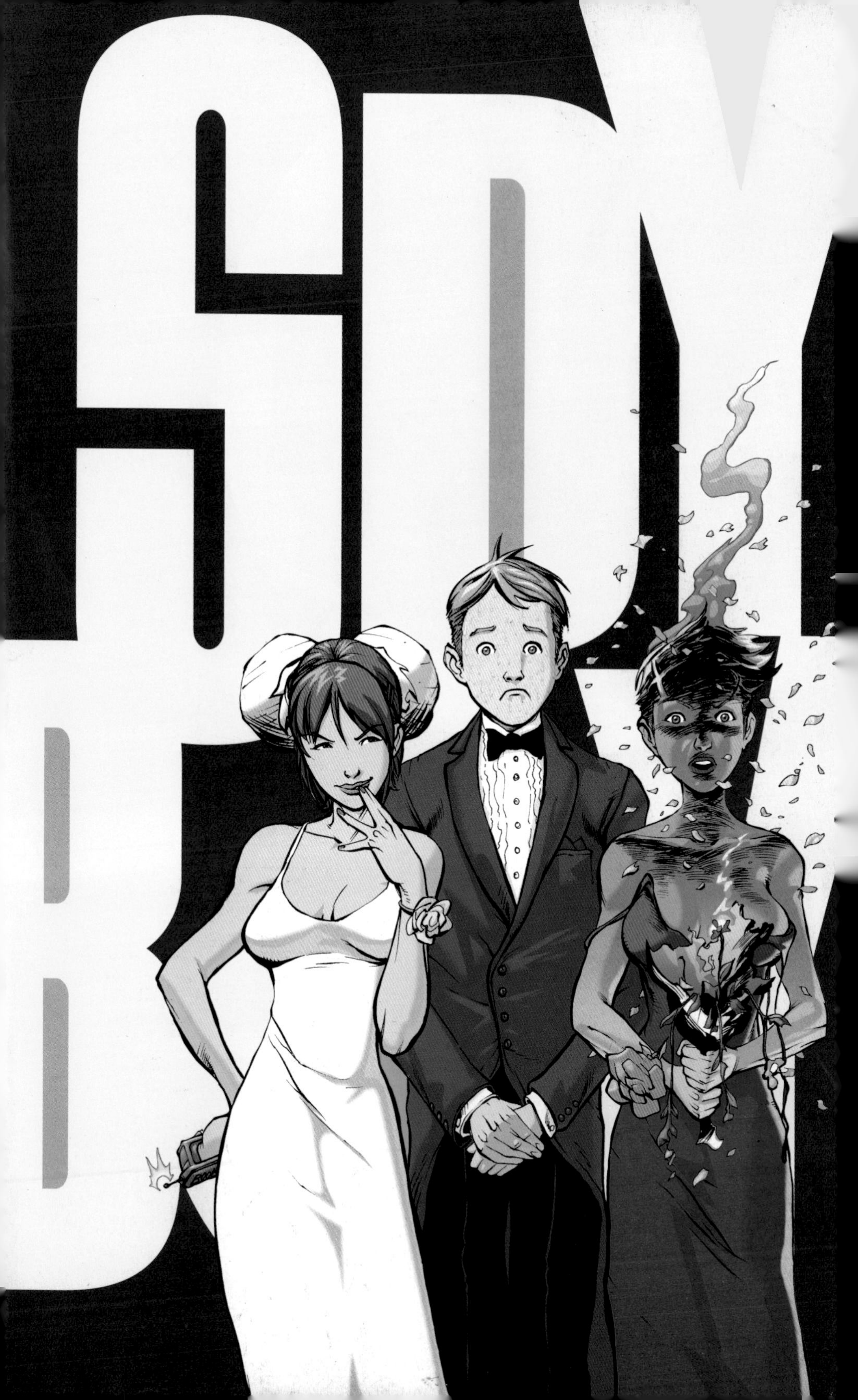

SPY BOY™

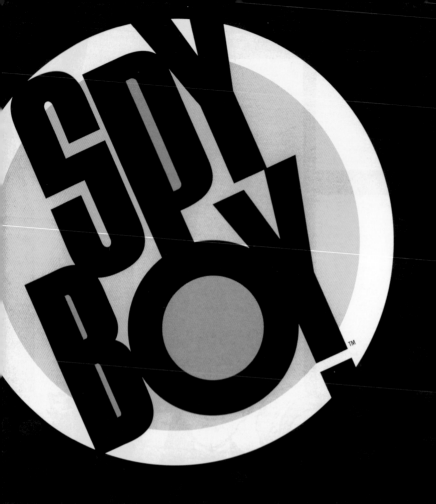

Part 1

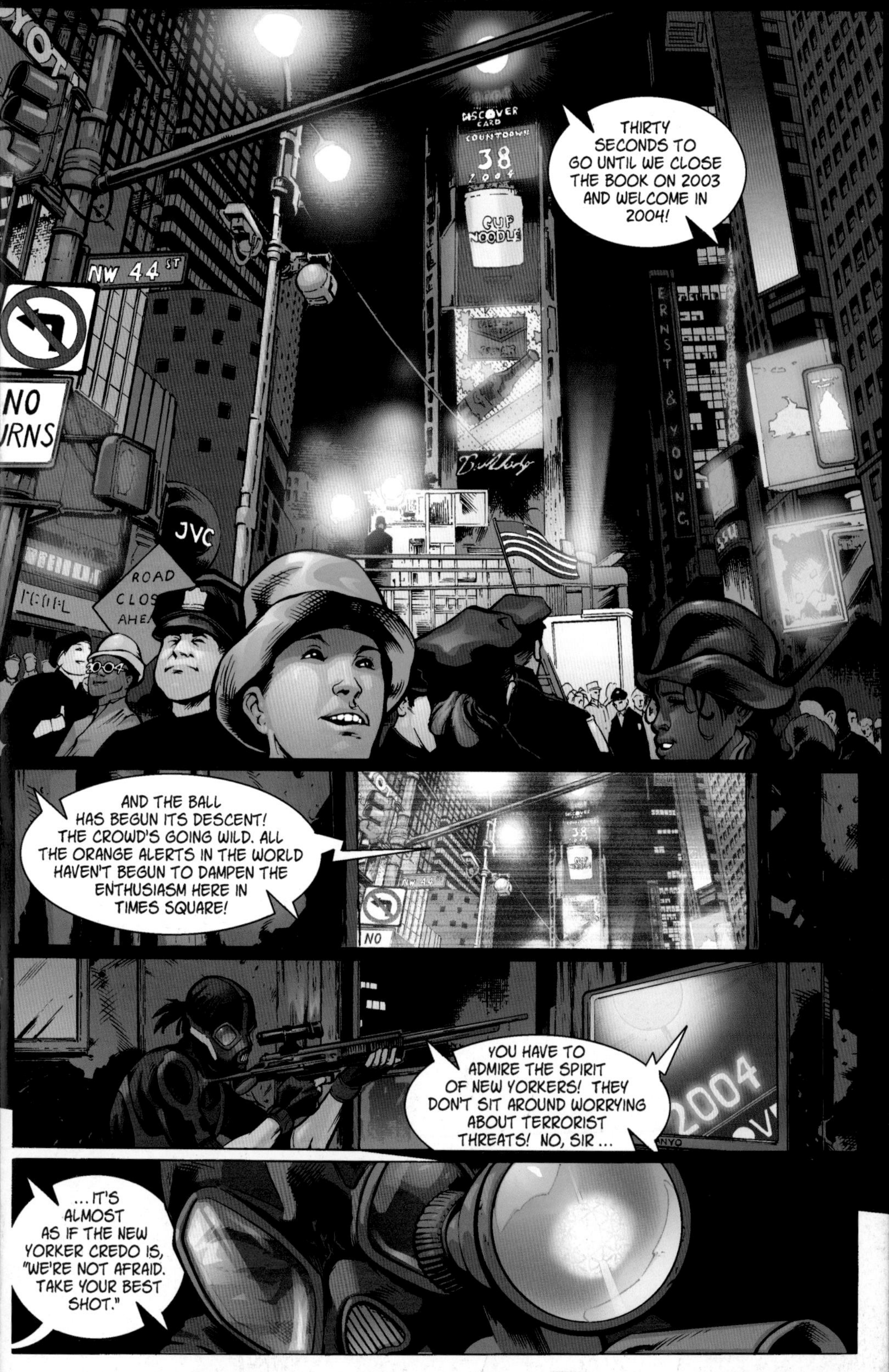

DISCOVER CARD
COUNTDOWN
38
2004
CUP NOODLES
NW 44 ST
NO TURNS
JVC
ROAD CLOS AHEA
THIRTY SECONDS TO GO UNTIL WE CLOSE THE BOOK ON 2003 AND WELCOME IN 2004!
ERNST & YOUNG
AND THE BALL HAS BEGUN ITS DESCENT! THE CROWD'S GOING WILD. ALL THE ORANGE ALERTS IN THE WORLD HAVEN'T BEGUN TO DAMPEN THE ENTHUSIASM HERE IN TIMES SQUARE!
YOU HAVE TO ADMIRE THE SPIRIT OF NEW YORKERS! THEY DON'T SIT AROUND WORRYING ABOUT TERRORIST THREATS! NO, SIR ...
2004
... IT'S ALMOST AS IF THE NEW YORKER CREDO IS, "WE'RE NOT AFRAID. TAKE YOUR BEST SHOT."

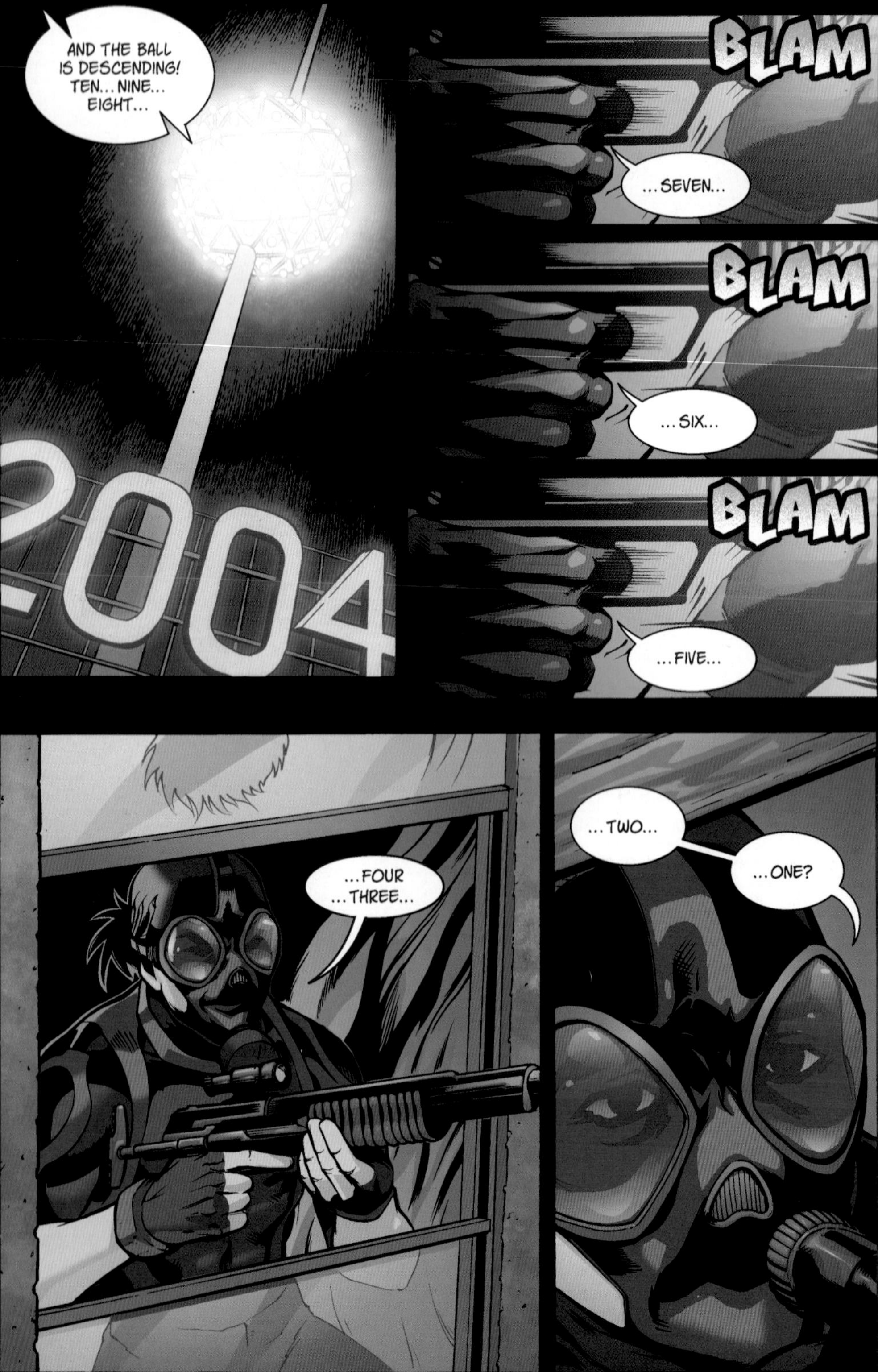
AND THE BALL IS DESCENDING! TEN... NINE... EIGHT...
BLAM
...SEVEN...
BLAM
...SIX...
BLAM
...FIVE...
...FOUR ...THREE...
...TWO...
...ONE?

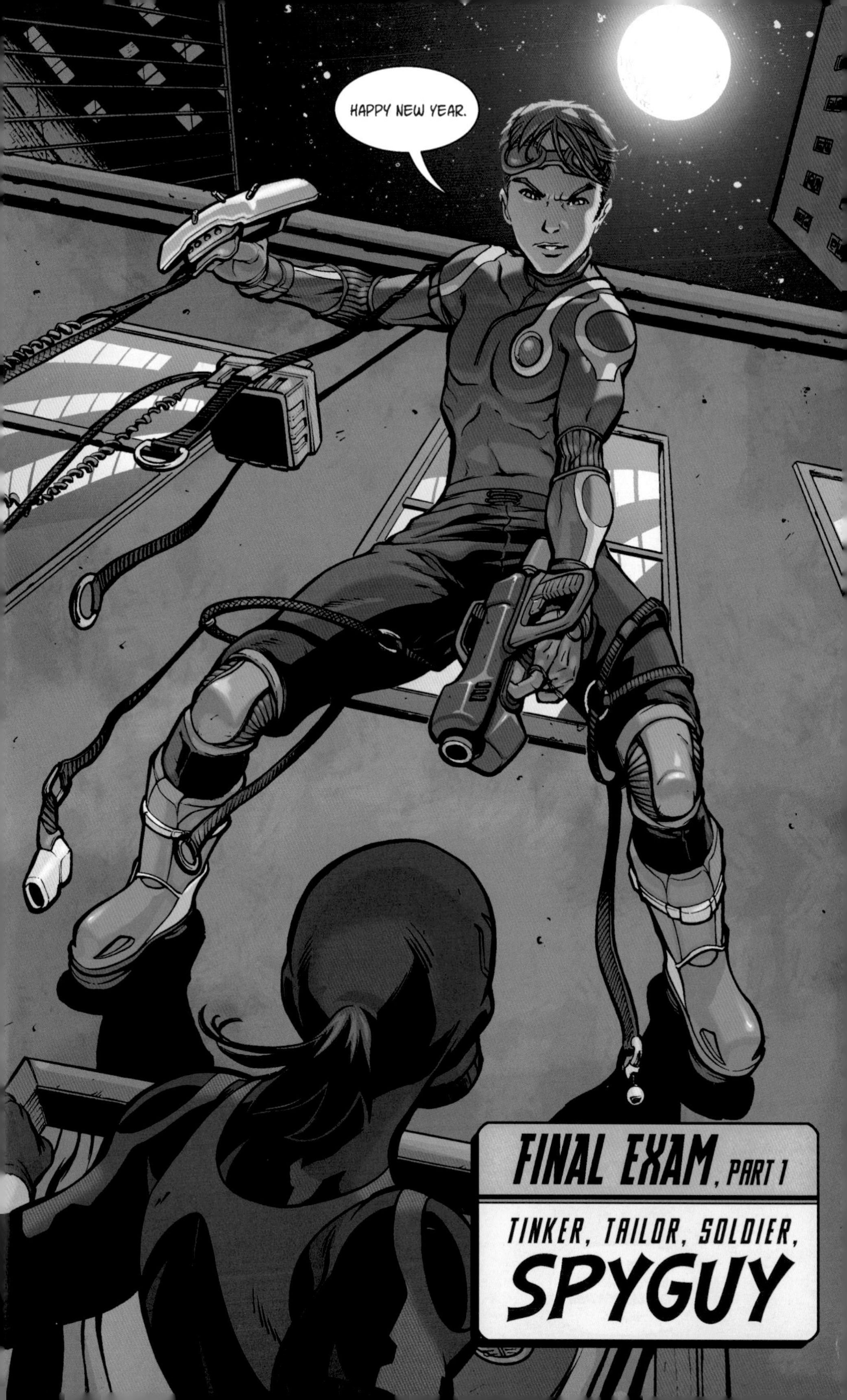
HAPPY NEW YEAR.
FINAL EXAM, PART 1
TINKER, TAILOR, SOLDIER,
SPYGUY

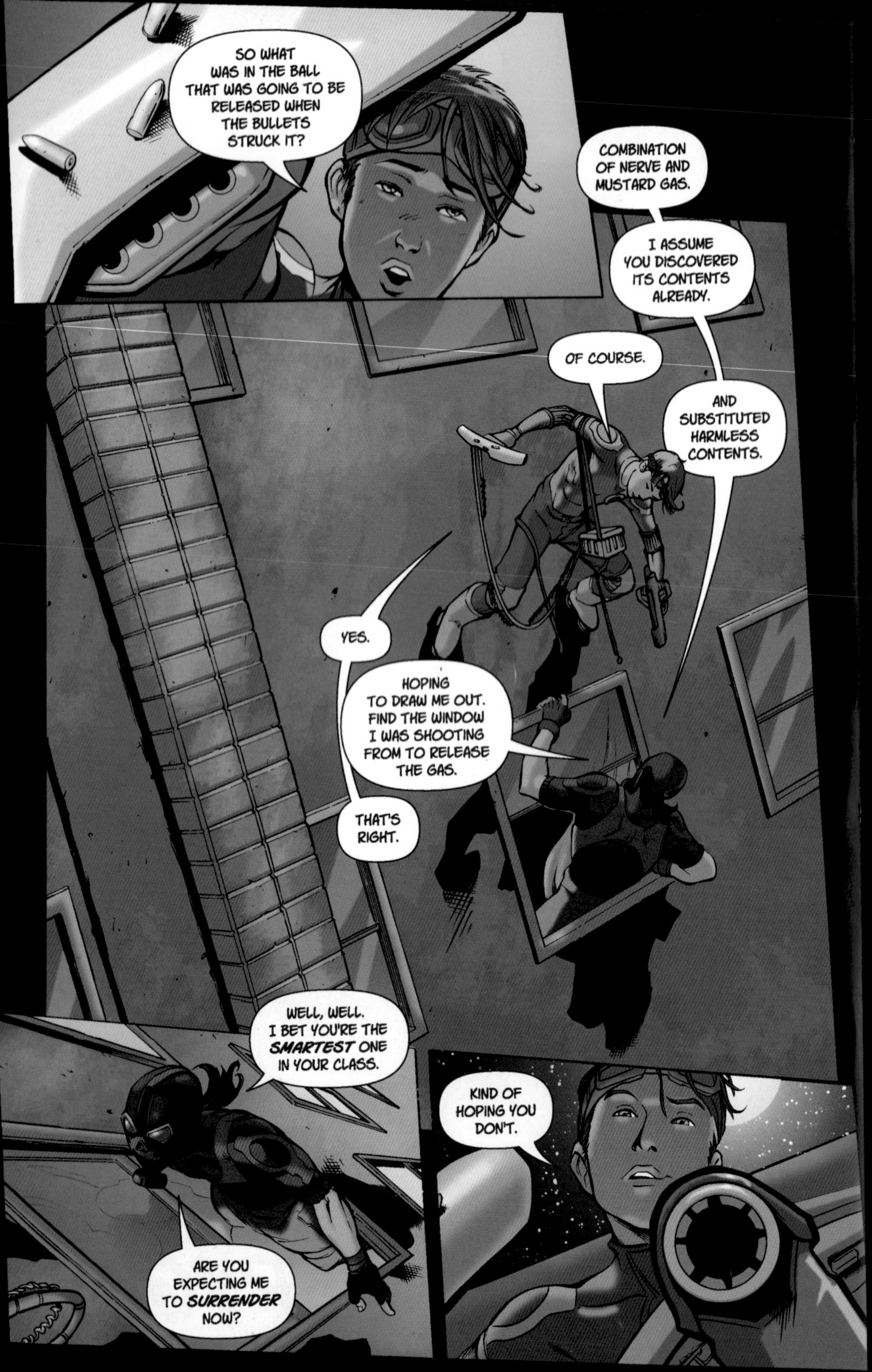
SO WHAT WAS IN THE BALL THAT WAS GOING TO BE RELEASED WHEN THE BULLETS STRUCK IT?
COMBINATION OF NERVE AND MUSTARD GAS.
I ASSUME YOU DISCOVERED ITS CONTENTS ALREADY.
OF COURSE.
AND SUBSTITUTED HARMLESS CONTENTS.
YES.
HOPING TO DRAW ME OUT. FIND THE WINDOW I WAS SHOOTING FROM TO RELEASE THE GAS.
THAT'S RIGHT.
WELL, WELL. I BET YOU'RE THE **SMARTEST** ONE IN YOUR CLASS.
KIND OF HOPING YOU DON'T.
ARE YOU EXPECTING ME TO **SURRENDER** NOW?

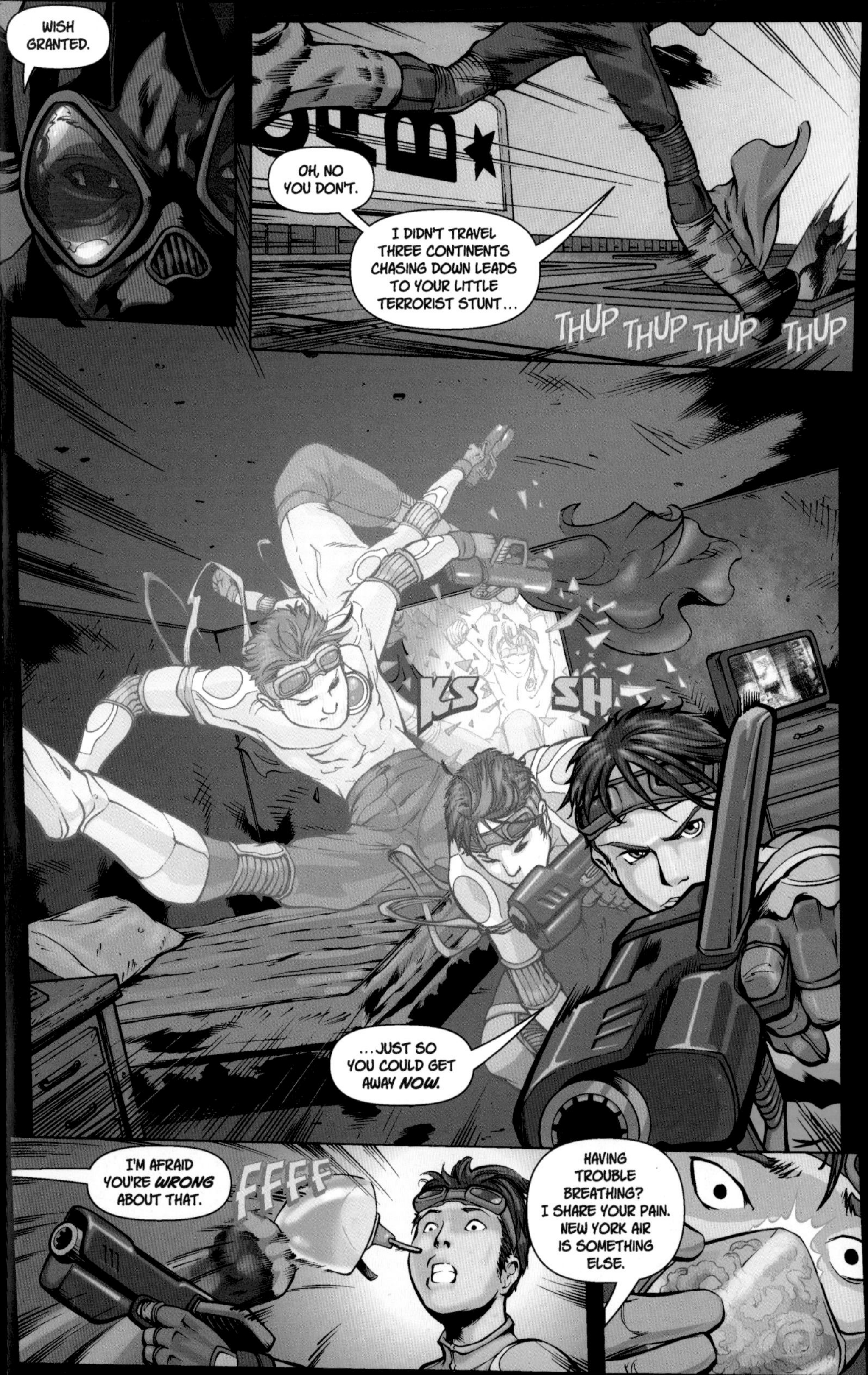
WISH GRANTED.
OH, NO YOU DON'T.
I DIDN'T TRAVEL THREE CONTINENTS CHASING DOWN LEADS TO YOUR LITTLE TERRORIST STUNT...
THUP THUP THUP THUP
KS SH
...JUST SO YOU COULD GET AWAY NOW.
I'M AFRAID YOU'RE WRONG ABOUT THAT.
FFFF
HAVING TROUBLE BREATHING? I SHARE YOUR PAIN. NEW YORK AIR IS SOMETHING ELSE.

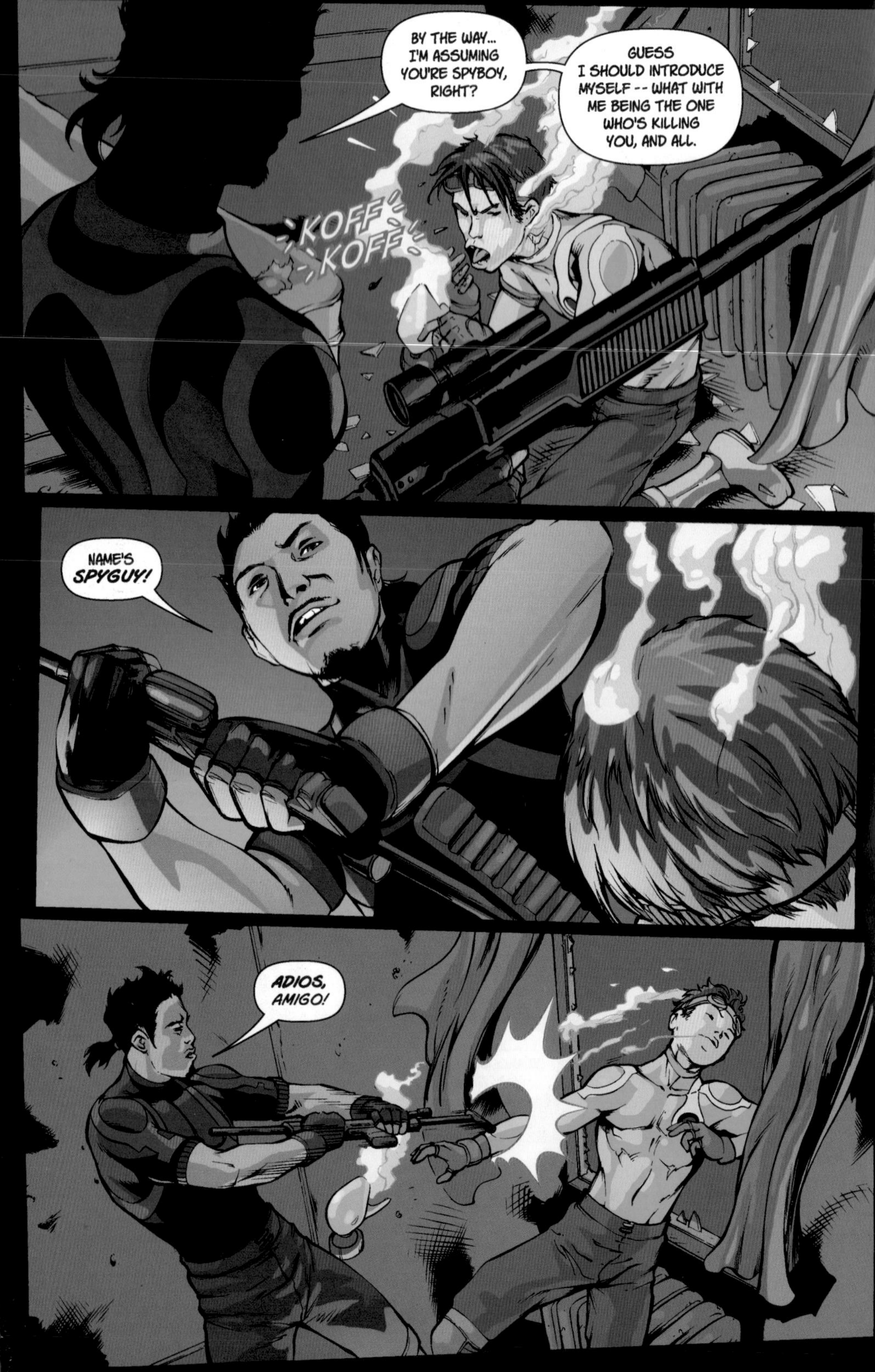
BY THE WAY... I'M ASSUMING YOU'RE SPYBOY, RIGHT?
GUESS I SHOULD INTRODUCE MYSELF -- WHAT WITH ME BEING THE ONE WHO'S KILLING YOU, AND ALL.
KOFF KOFF
NAME'S SPYGUY!
ADIOS, AMIGO!

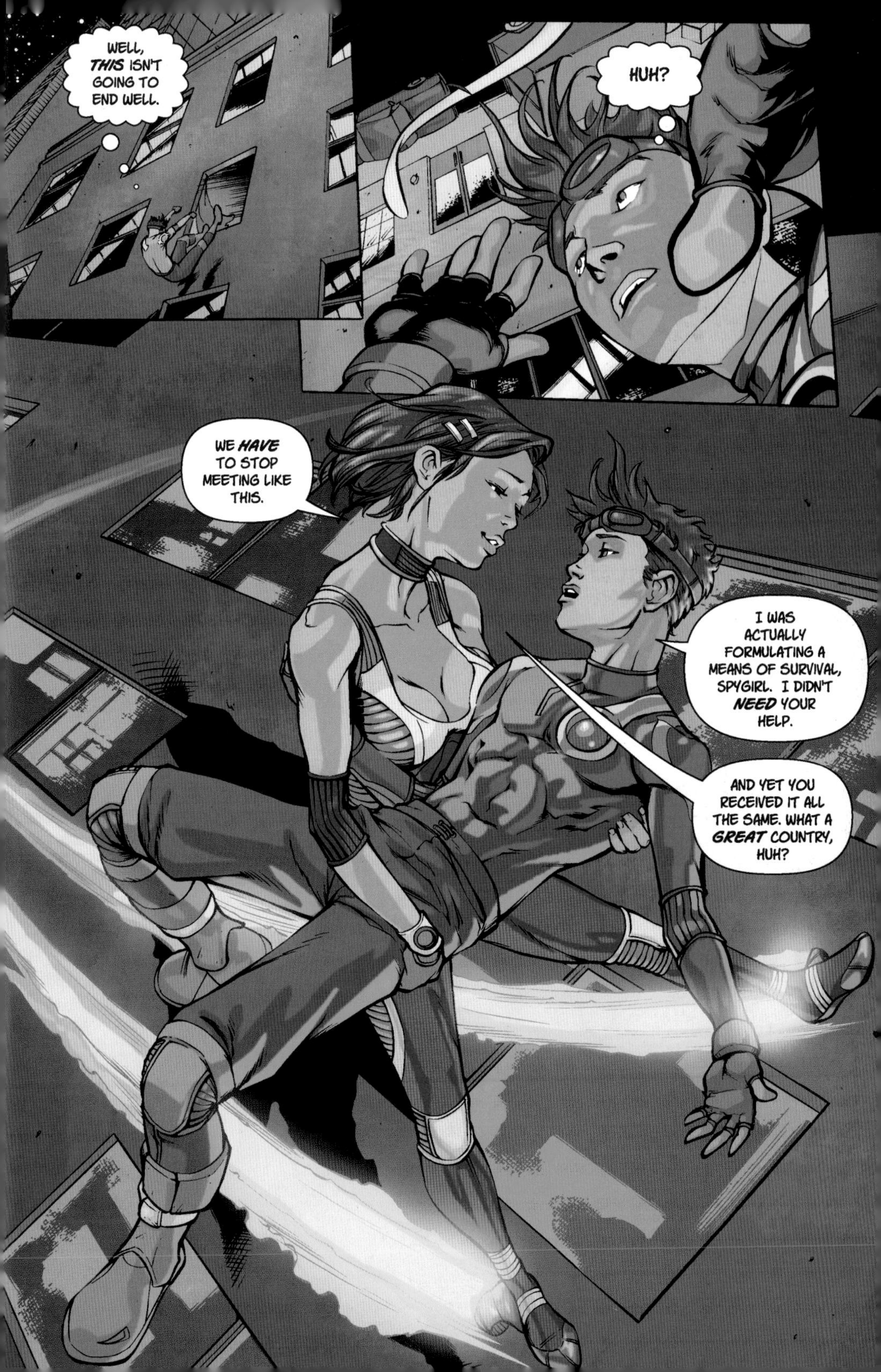
WELL, THIS ISN'T GOING TO END WELL.
HUH?
WE HAVE TO STOP MEETING LIKE THIS.
I WAS ACTUALLY FORMULATING A MEANS OF SURVIVAL, SPYGIRL. I DIDN'T NEED YOUR HELP.
AND YET YOU RECEIVED IT ALL THE SAME. WHAT A GREAT COUNTRY, HUH?

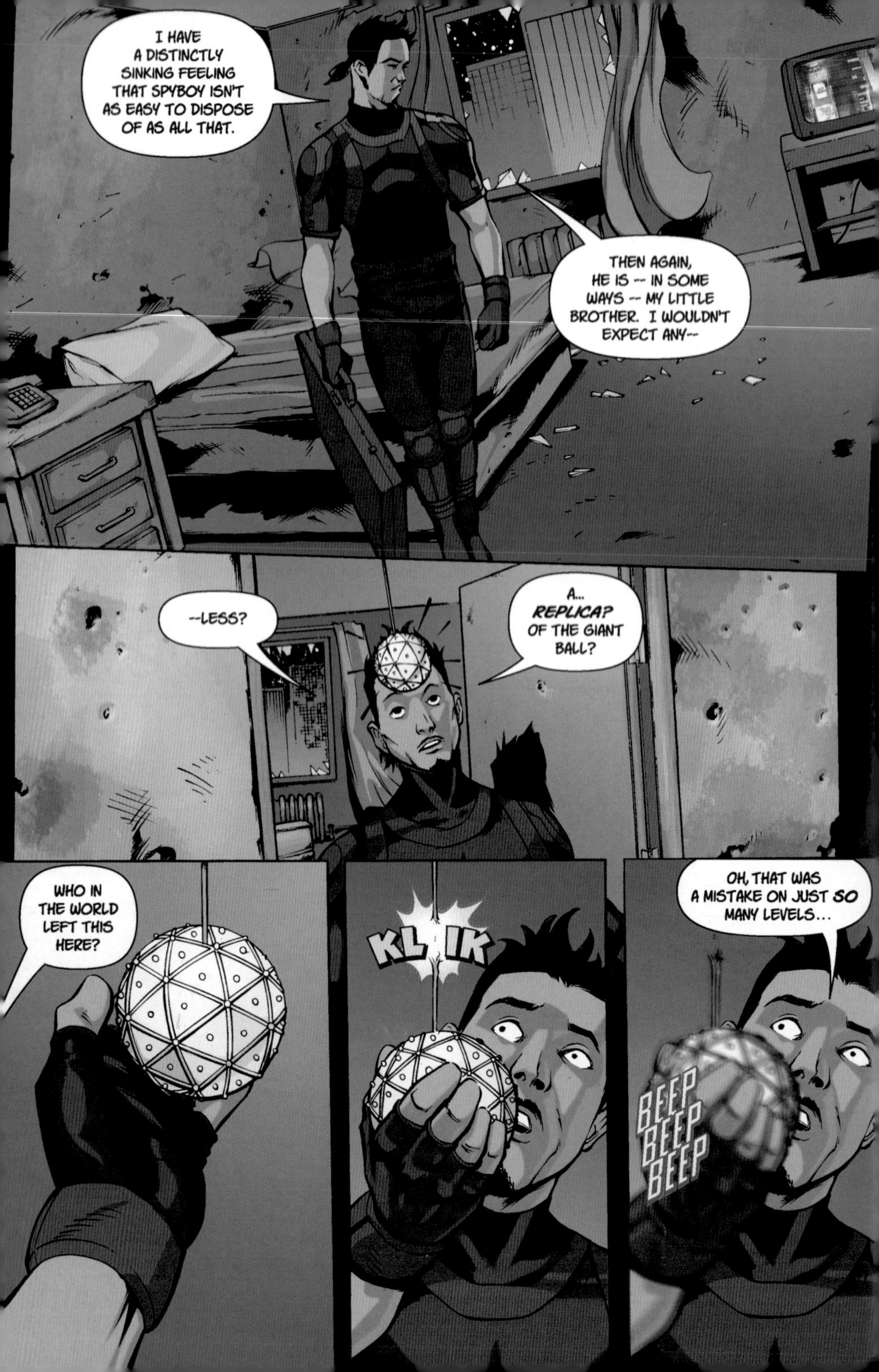
I HAVE A DISTINCTLY SINKING FEELING THAT SPYBOY ISN'T AS EASY TO DISPOSE OF AS ALL THAT.
THEN AGAIN, HE IS -- IN SOME WAYS -- MY LITTLE BROTHER. I WOULDN'T EXPECT ANY--
--LESS?
A... REPLICA? OF THE GIANT BALL?
WHO IN THE WORLD LEFT THIS HERE?
KLIK
OH, THAT WAS A MISTAKE ON JUST SO MANY LEVELS...
BEEP BEEP BEEP

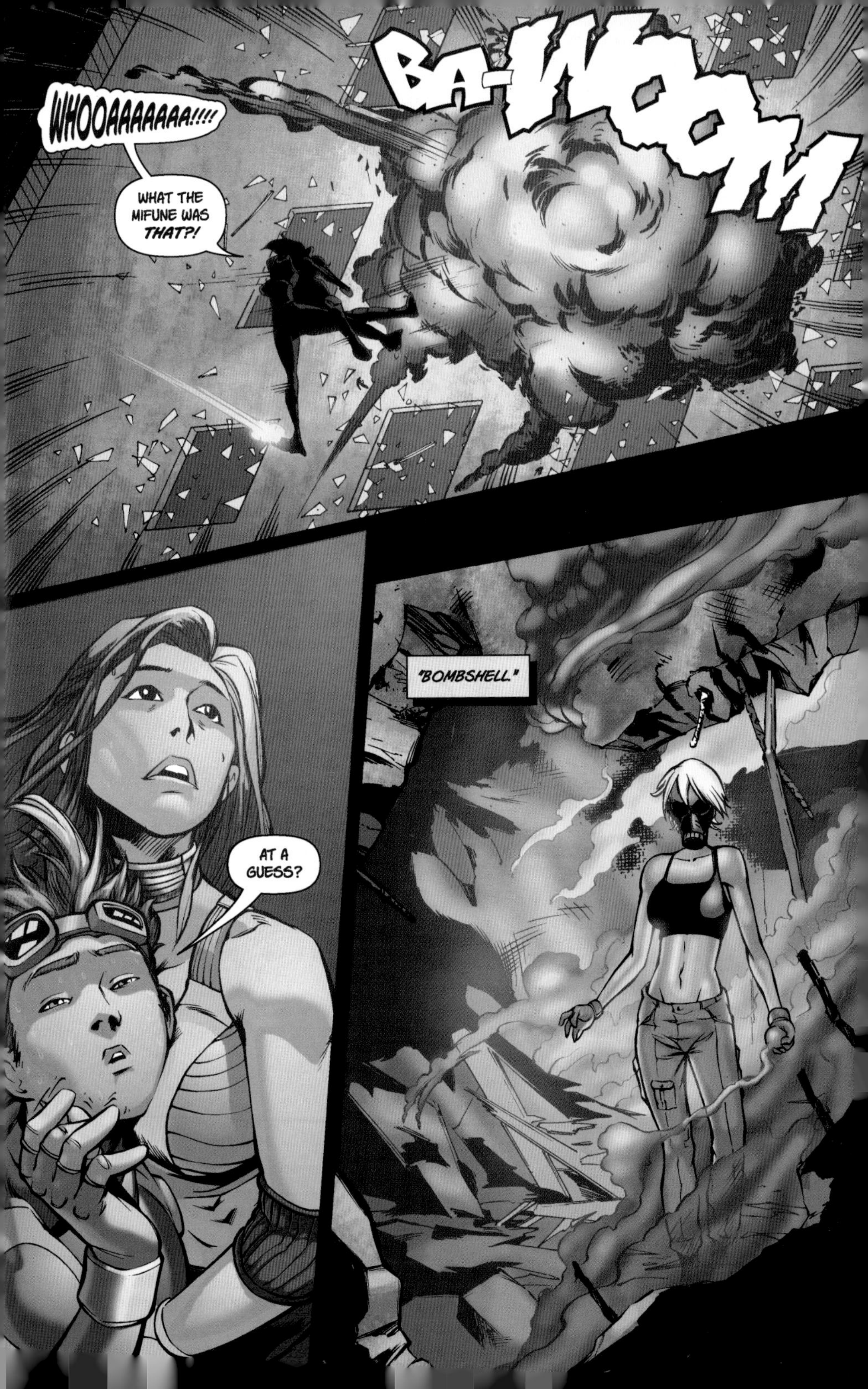
WHOOAAAAAAA!!!!
WHAT THE MIFUNE WAS THAT?!
BA-WOOM
AT A GUESS?
"BOMBSHELL."

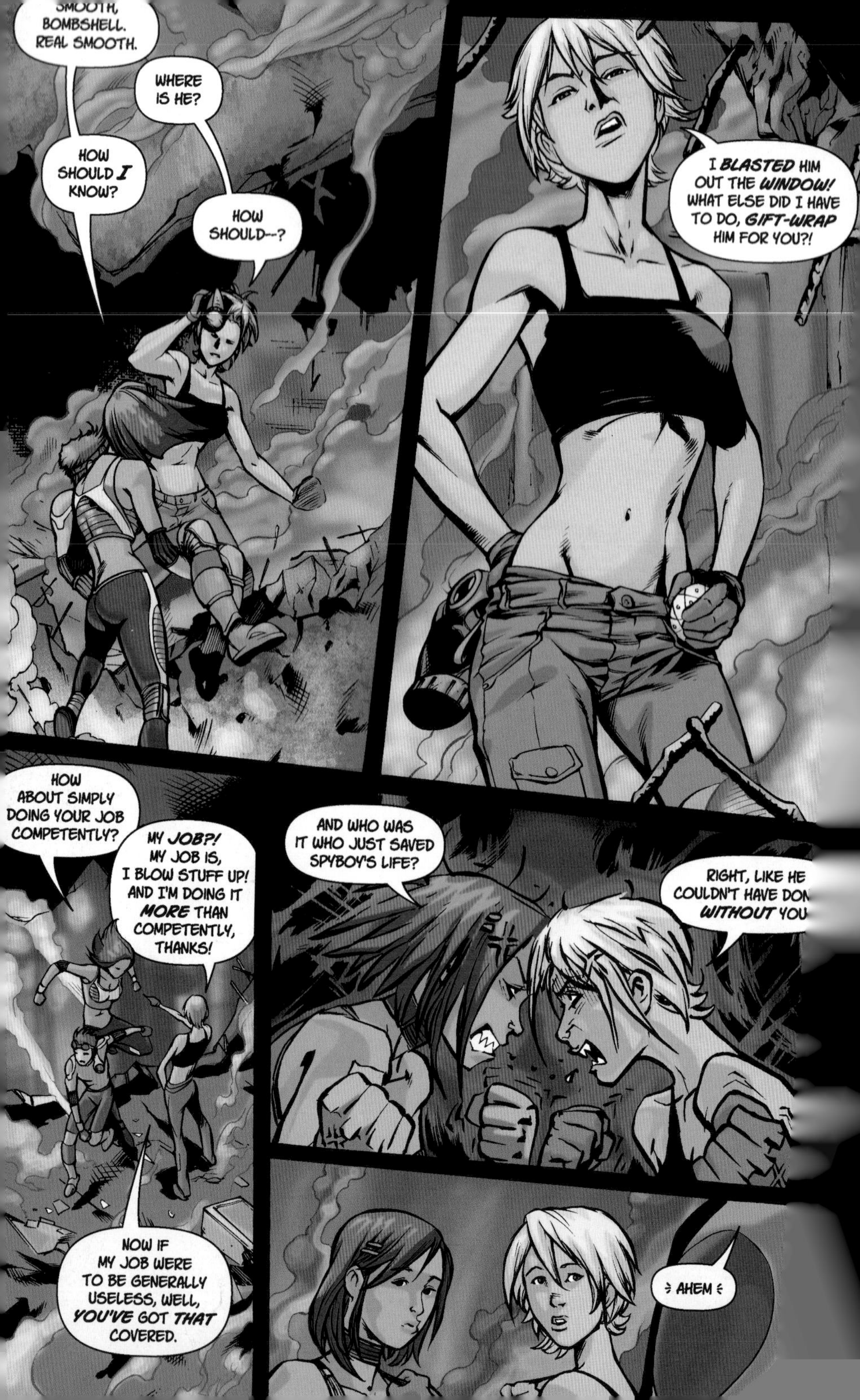
SMOOTH, BOMBSHELL. REAL SMOOTH.
WHERE IS HE?
HOW SHOULD I KNOW?
HOW SHOULD--?
I BLASTED HIM OUT THE WINDOW! WHAT ELSE DID I HAVE TO DO, GIFT-WRAP HIM FOR YOU?!
HOW ABOUT SIMPLY DOING YOUR JOB COMPETENTLY?
MY JOB?! MY JOB IS, I BLOW STUFF UP! AND I'M DOING IT MORE THAN COMPETENTLY, THANKS!
NOW IF MY JOB WERE TO BE GENERALLY USELESS, WELL, YOU'VE GOT THAT COVERED.
AND WHO WAS IT WHO JUST SAVED SPYBOY'S LIFE?
RIGHT, LIKE HE COULDN'T HAVE DON WITHOUT YOU
AHEM

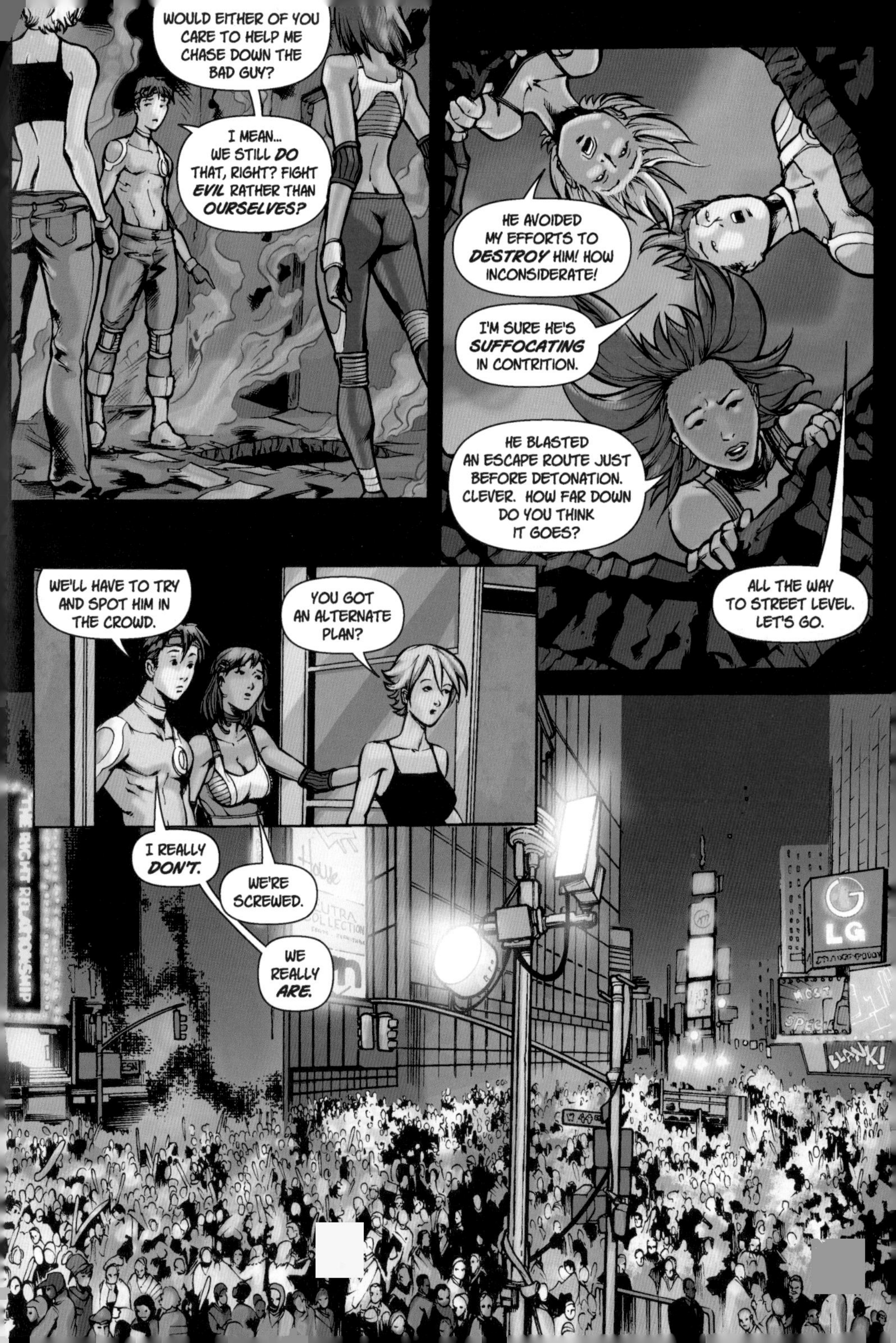

WOULD EITHER OF YOU CARE TO HELP ME CHASE DOWN THE BAD GUY?
I MEAN... WE STILL DO THAT, RIGHT? FIGHT EVIL RATHER THAN OURSELVES?
HE AVOIDED MY EFFORTS TO DESTROY HIM! HOW INCONSIDERATE!
I'M SURE HE'S SUFFOCATING IN CONTRITION.
HE BLASTED AN ESCAPE ROUTE JUST BEFORE DETONATION. CLEVER. HOW FAR DOWN DO YOU THINK IT GOES?
ALL THE WAY TO STREET LEVEL. LET'S GO.
WE'LL HAVE TO TRY AND SPOT HIM IN THE CROWD.
YOU GOT AN ALTERNATE PLAN?
I REALLY DON'T.
WE'RE SCREWED.
WE REALLY ARE.
THE RIGHT RELATIONSHIP
LG
BLANK!

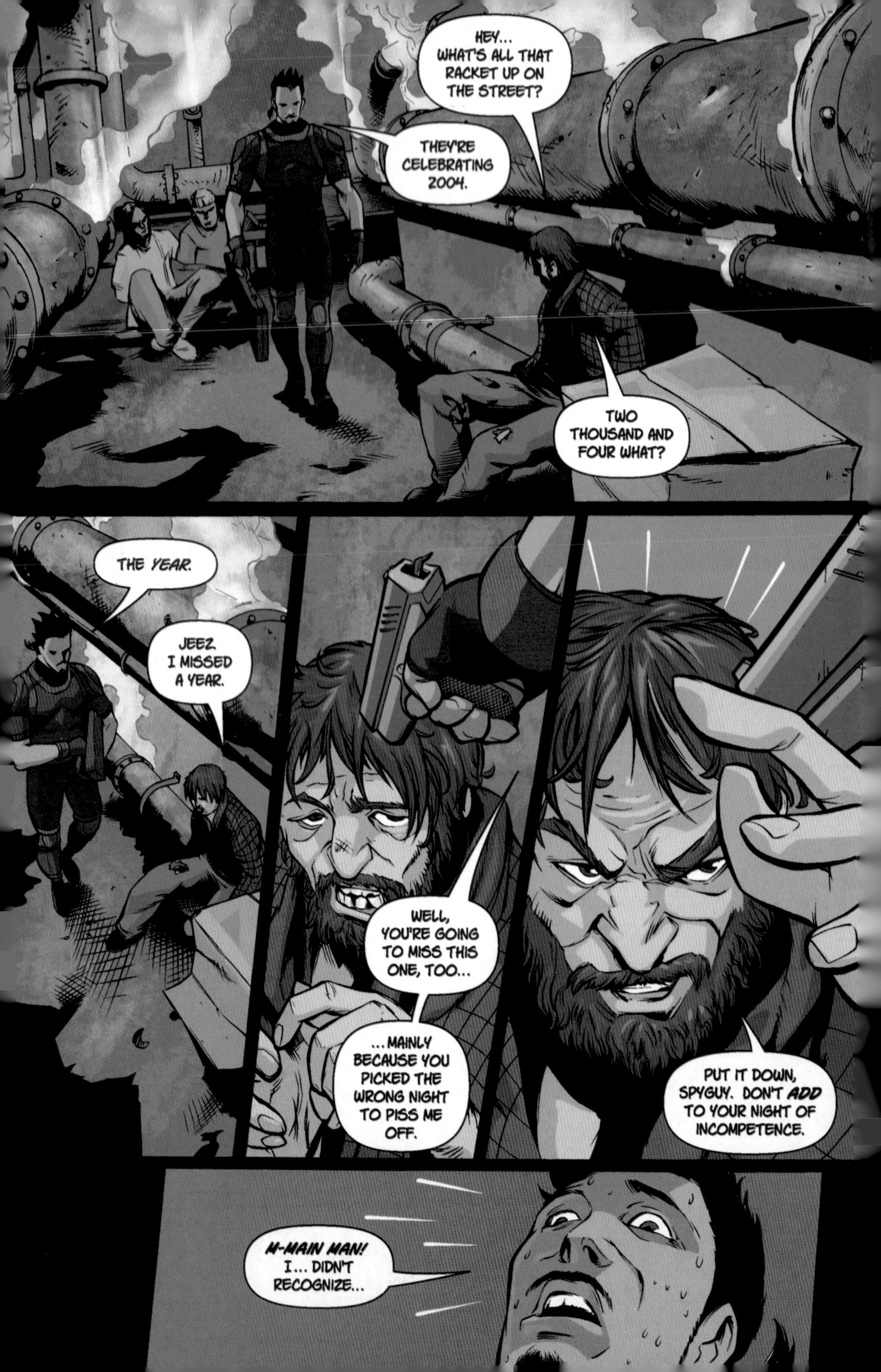
HEY... WHAT'S ALL THAT RACKET UP ON THE STREET?
THEY'RE CELEBRATING 2004.
TWO THOUSAND AND FOUR WHAT?
THE *YEAR.*
JEEZ. I MISSED A YEAR.
WELL, YOU'RE GOING TO MISS THIS ONE, TOO...
...MAINLY BECAUSE YOU PICKED THE WRONG NIGHT TO PISS ME OFF.
PUT IT DOWN, SPYGUY. DON'T *ADD* TO YOUR NIGHT OF INCOMPETENCE.
M-MAIN MAN! I... DIDN'T RECOGNIZE...

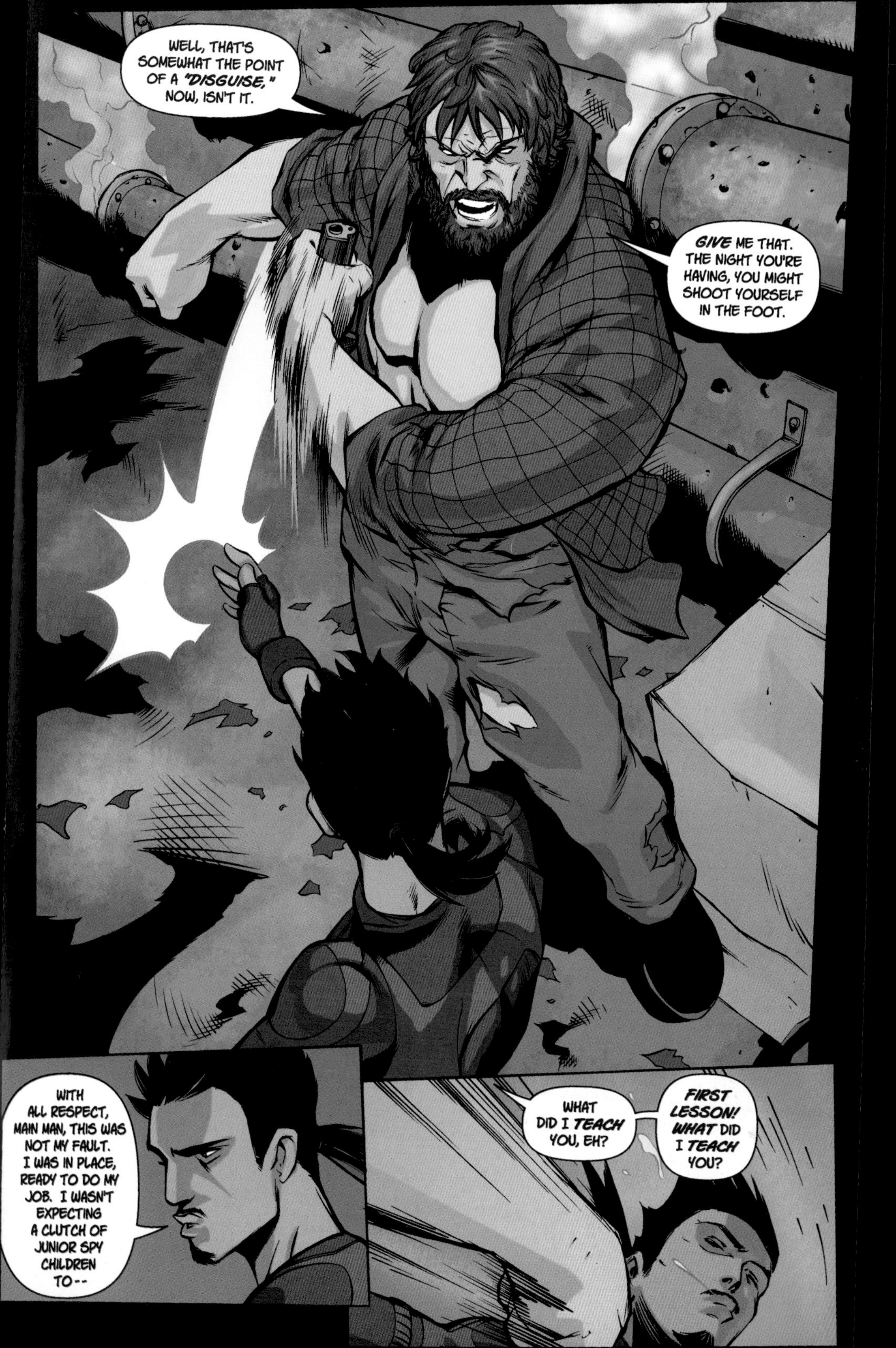
WELL, THAT'S SOMEWHAT THE POINT OF A "DISGUISE," NOW, ISN'T IT.
GIVE ME THAT. THE NIGHT YOU'RE HAVING, YOU MIGHT SHOOT YOURSELF IN THE FOOT.
WITH ALL RESPECT, MAIN MAN, THIS WAS NOT MY FAULT. I WAS IN PLACE, READY TO DO MY JOB. I WASN'T EXPECTING A CLUTCH OF JUNIOR SPY CHILDREN TO--
WHAT DID I TEACH YOU, EH?
FIRST LESSON! WHAT DID I TEACH YOU?

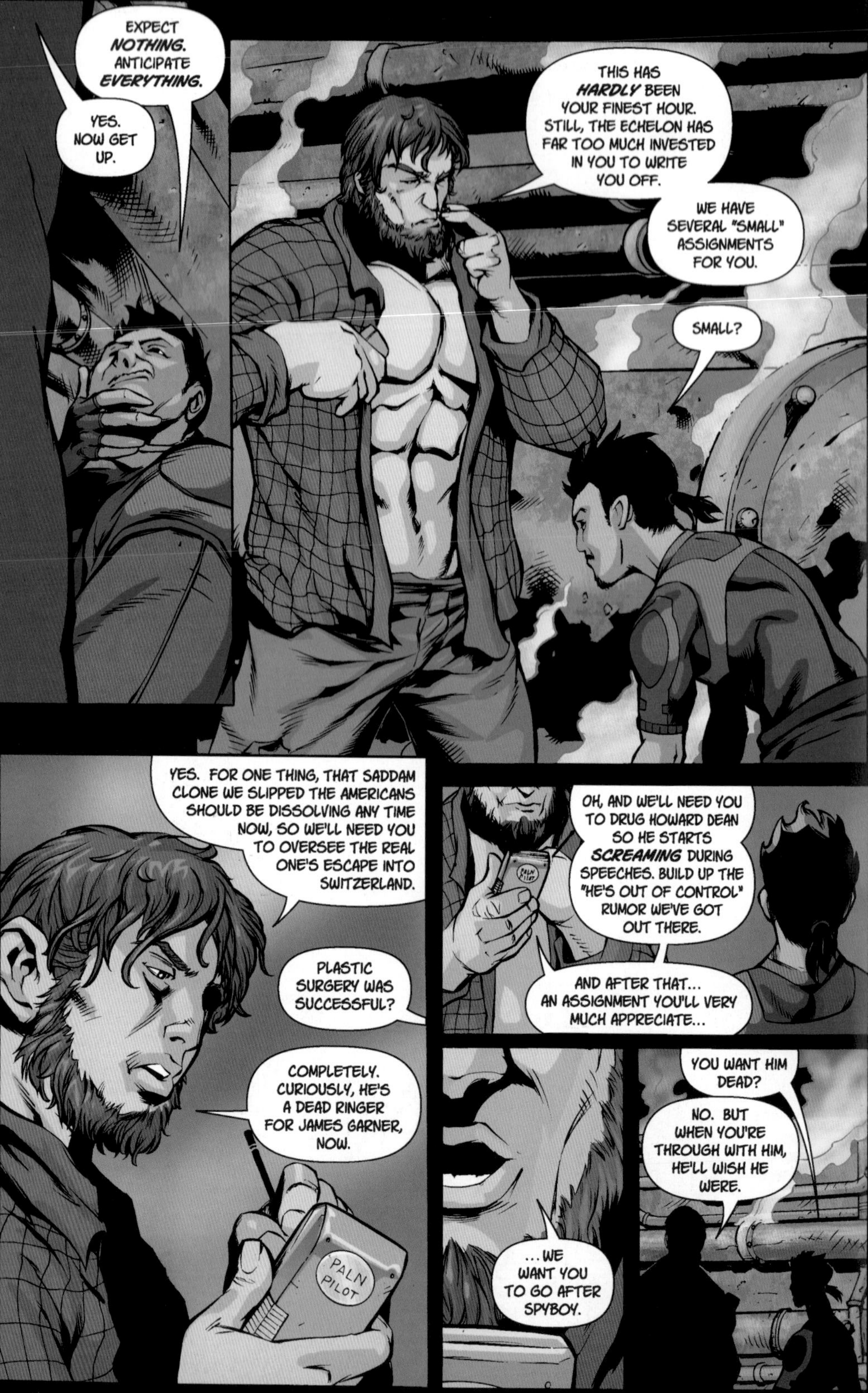

EXPECT NOTHING. ANTICIPATE EVERYTHING.
YES. NOW GET UP.
THIS HAS HARDLY BEEN YOUR FINEST HOUR. STILL, THE ECHELON HAS FAR TOO MUCH INVESTED IN YOU TO WRITE YOU OFF.
WE HAVE SEVERAL "SMALL" ASSIGNMENTS FOR YOU.
SMALL?
YES. FOR ONE THING, THAT SADDAM CLONE WE SLIPPED THE AMERICANS SHOULD BE DISSOLVING ANY TIME NOW, SO WE'LL NEED YOU TO OVERSEE THE REAL ONE'S ESCAPE INTO SWITZERLAND.
PLASTIC SURGERY WAS SUCCESSFUL?
COMPLETELY. CURIOUSLY, HE'S A DEAD RINGER FOR JAMES GARNER, NOW.
PALN PILOT
OH, AND WE'LL NEED YOU TO DRUG HOWARD DEAN SO HE STARTS SCREAMING DURING SPEECHES. BUILD UP THE "HE'S OUT OF CONTROL" RUMOR WE'VE GOT OUT THERE.
AND AFTER THAT... AN ASSIGNMENT YOU'LL VERY MUCH APPRECIATE...
...WE WANT YOU TO GO AFTER SPYBOY.
YOU WANT HIM DEAD?
NO. BUT WHEN YOU'RE THROUGH WITH HIM, HE'LL WISH HE WERE.

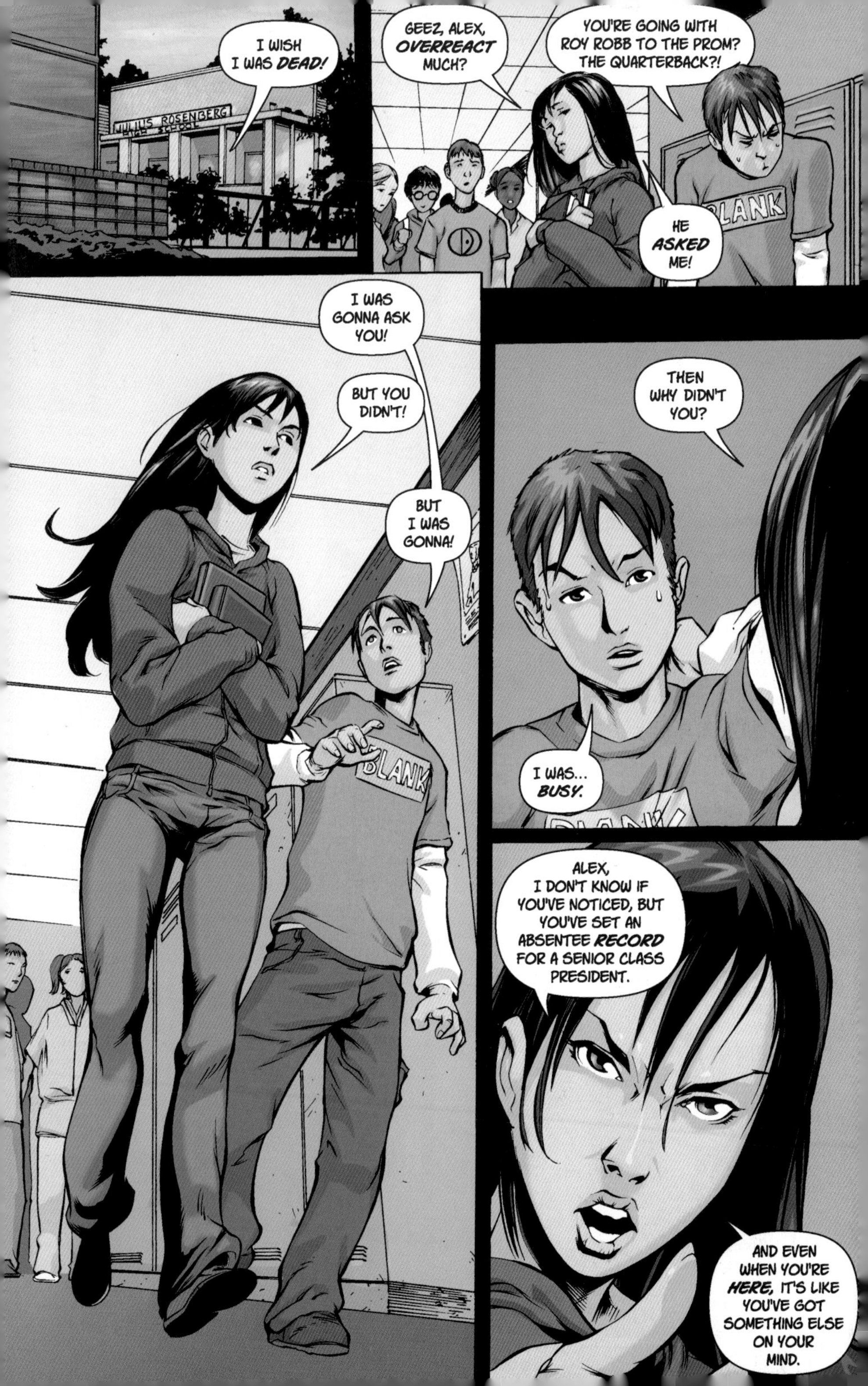
JULIUS ROSENBERG HIGH SCHOOL
I WISH I WAS DEAD!
GEEZ, ALEX, OVERREACT MUCH?
YOU'RE GOING WITH ROY ROBB TO THE PROM? THE QUARTERBACK?!
HE ASKED ME!
BLANK
I WAS GONNA ASK YOU!
BUT YOU DIDN'T!
BUT I WAS GONNA!
BLANK
THEN WHY DIDN'T YOU?
I WAS... BUSY.
ALEX, I DON'T KNOW IF YOU'VE NOTICED, BUT YOU'VE SET AN ABSENTEE RECORD FOR A SENIOR CLASS PRESIDENT.
AND EVEN WHEN YOU'RE HERE, IT'S LIKE YOU'VE GOT SOMETHING ELSE ON YOUR MIND.

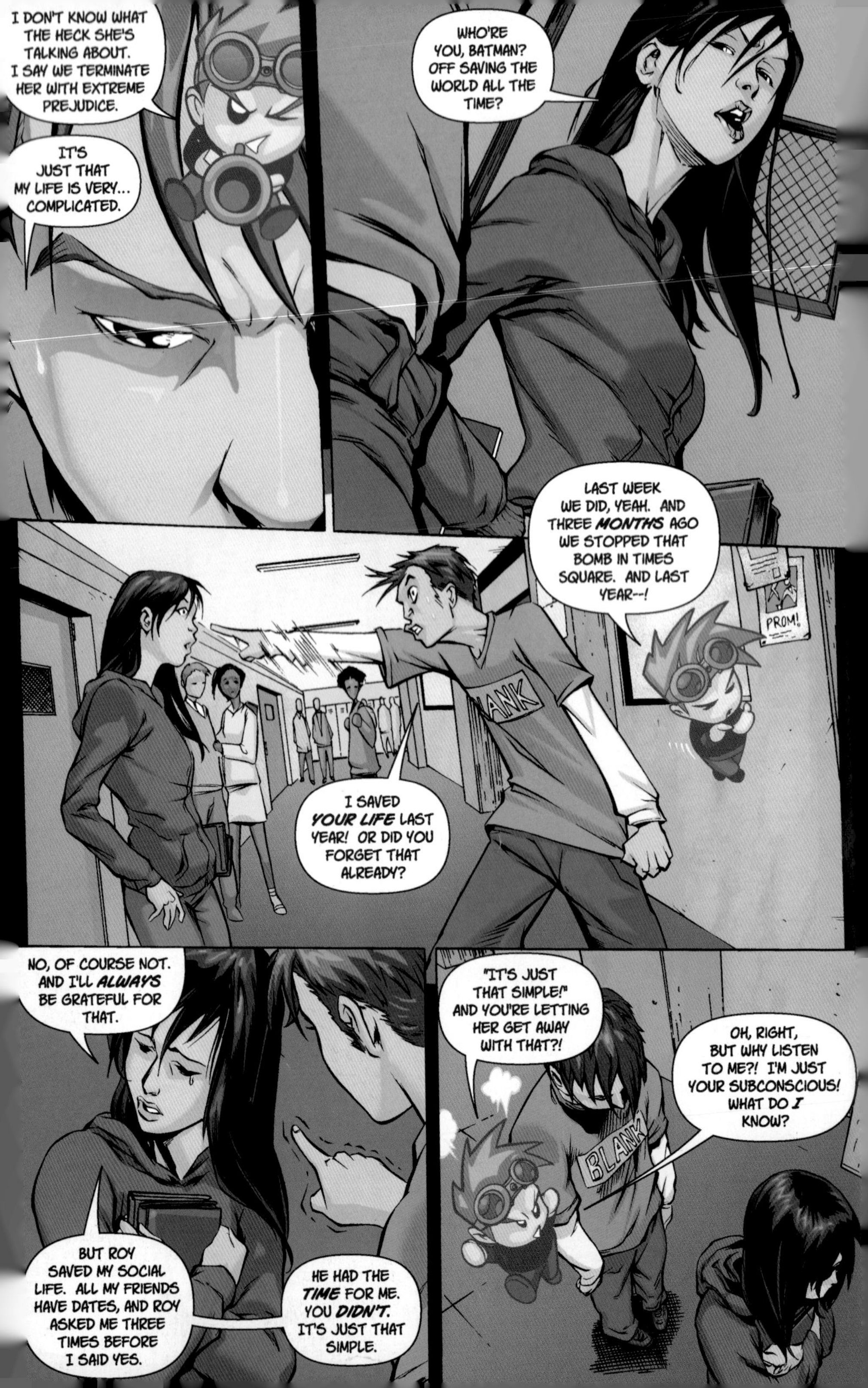
I DON'T KNOW WHAT THE HECK SHE'S TALKING ABOUT. I SAY WE TERMINATE HER WITH EXTREME PREJUDICE.
IT'S JUST THAT MY LIFE IS VERY... COMPLICATED.
WHO'RE YOU, BATMAN? OFF SAVING THE WORLD ALL THE TIME?
LAST WEEK WE DID, YEAH. AND THREE MONTHS AGO WE STOPPED THAT BOMB IN TIMES SQUARE. AND LAST YEAR--!
PROM!
BLANK
I SAVED YOUR LIFE LAST YEAR! OR DID YOU FORGET THAT ALREADY?
NO, OF COURSE NOT. AND I'LL ALWAYS BE GRATEFUL FOR THAT.
BUT ROY SAVED MY SOCIAL LIFE. ALL MY FRIENDS HAVE DATES, AND ROY ASKED ME THREE TIMES BEFORE I SAID YES.
HE HAD THE TIME FOR ME. YOU DIDN'T. IT'S JUST THAT SIMPLE.
"IT'S JUST THAT SIMPLE!" AND YOU'RE LETTING HER GET AWAY WITH THAT?!
OH, RIGHT, BUT WHY LISTEN TO ME?! I'M JUST YOUR SUBCONSCIOUS! WHAT DO I KNOW?
BLANK

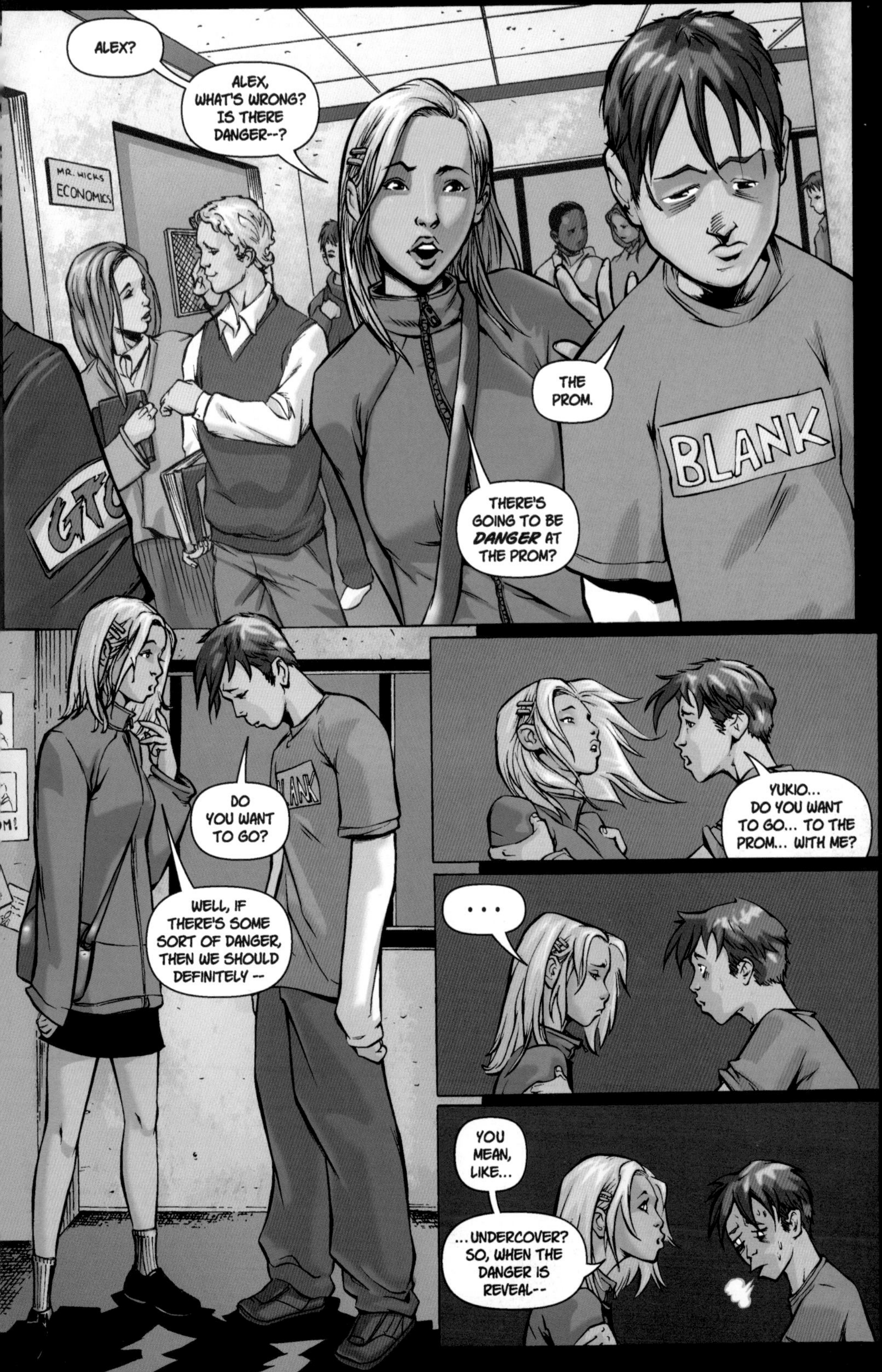

ALEX?
ALEX, WHAT'S WRONG? IS THERE DANGER--?
MR. HICKS ECONOMICS
THE PROM.
BLANK
THERE'S GOING TO BE *DANGER* AT THE PROM?
DO YOU WANT TO GO?
WELL, IF THERE'S SOME SORT OF DANGER, THEN WE SHOULD DEFINITELY --
YUKIO... DO YOU WANT TO GO... TO THE PROM... WITH ME?
. . .
YOU MEAN, LIKE...
...UNDERCOVER? SO, WHEN THE DANGER IS REVEAL--

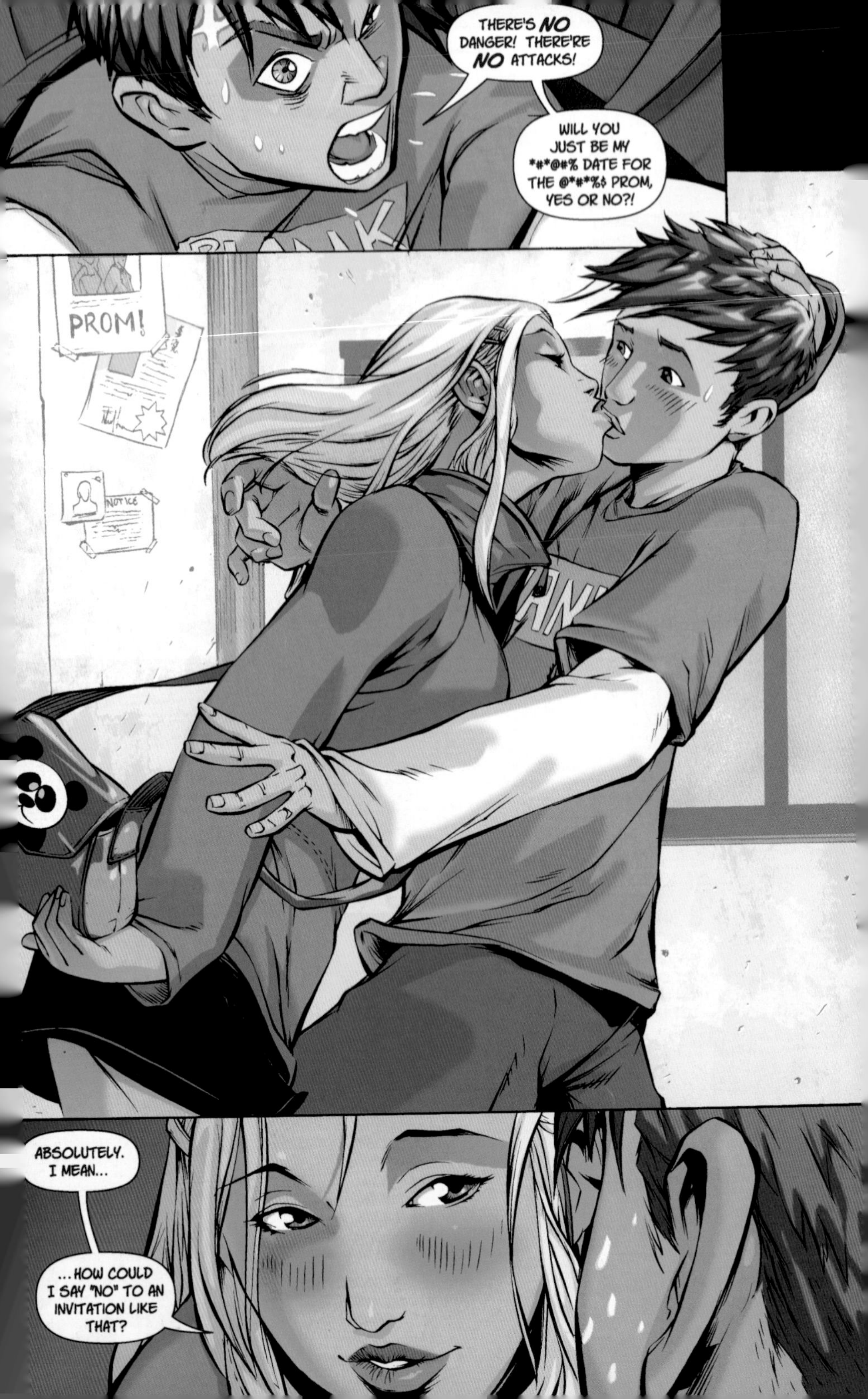
THERE'S NO DANGER! THERE'RE NO ATTACKS!
WILL YOU JUST BE MY *#*@#% DATE FOR THE @*#*%$ PROM, YES OR NO?!
PROM!
NOTICE
ABSOLUTELY. I MEAN...
...HOW COULD I SAY "NO" TO AN INVITATION LIKE THAT?

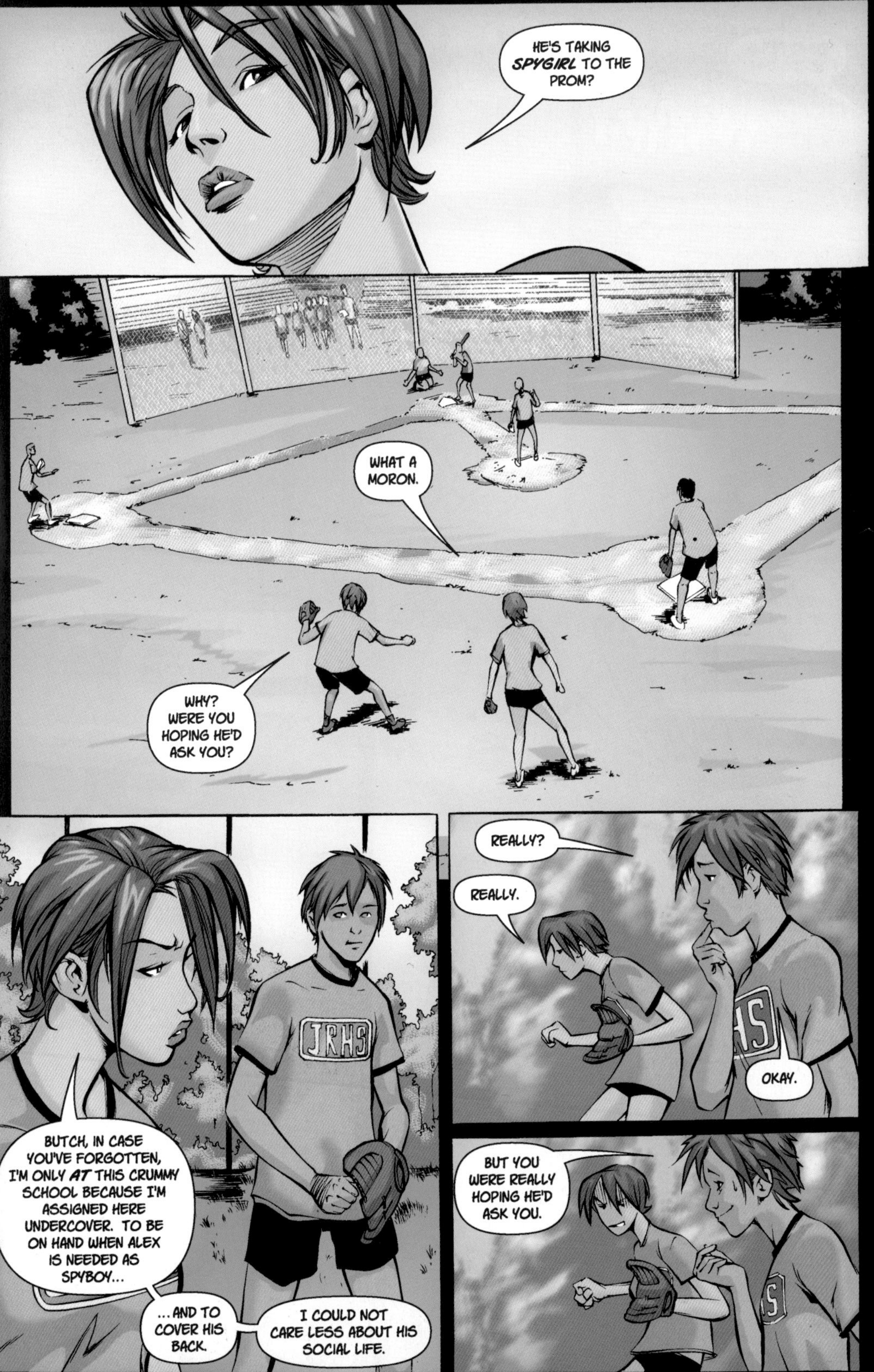
HE'S TAKING *SPYGIRL* TO THE PROM?
WHAT A MORON.
WHY? WERE YOU HOPING HE'D ASK YOU?
BUTCH, IN CASE YOU'VE FORGOTTEN, I'M ONLY *AT* THIS CRUMMY SCHOOL BECAUSE I'M ASSIGNED HERE UNDERCOVER. TO BE ON HAND WHEN ALEX IS NEEDED AS SPYBOY...
...AND TO COVER HIS BACK.
I COULD NOT CARE LESS ABOUT HIS SOCIAL LIFE.
JRHS
REALLY?
REALLY.
OKAY.
BUT YOU WERE REALLY HOPING HE'D ASK YOU.

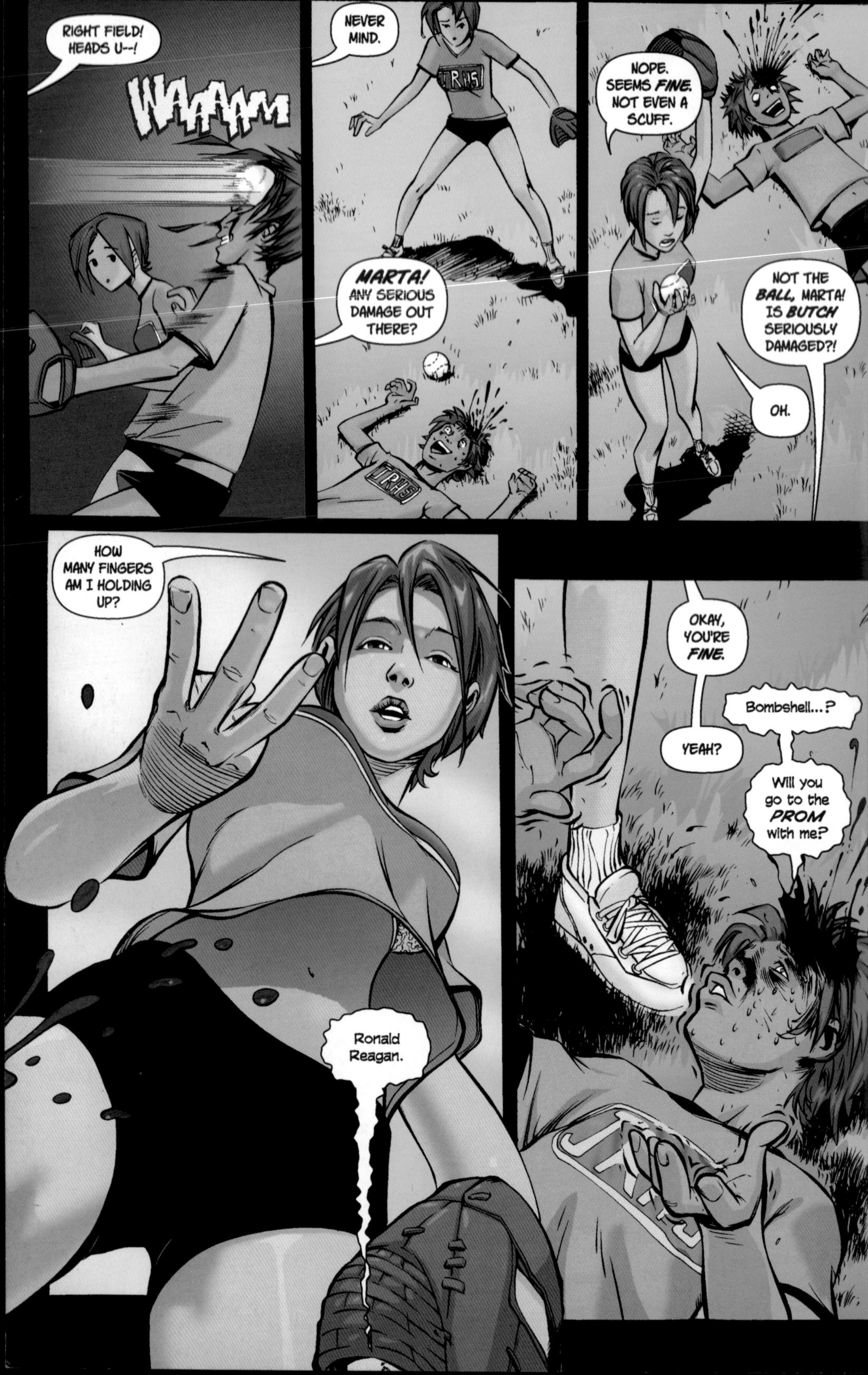
RIGHT FIELD! HEADS U--!
WAAAAM
NEVER MIND.
MARTA! ANY SERIOUS DAMAGE OUT THERE?
NOPE. SEEMS FINE. NOT EVEN A SCUFF.
NOT THE BALL, MARTA! IS BUTCH SERIOUSLY DAMAGED?!
OH.
HOW MANY FINGERS AM I HOLDING UP?
Ronald Reagan.
OKAY, YOU'RE FINE.
Bombshell...?
YEAH?
Will you go to the PROM with me?

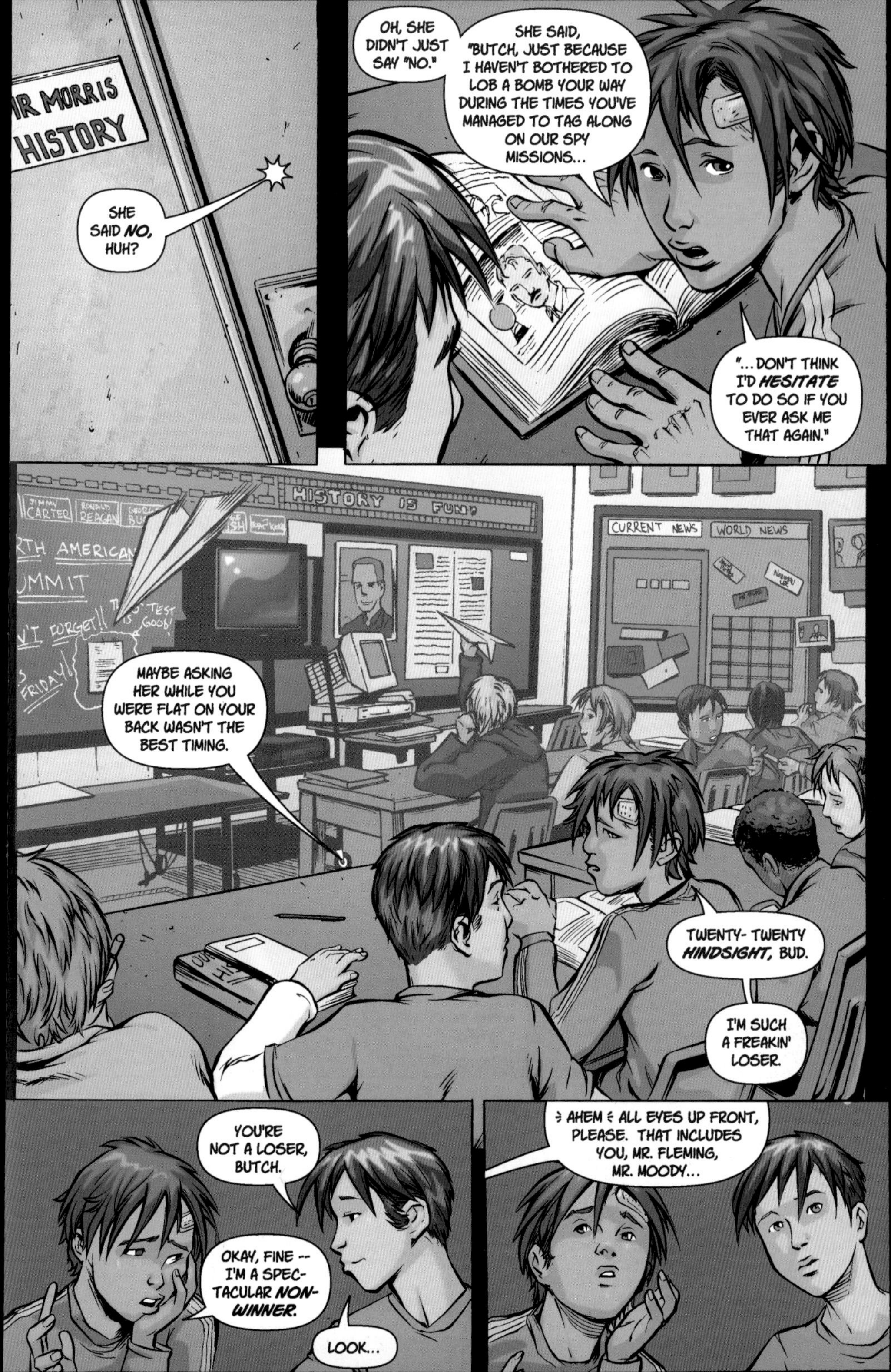
R MORRIS
HISTORY
SHE SAID *NO,* HUH?
OH, SHE DIDN'T JUST SAY "NO."
SHE SAID, "BUTCH, JUST BECAUSE I HAVEN'T BOTHERED TO LOB A BOMB YOUR WAY DURING THE TIMES YOU'VE MANAGED TO TAG ALONG ON OUR SPY MISSIONS...
"... DON'T THINK I'D *HESITATE* TO DO SO IF YOU EVER ASK ME THAT AGAIN."
HISTORY IS FUN!
JIMMY CARTER
RONALD REAGAN
CURRENT NEWS
WORLD NEWS
MAYBE ASKING HER WHILE YOU WERE FLAT ON YOUR BACK WASN'T THE BEST TIMING.
TWENTY- TWENTY *HINDSIGHT,* BUD.
I'M SUCH A FREAKIN' LOSER.
YOU'RE NOT A LOSER, BUTCH.
OKAY, FINE -- I'M A SPEC-TACULAR ***NON-WINNER.***
LOOK...
⋟ AHEM ⋞ ALL EYES UP FRONT, PLEASE. THAT INCLUDES YOU, MR. FLEMING, MR. MOODY...

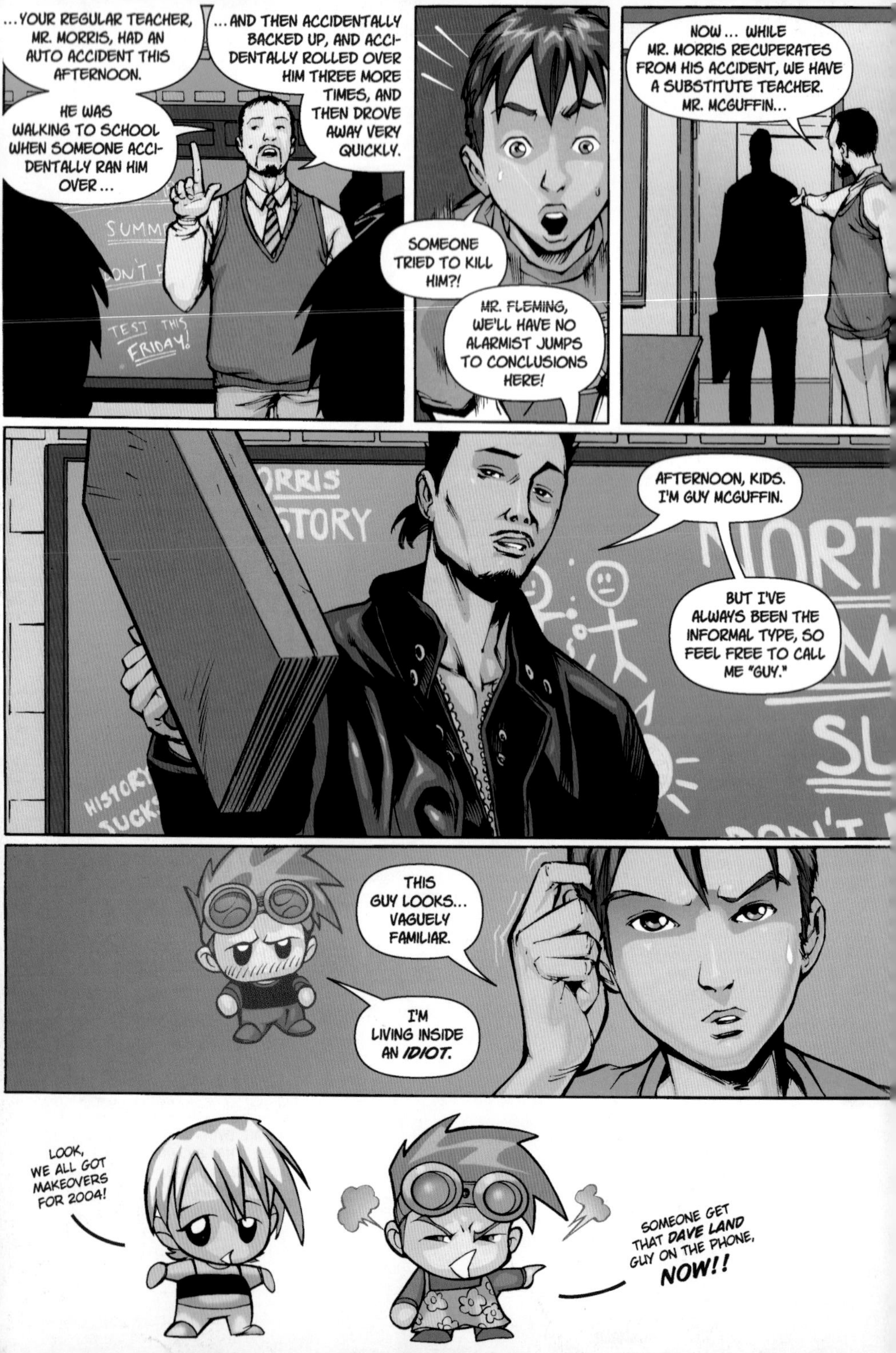
...YOUR REGULAR TEACHER, MR. MORRIS, HAD AN AUTO ACCIDENT THIS AFTERNOON.
HE WAS WALKING TO SCHOOL WHEN SOMEONE ACCIDENTALLY RAN HIM OVER...
...AND THEN ACCIDENTALLY BACKED UP, AND ACCIDENTALLY ROLLED OVER HIM THREE MORE TIMES, AND THEN DROVE AWAY VERY QUICKLY.
SUMM
DON'T
TEST THIS FRIDAY!
SOMEONE TRIED TO KILL HIM?!
MR. FLEMING, WE'LL HAVE NO ALARMIST JUMPS TO CONCLUSIONS HERE!
NOW... WHILE MR. MORRIS RECUPERATES FROM HIS ACCIDENT, WE HAVE A SUBSTITUTE TEACHER. MR. MCGUFFIN...
ORRIS
STORY
HISTORY SUCKS
AFTERNOON, KIDS. I'M GUY MCGUFFIN.
BUT I'VE ALWAYS BEEN THE INFORMAL TYPE, SO FEEL FREE TO CALL ME "GUY."
THIS GUY LOOKS... VAGUELY FAMILIAR.
I'M LIVING INSIDE AN *IDIOT*.
LOOK, WE ALL GOT MAKEOVERS FOR 2004!
SOMEONE GET THAT *DAVE LAND* GUY ON THE PHONE, *NOW!!*

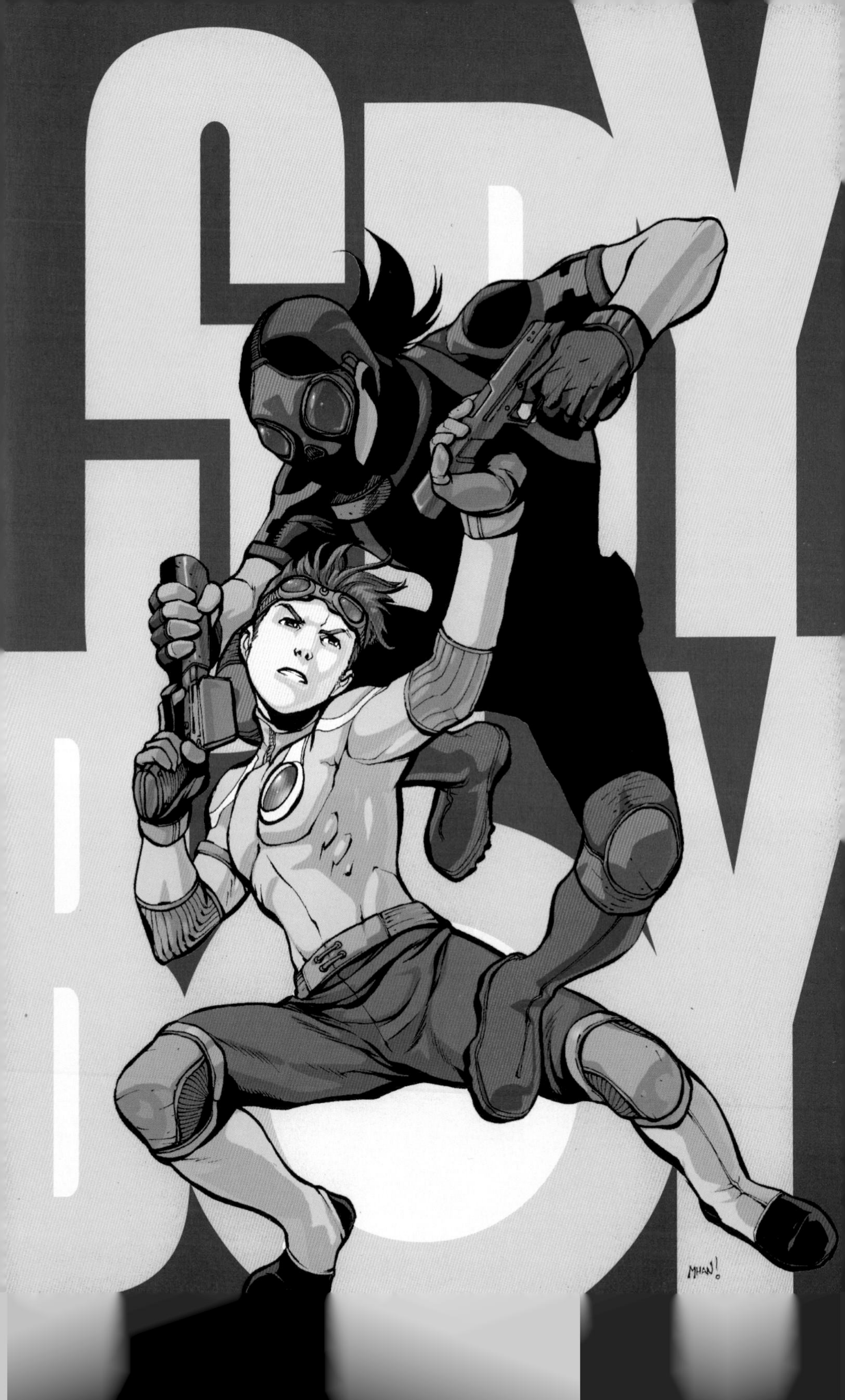
MHAN!

SPY BOY™

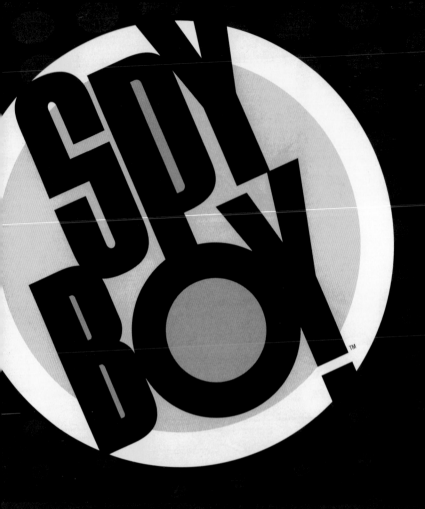

Part 2

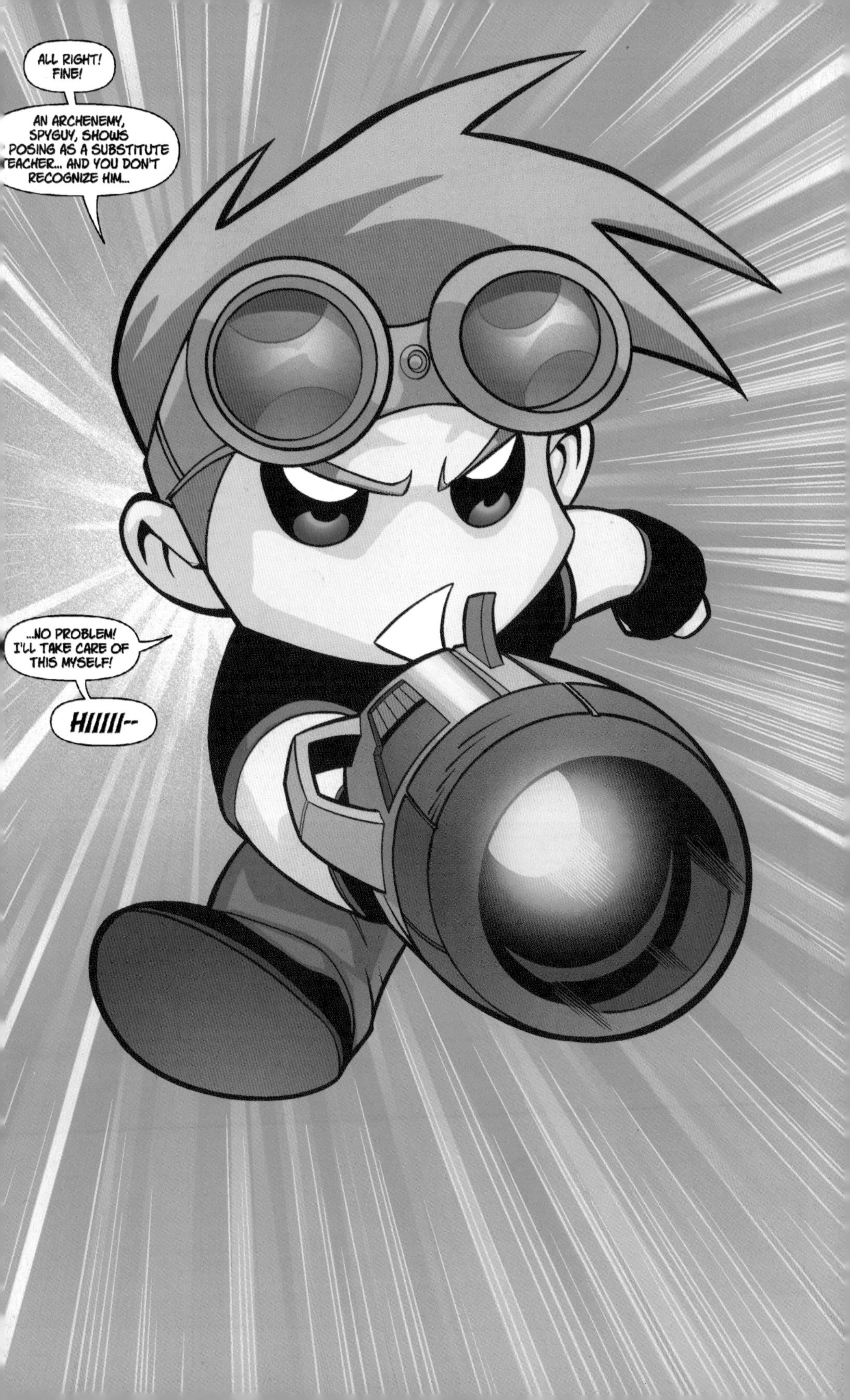
ALL RIGHT! FINE!
AN ARCHENEMY, SPYGUY, SHOWS POSING AS A SUBSTITUTE TEACHER... AND YOU DON'T RECOGNIZE HIM...
...NO PROBLEM! I'LL TAKE CARE OF THIS MYSELF!
HIIIII--

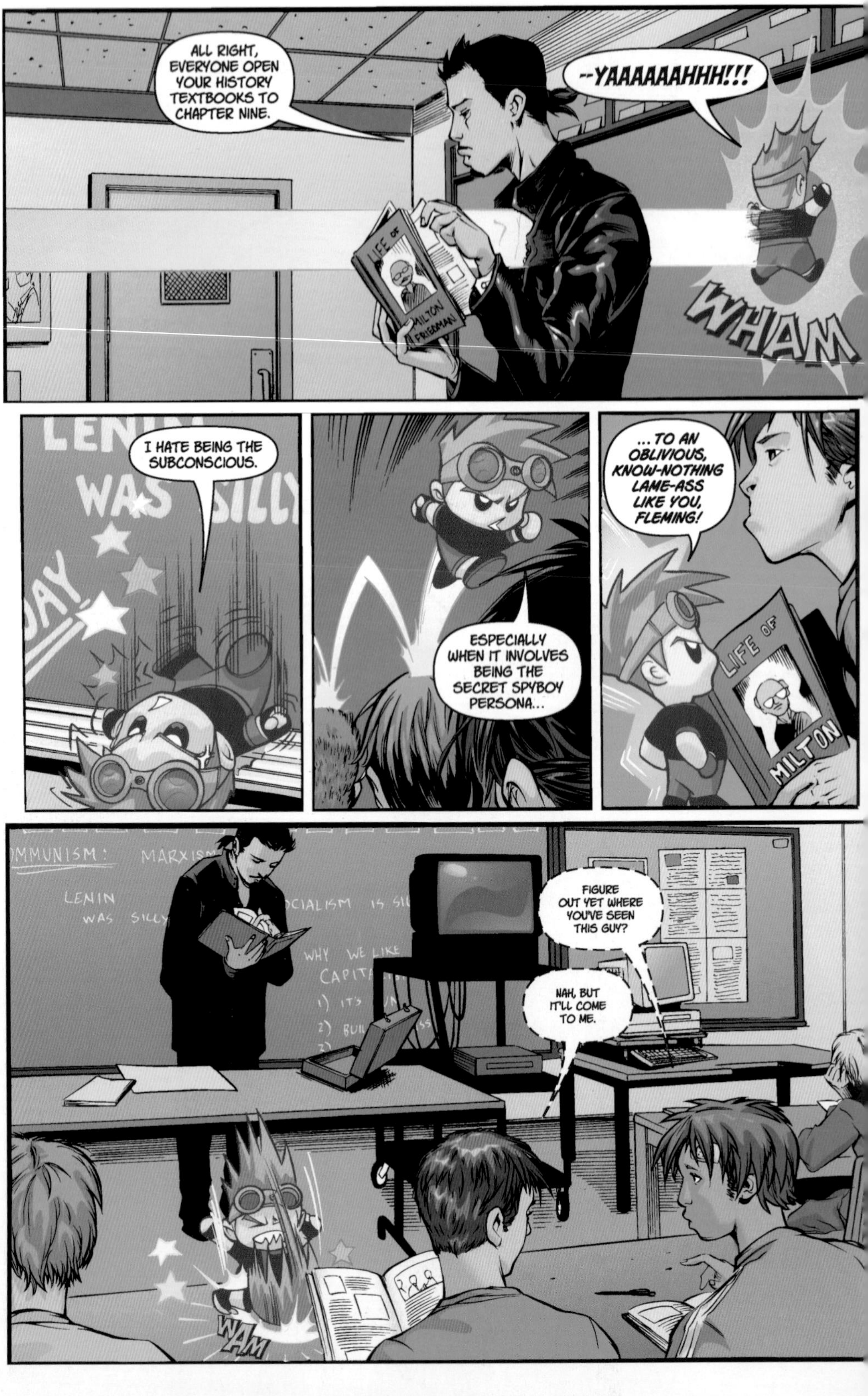
ALL RIGHT, EVERYONE OPEN YOUR HISTORY TEXTBOOKS TO CHAPTER NINE.
--YAAAAAAHHH!!!
LIFE OF MILTON FRIEDMAN
WHAM
I HATE BEING THE SUBCONSCIOUS.
ESPECIALLY WHEN IT INVOLVES BEING THE SECRET SPYBOY PERSONA...
...TO AN OBLIVIOUS, KNOW-NOTHING LAME-ASS LIKE YOU, FLEMING!
LIFE OF MILTON
LENIN WAS SILLY
FIGURE OUT YET WHERE YOU'VE SEEN THIS GUY?
NAH, BUT IT'LL COME TO ME.
WAM

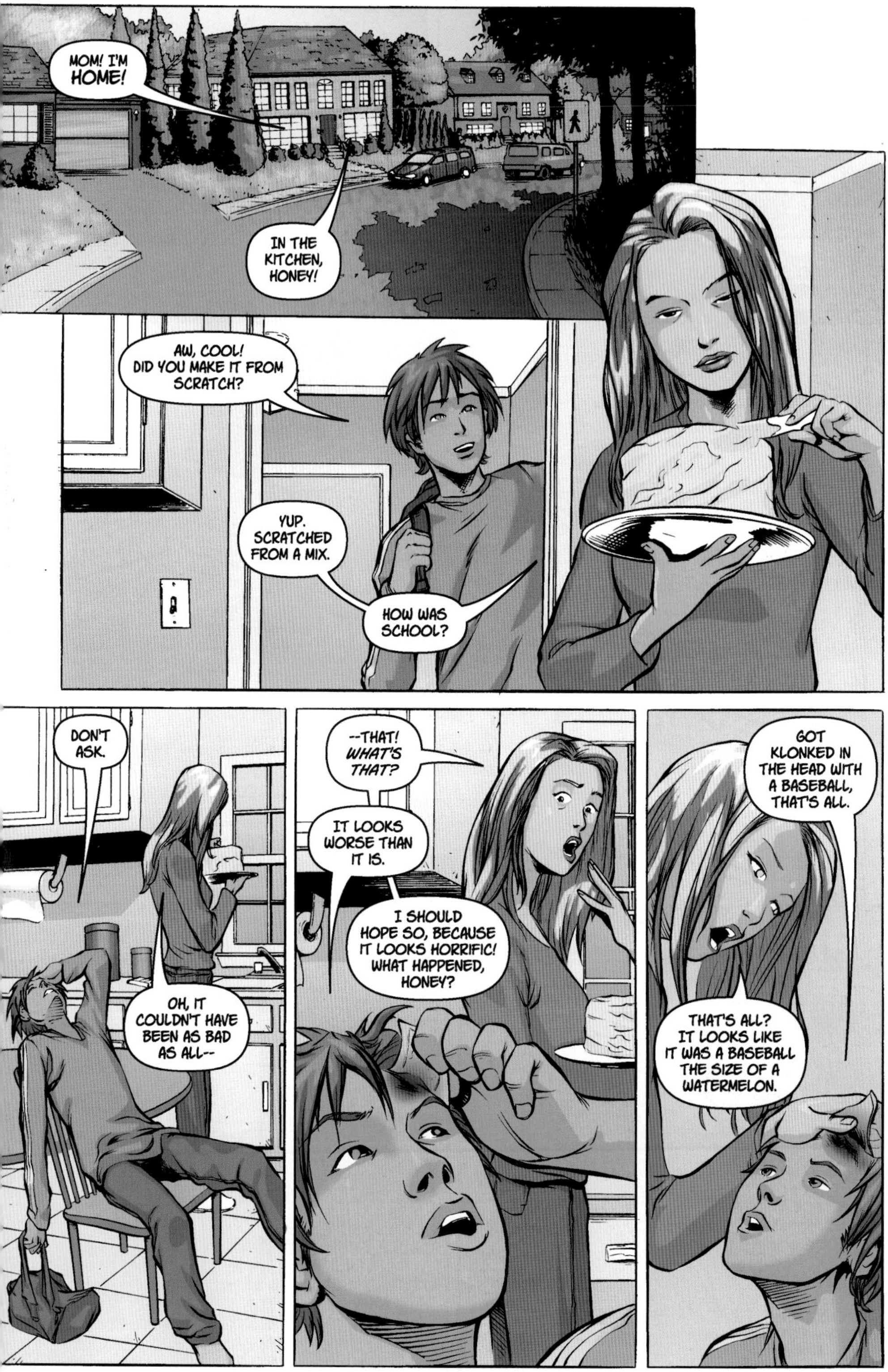
MOM! I'M HOME!
IN THE KITCHEN, HONEY!
AW, COOL! DID YOU MAKE IT FROM SCRATCH?
YUP. SCRATCHED FROM A MIX.
HOW WAS SCHOOL?
DON'T ASK.
OH, IT COULDN'T HAVE BEEN AS BAD AS ALL--
--THAT! WHAT'S THAT?
IT LOOKS WORSE THAN IT IS.
I SHOULD HOPE SO, BECAUSE IT LOOKS HORRIFIC! WHAT HAPPENED, HONEY?
GOT KLONKED IN THE HEAD WITH A BASEBALL, THAT'S ALL.
THAT'S ALL? IT LOOKS LIKE IT WAS A BASEBALL THE SIZE OF A WATERMELON.

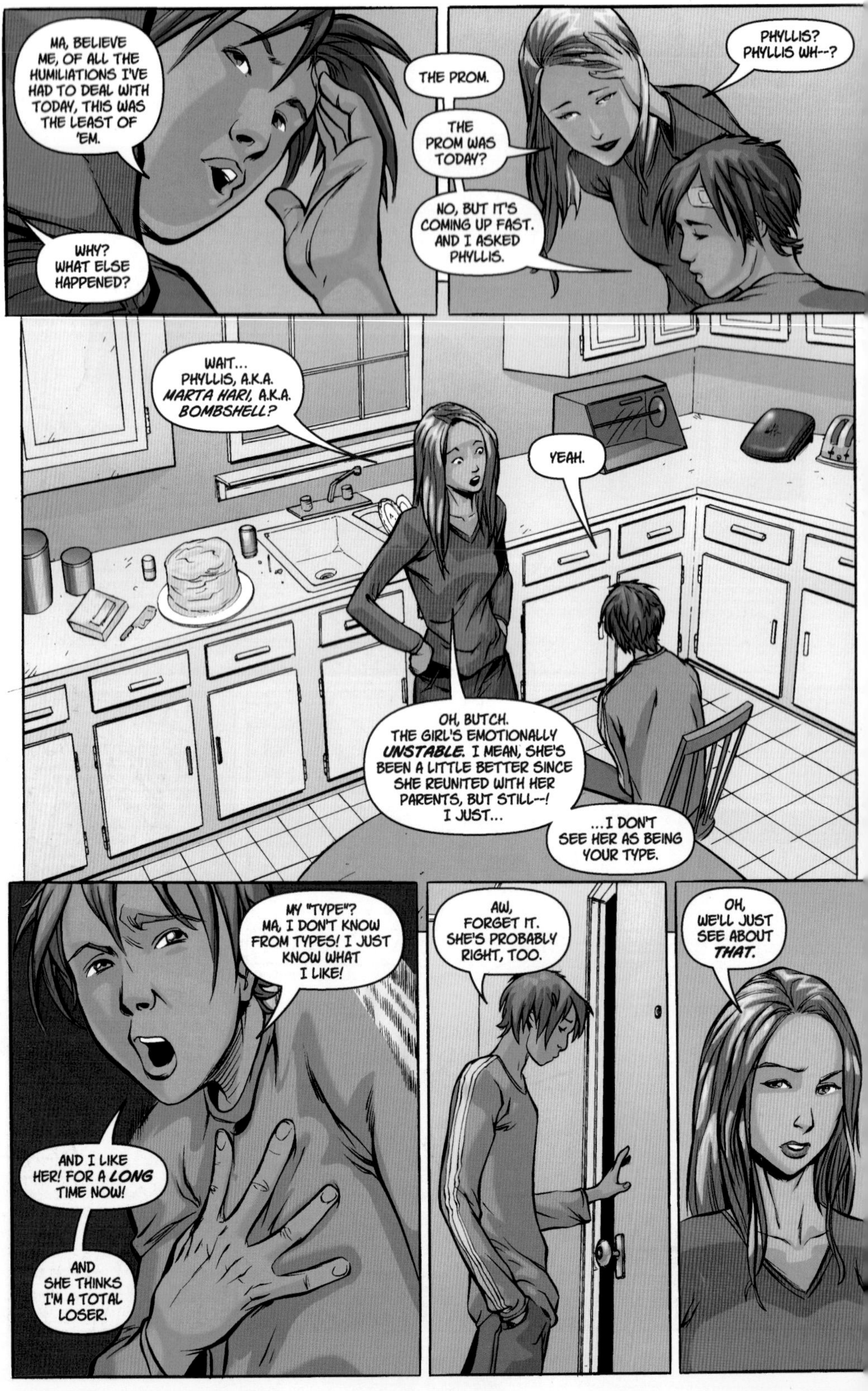
MA, BELIEVE ME, OF ALL THE HUMILIATIONS I'VE HAD TO DEAL WITH TODAY, THIS WAS THE LEAST OF 'EM.
WHY? WHAT ELSE HAPPENED?
THE PROM.
THE PROM WAS TODAY?
NO, BUT IT'S COMING UP FAST. AND I ASKED PHYLLIS.
PHYLLIS? PHYLLIS WH--?
WAIT... PHYLLIS, A.K.A. MARTA HARI, A.K.A. BOMBSHELL?
YEAH.
OH, BUTCH. THE GIRL'S EMOTIONALLY UNSTABLE. I MEAN, SHE'S BEEN A LITTLE BETTER SINCE SHE REUNITED WITH HER PARENTS, BUT STILL--! I JUST...
...I DON'T SEE HER AS BEING YOUR TYPE.
MY "TYPE"? MA, I DON'T KNOW FROM TYPES! I JUST KNOW WHAT I LIKE!
AND I LIKE HER! FOR A LONG TIME NOW!
AND SHE THINKS I'M A TOTAL LOSER.
AW, FORGET IT. SHE'S PROBABLY RIGHT, TOO.
OH, WE'LL JUST SEE ABOUT THAT.

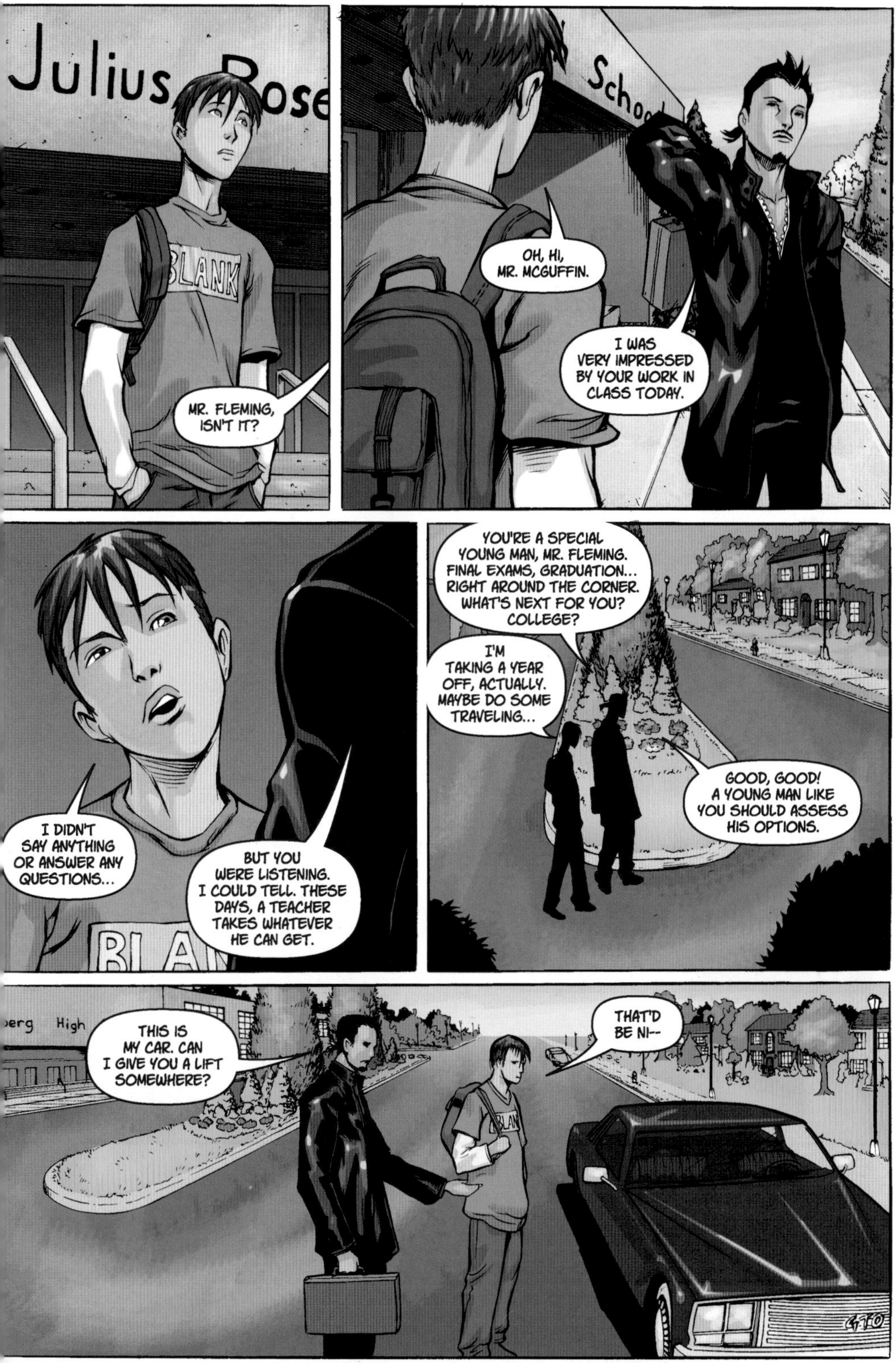
Julius Rose
BLANK
MR. FLEMING, ISN'T IT?
School
OH, HI, MR. MCGUFFIN.
I WAS VERY IMPRESSED BY YOUR WORK IN CLASS TODAY.
I DIDN'T SAY ANYTHING OR ANSWER ANY QUESTIONS...
BUT YOU WERE LISTENING. I COULD TELL. THESE DAYS, A TEACHER TAKES WHATEVER HE CAN GET.
YOU'RE A SPECIAL YOUNG MAN, MR. FLEMING. FINAL EXAMS, GRADUATION... RIGHT AROUND THE CORNER. WHAT'S NEXT FOR YOU? COLLEGE?
I'M TAKING A YEAR OFF, ACTUALLY. MAYBE DO SOME TRAVELING...
GOOD, GOOD! A YOUNG MAN LIKE YOU SHOULD ASSESS HIS OPTIONS.
High
THIS IS MY CAR. CAN I GIVE YOU A LIFT SOMEWHERE?
THAT'D BE NI--

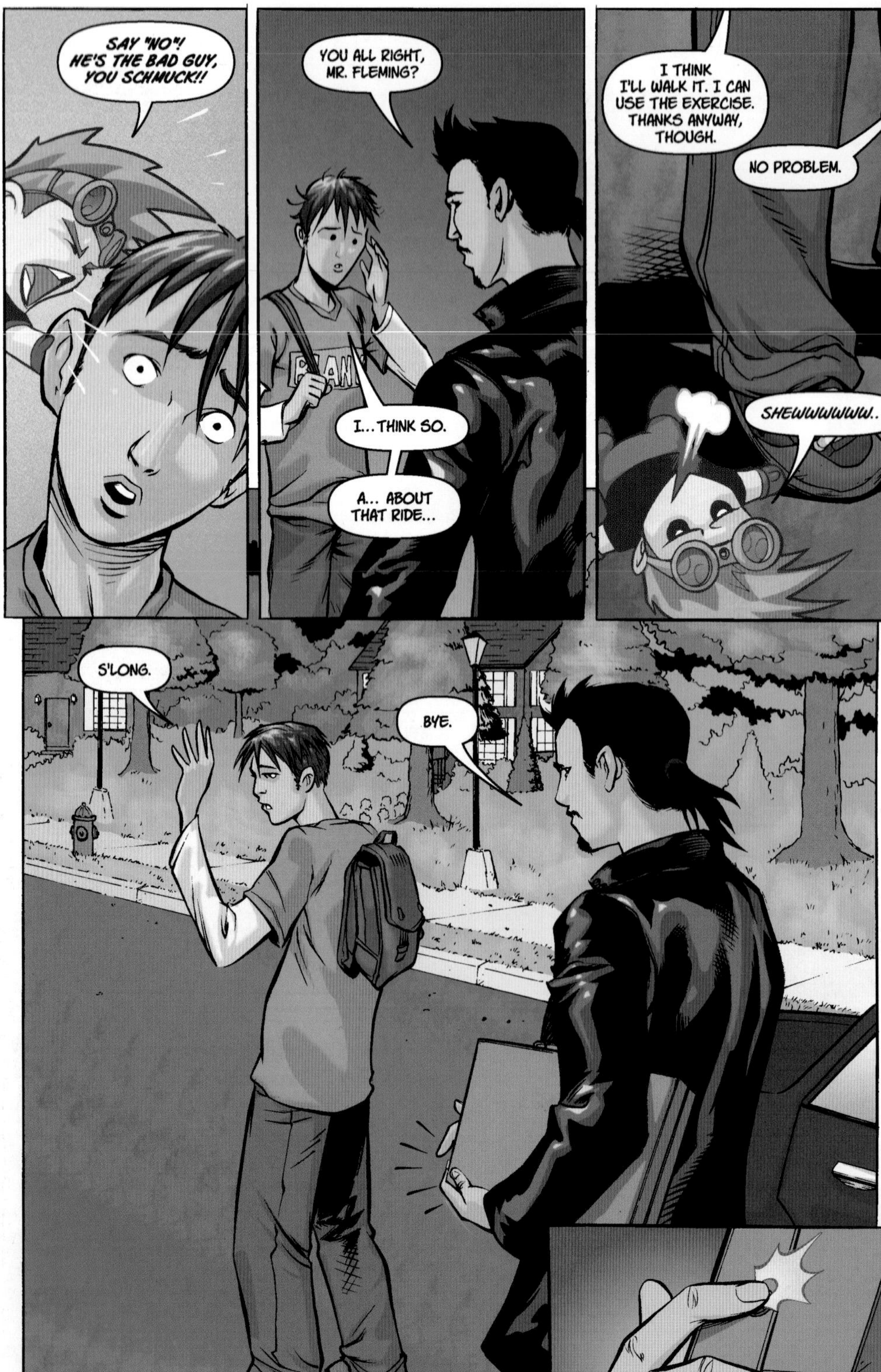
SAY "NO"! HE'S THE BAD GUY, YOU SCHMUCK!!
YOU ALL RIGHT, MR. FLEMING?
I... THINK SO.
A... ABOUT THAT RIDE...
I THINK I'LL WALK IT. I CAN USE THE EXERCISE. THANKS ANYWAY, THOUGH.
NO PROBLEM.
SHEWWWWWW...
S'LONG.
BYE.

THE THINGS A SUBCONSCIOUS HAS TO DO TO KEEP YOU SAFE.

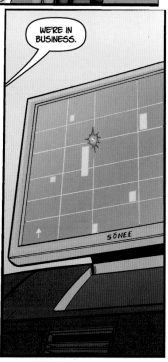

WE'RE IN BUSINESS.

SŌNEE

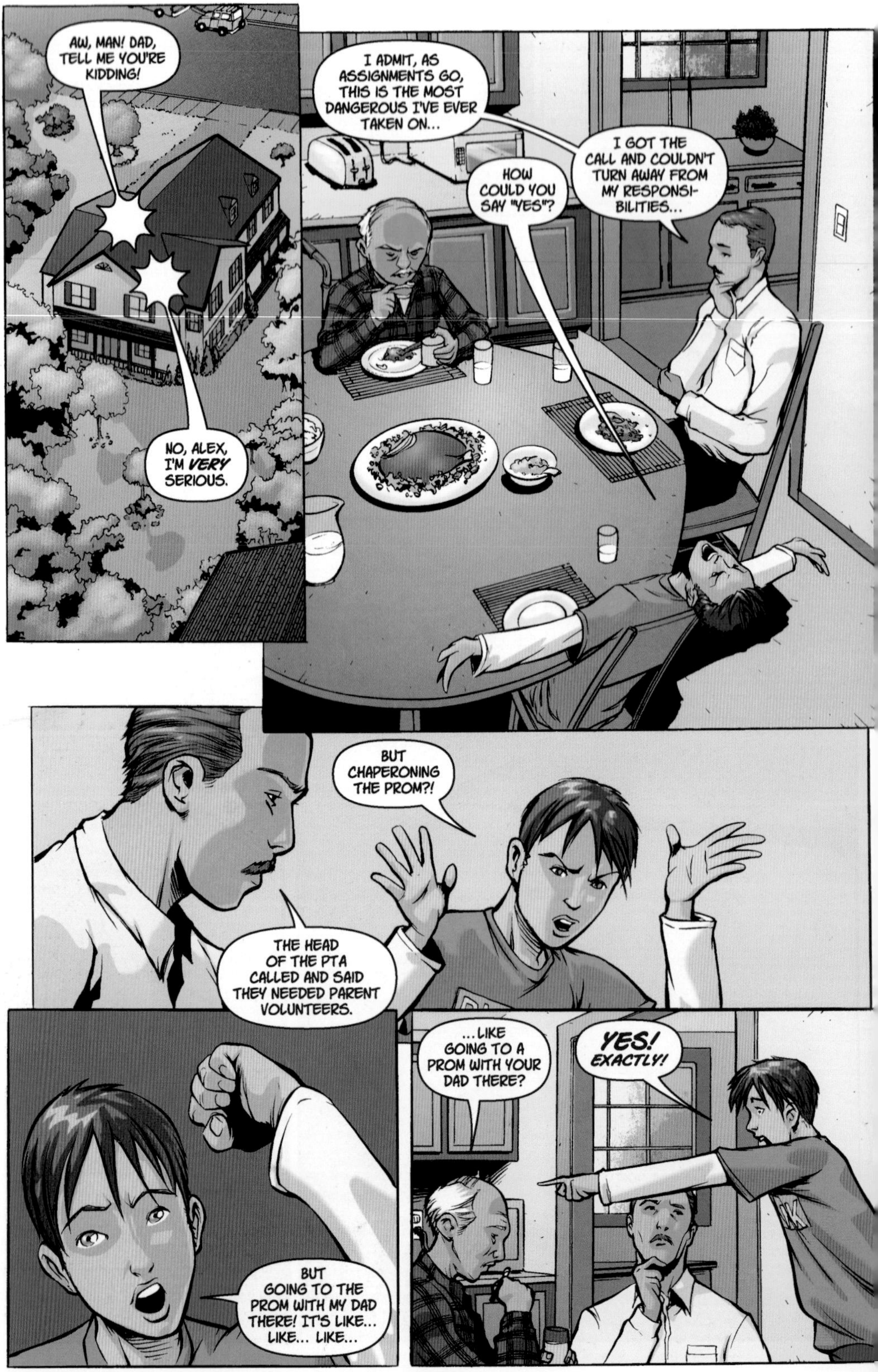
AW, MAN! DAD, TELL ME YOU'RE KIDDING!
NO, ALEX, I'M *VERY* SERIOUS.
I ADMIT, AS ASSIGNMENTS GO, THIS IS THE MOST DANGEROUS I'VE EVER TAKEN ON...
I GOT THE CALL AND COULDN'T TURN AWAY FROM MY RESPONSI-BILITIES...
HOW COULD YOU SAY "YES"?
BUT CHAPERONING THE PROM?!
THE HEAD OF THE PTA CALLED AND SAID THEY NEEDED PARENT VOLUNTEERS.
BUT GOING TO THE PROM WITH MY DAD THERE! IT'S LIKE... LIKE... LIKE...
...LIKE GOING TO A PROM WITH YOUR DAD THERE?
YES! EXACTLY!

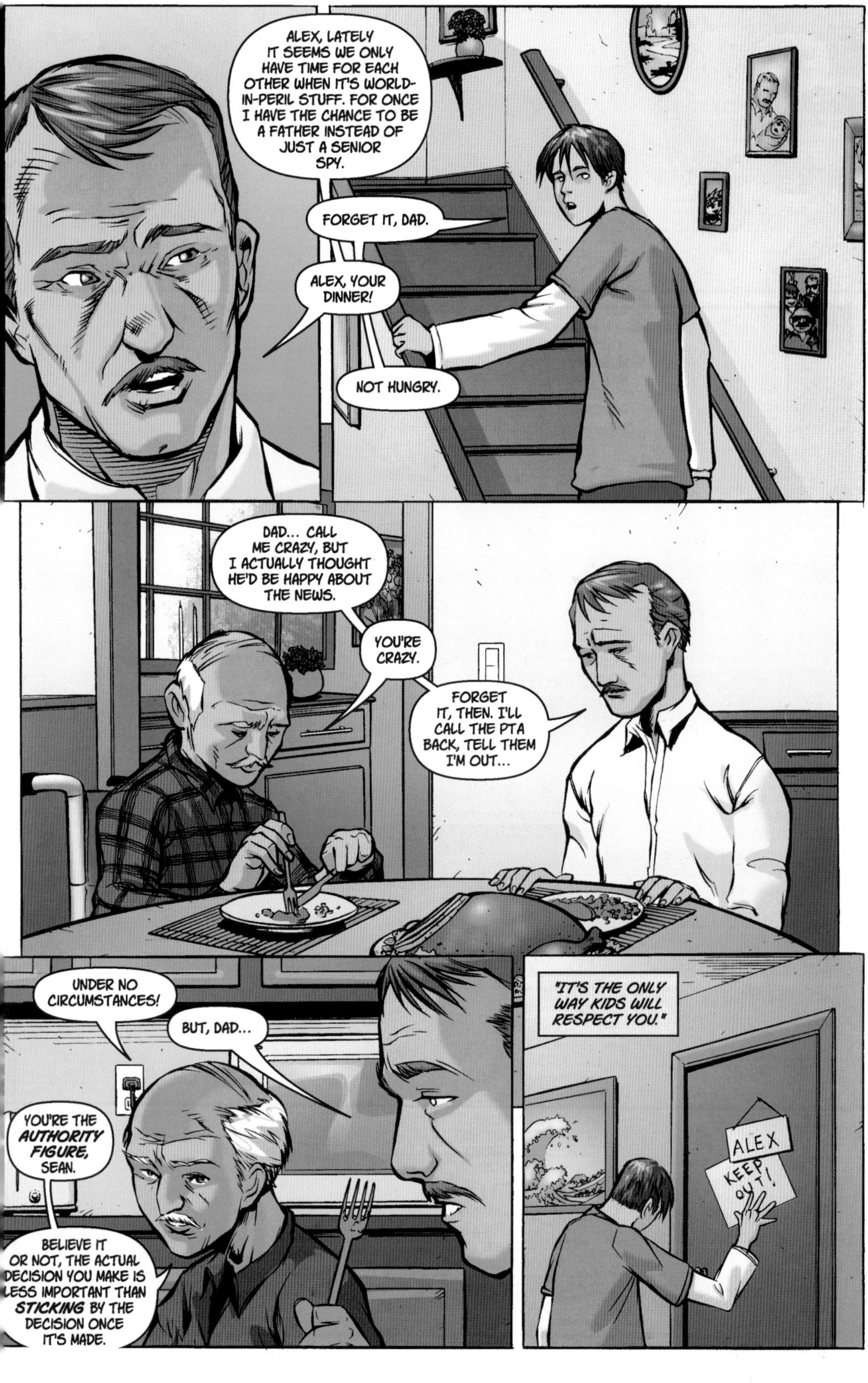
ALEX, LATELY IT SEEMS WE ONLY HAVE TIME FOR EACH OTHER WHEN IT'S WORLD-IN-PERIL STUFF. FOR ONCE I HAVE THE CHANCE TO BE A FATHER INSTEAD OF JUST A SENIOR SPY.
FORGET IT, DAD.
ALEX, YOUR DINNER!
NOT HUNGRY.
DAD... CALL ME CRAZY, BUT I ACTUALLY THOUGHT HE'D BE HAPPY ABOUT THE NEWS.
YOU'RE CRAZY.
FORGET IT, THEN. I'LL CALL THE PTA BACK, TELL THEM I'M OUT...
UNDER NO CIRCUMSTANCES!
BUT, DAD...
YOU'RE THE AUTHORITY FIGURE, SEAN.
BELIEVE IT OR NOT, THE ACTUAL DECISION YOU MAKE IS LESS IMPORTANT THAN STICKING BY THE DECISION ONCE IT'S MADE.
"IT'S THE ONLY WAY KIDS WILL RESPECT YOU."
ALEX
KEEP OUT!

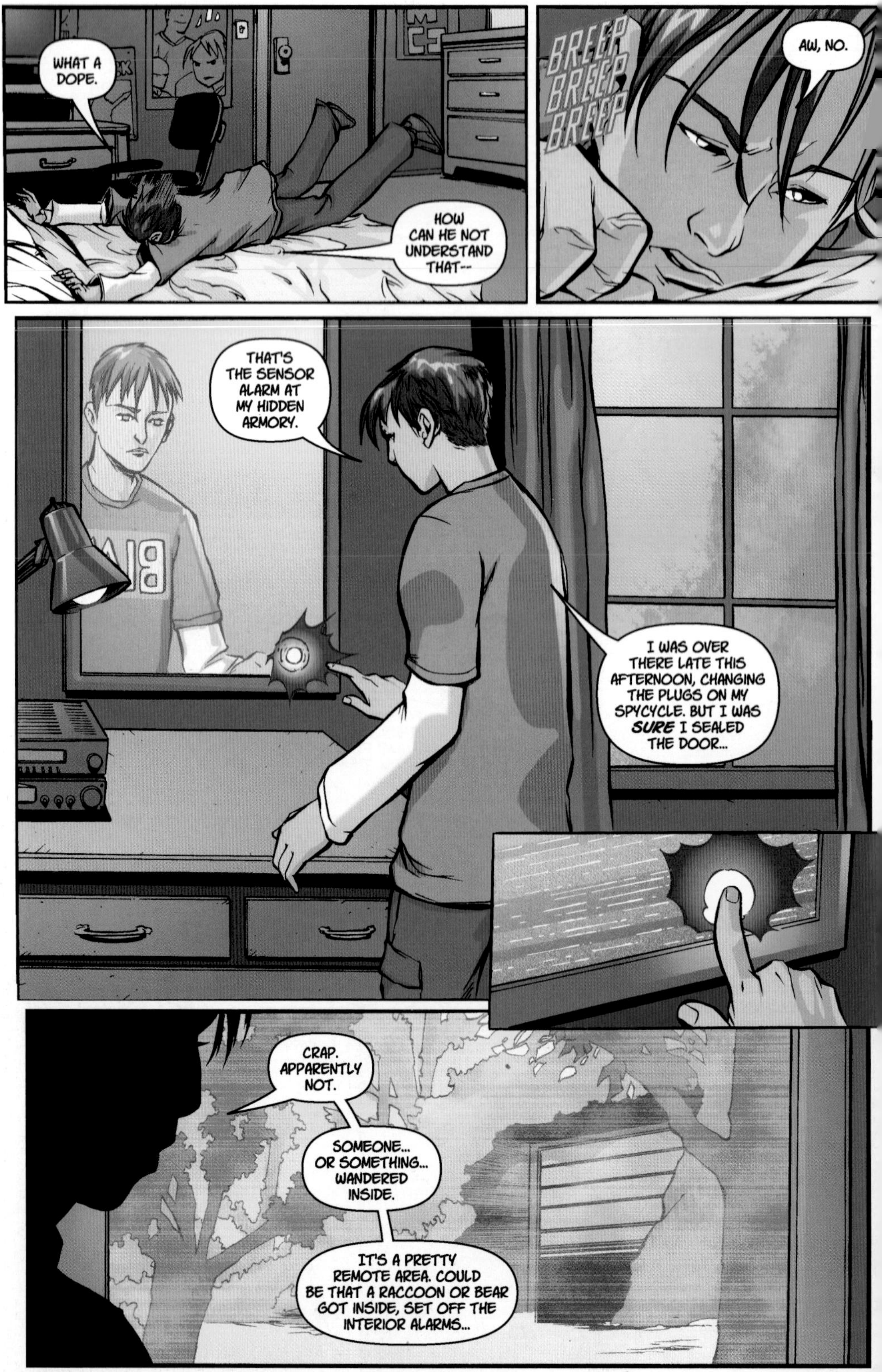
WHAT A DOPE.
HOW CAN HE NOT UNDERSTAND THAT--
BREEP BREEP BREEP
AW, NO.
THAT'S THE SENSOR ALARM AT MY HIDDEN ARMORY.
I WAS OVER THERE LATE THIS AFTERNOON, CHANGING THE PLUGS ON MY SPYCYCLE. BUT I WAS SURE I SEALED THE DOOR...
CRAP. APPARENTLY NOT.
SOMEONE... OR SOMETHING... WANDERED INSIDE.
IT'S A PRETTY REMOTE AREA. COULD BE THAT A RACCOON OR BEAR GOT INSIDE, SET OFF THE INTERIOR ALARMS...

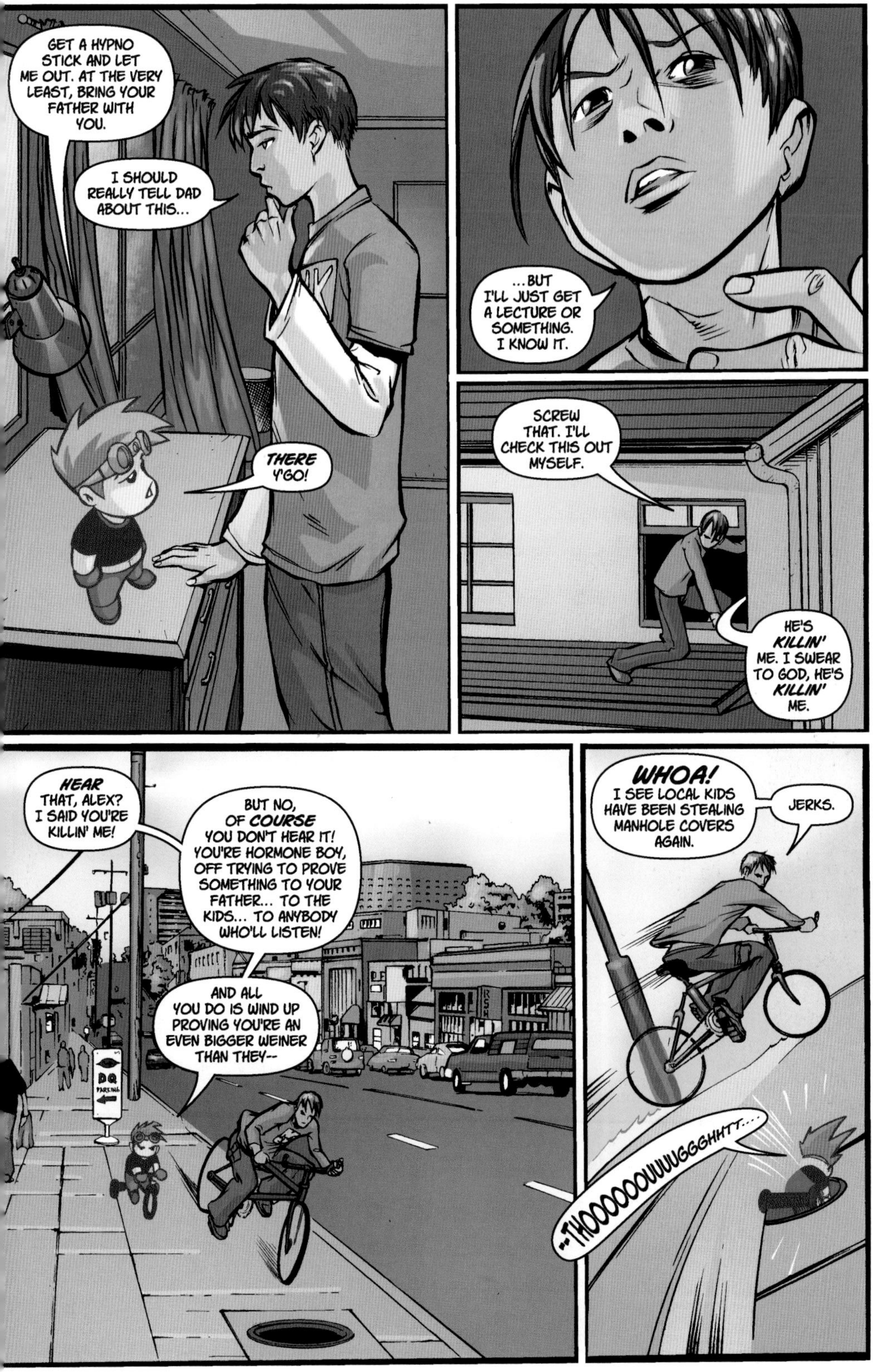
GET A HYPNO STICK AND LET ME OUT. AT THE VERY LEAST, BRING YOUR FATHER WITH YOU.
I SHOULD REALLY TELL DAD ABOUT THIS...
THERE Y'GO!
...BUT I'LL JUST GET A LECTURE OR SOMETHING. I KNOW IT.
SCREW THAT. I'LL CHECK THIS OUT MYSELF.
HE'S KILLIN' ME. I SWEAR TO GOD, HE'S KILLIN' ME.
HEAR THAT, ALEX? I SAID YOU'RE KILLIN' ME!
BUT NO, OF COURSE YOU DON'T HEAR IT! YOU'RE HORMONE BOY, OFF TRYING TO PROVE SOMETHING TO YOUR FATHER... TO THE KIDS... TO ANYBODY WHO'LL LISTEN!
AND ALL YOU DO IS WIND UP PROVING YOU'RE AN EVEN BIGGER WEINER THAN THEY--
DQ PARKING
WHOA! I SEE LOCAL KIDS HAVE BEEN STEALING MANHOLE COVERS AGAIN.
JERKS.
--THOOOOOOUUUUGGGHHTT....

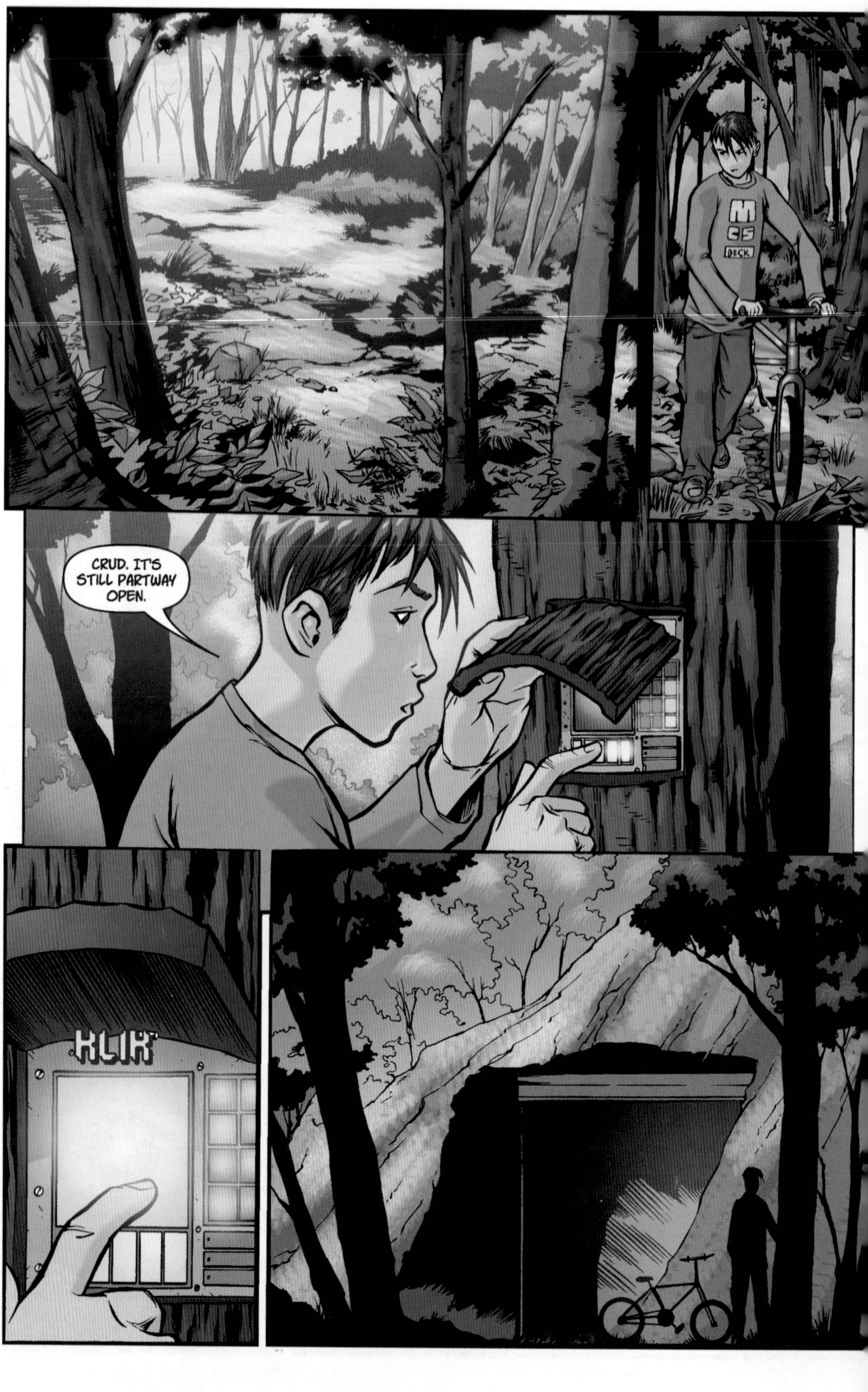
CRUD. IT'S STILL PARTWAY OPEN.
KLIK

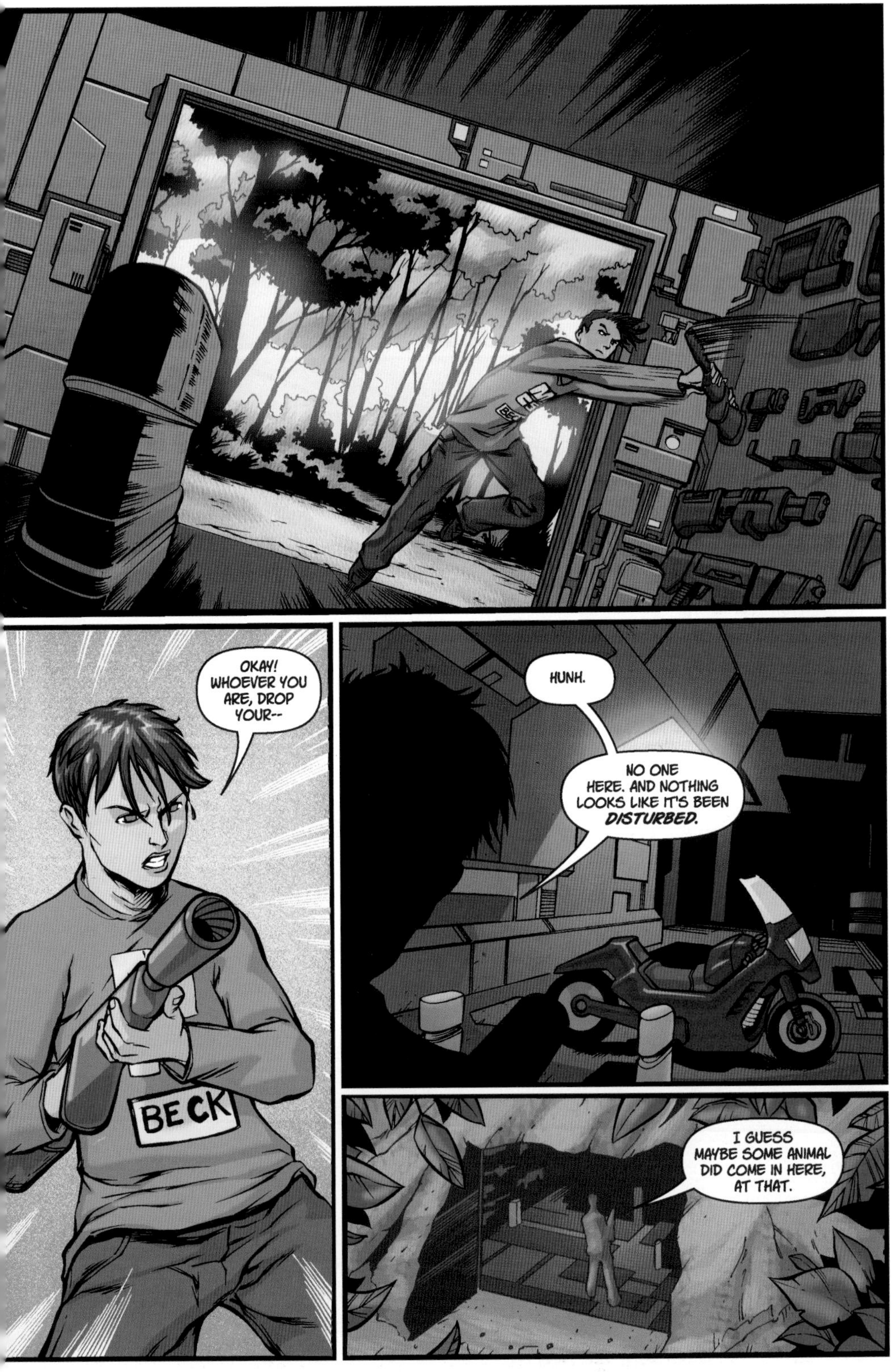
OKAY! WHOEVER YOU ARE, DROP YOUR--
BECK
HUNH.
NO ONE HERE. AND NOTHING LOOKS LIKE IT'S BEEN DISTURBED.
I GUESS MAYBE SOME ANIMAL DID COME IN HERE, AT THAT.

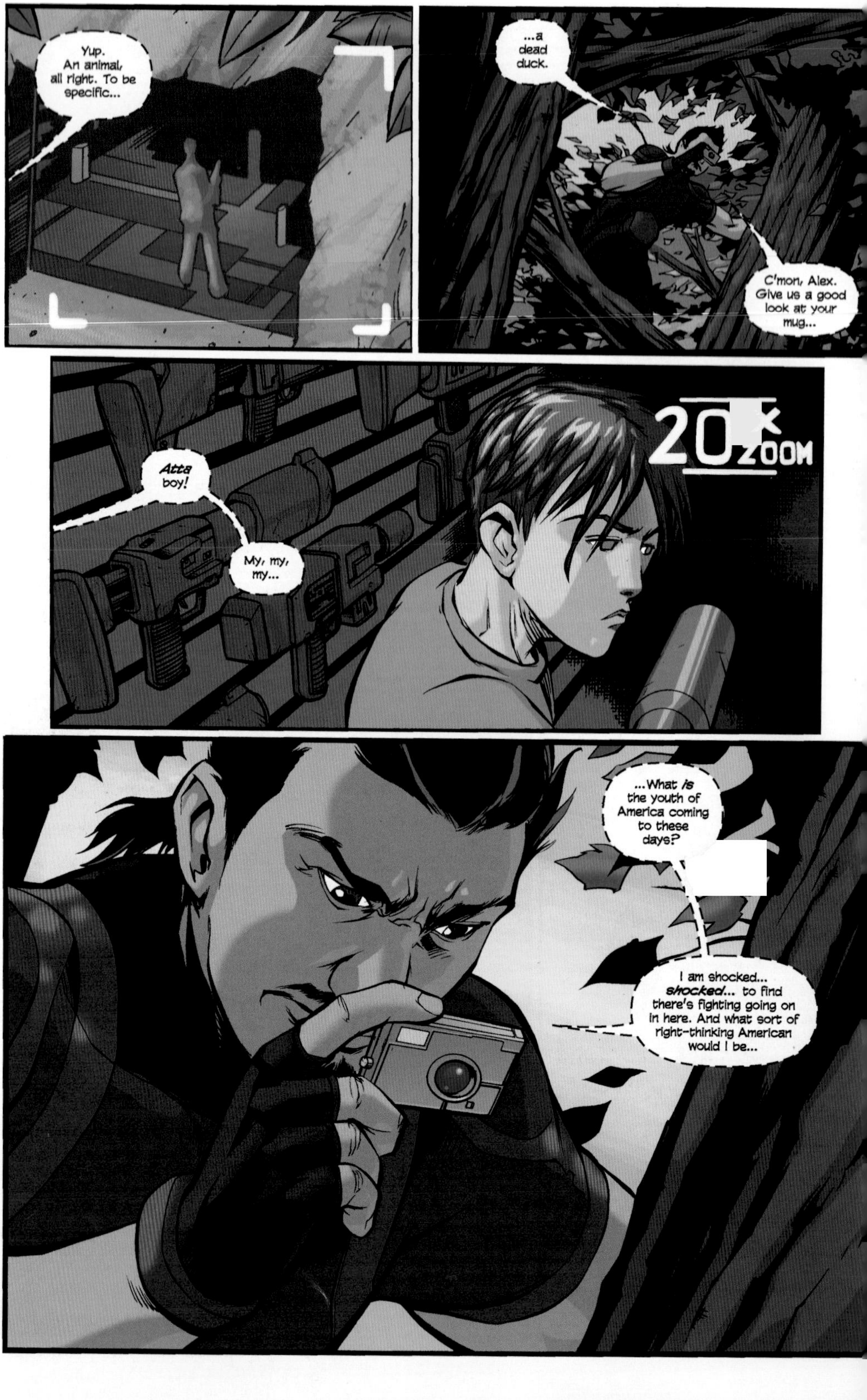
Yup. An animal, all right. To be specific...
...a dead duck.
C'mon, Alex. Give us a good look at your mug...
20x ZOOM
Atta boy!
My, my, my...
...What *is* the youth of America coming to these days?
I am shocked... ***shocked***... to find there's fighting going on in here. And what sort of right-thinking American would I be...

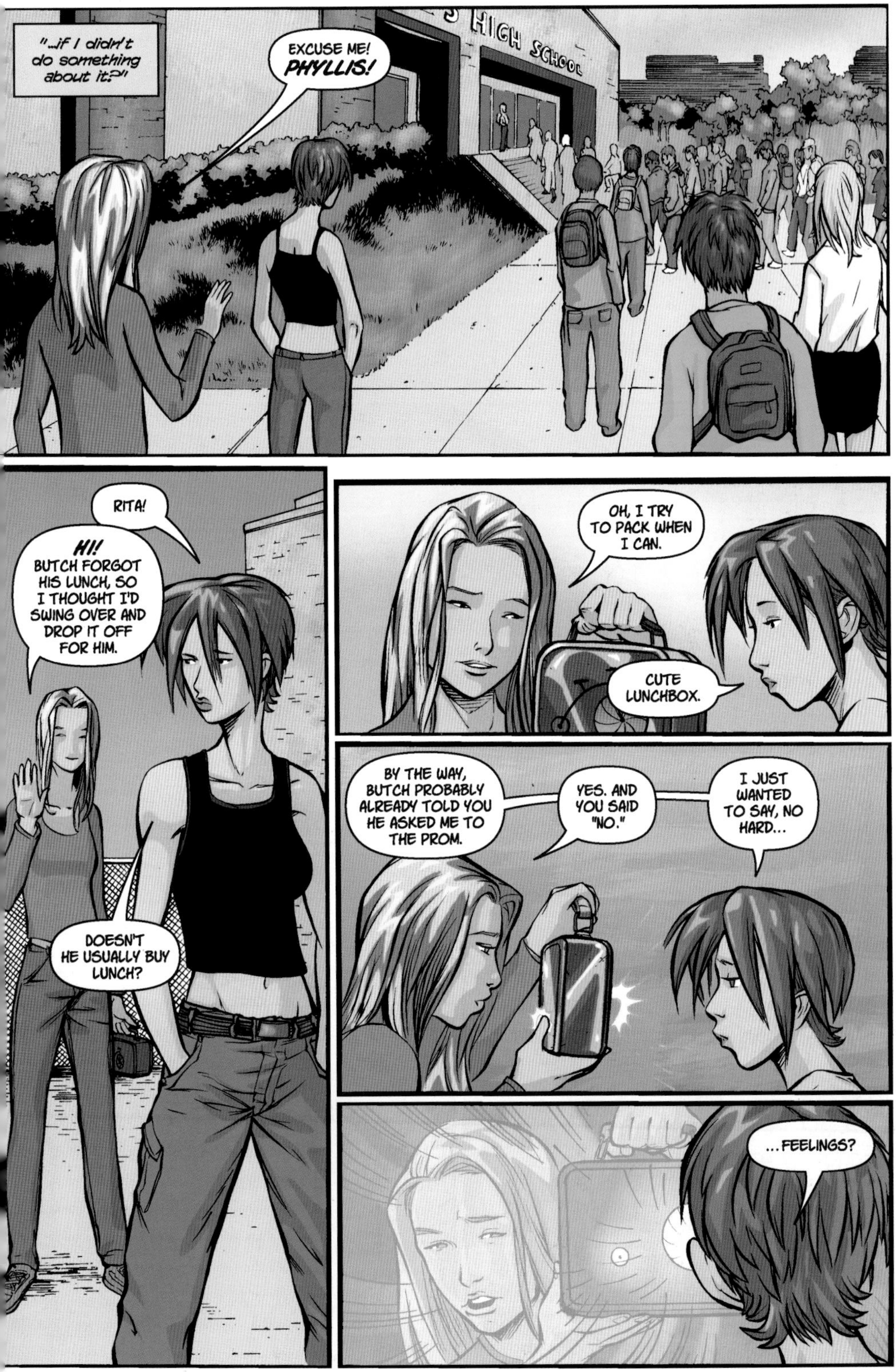
"...if I didn't do something about it?"
EXCUSE ME! PHYLLIS!
HIGH SCHOOL
RITA!
HI! BUTCH FORGOT HIS LUNCH, SO I THOUGHT I'D SWING OVER AND DROP IT OFF FOR HIM.
DOESN'T HE USUALLY BUY LUNCH?
OH, I TRY TO PACK WHEN I CAN.
CUTE LUNCHBOX.
BY THE WAY, BUTCH PROBABLY ALREADY TOLD YOU HE ASKED ME TO THE PROM.
YES. AND YOU SAID "NO."
I JUST WANTED TO SAY, NO HARD...
...FEELINGS?

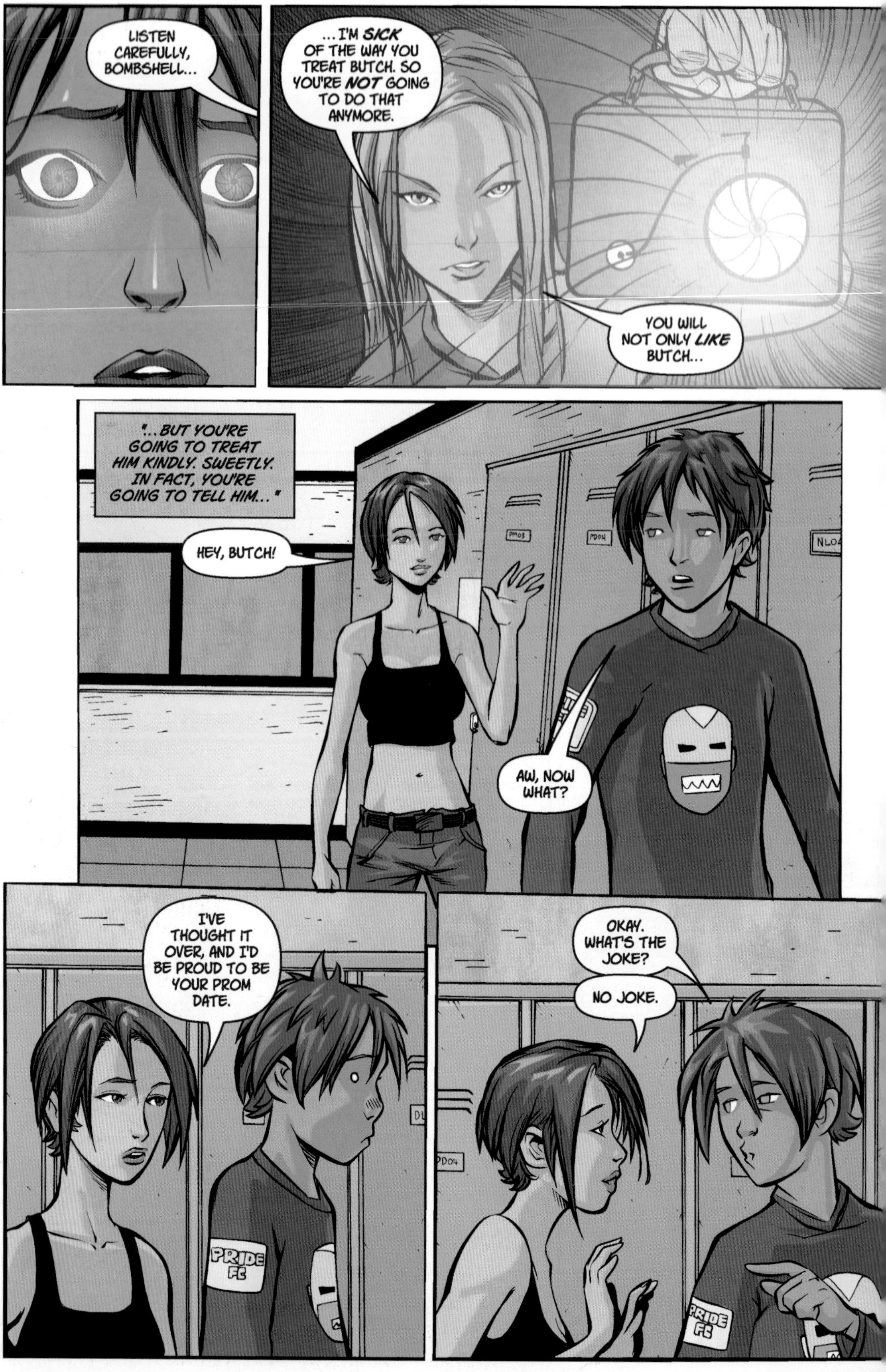
LISTEN CAREFULLY, BOMBSHELL...
...I'M *SICK* OF THE WAY YOU TREAT BUTCH. SO YOU'RE *NOT* GOING TO DO THAT ANYMORE.
YOU WILL NOT ONLY *LIKE* BUTCH...
"...BUT YOU'RE GOING TO TREAT HIM KINDLY. SWEETLY. IN FACT, YOU'RE GOING TO TELL HIM..."
HEY, BUTCH!
AW, NOW WHAT?
I'VE THOUGHT IT OVER, AND I'D BE PROUD TO BE YOUR PROM DATE.
OKAY. WHAT'S THE JOKE?
NO JOKE.

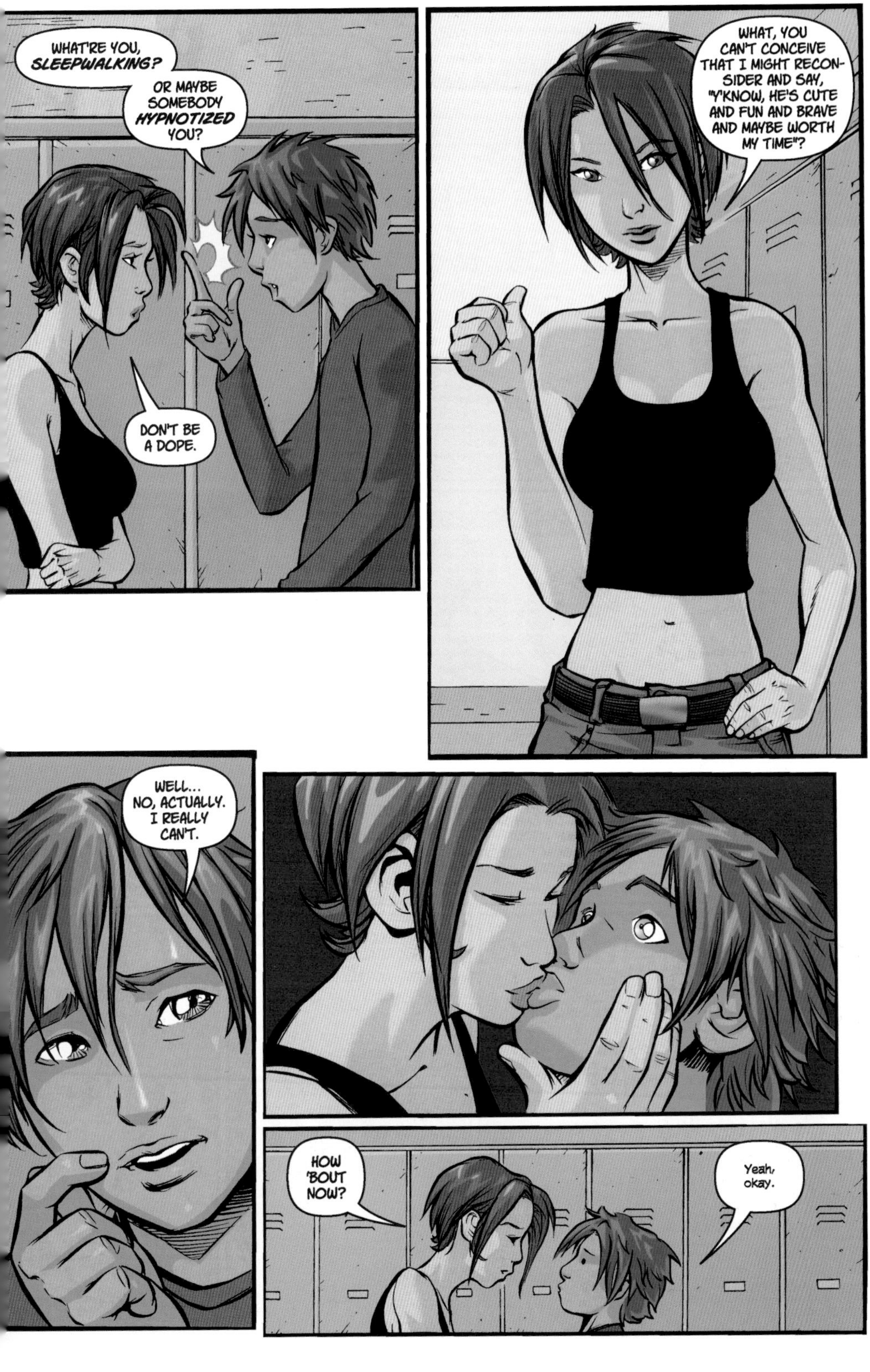

WHAT'RE YOU, SLEEPWALKING?
OR MAYBE SOMEBODY HYPNOTIZED YOU?
DON'T BE A DOPE.
WHAT, YOU CAN'T CONCEIVE THAT I MIGHT RECON-SIDER AND SAY, "Y'KNOW, HE'S CUTE AND FUN AND BRAVE AND MAYBE WORTH MY TIME"?
WELL... NO, ACTUALLY. I REALLY CAN'T.
HOW 'BOUT NOW?
Yeah, okay.

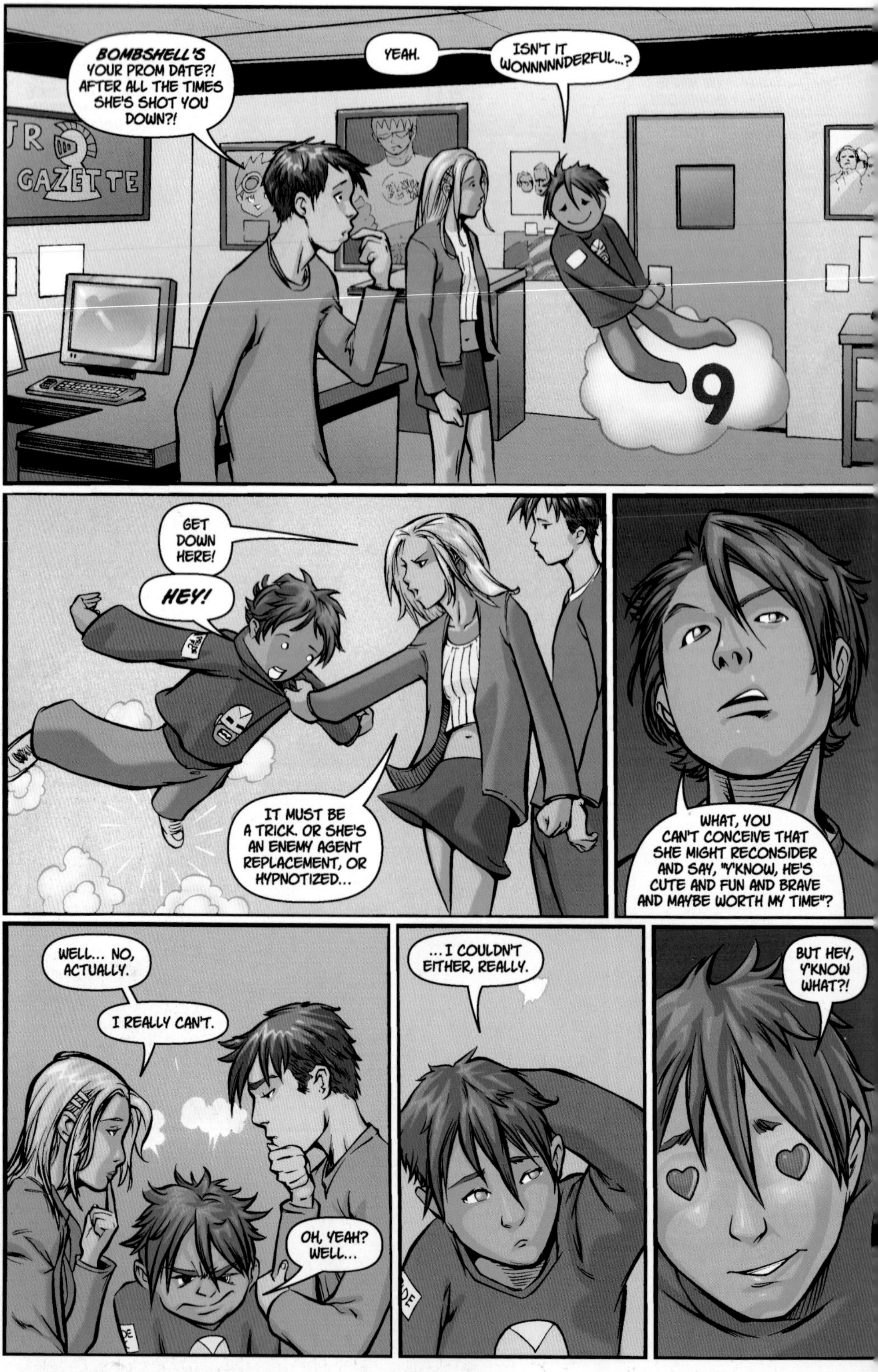

BOMBSHELL'S YOUR PROM DATE?! AFTER ALL THE TIMES SHE'S SHOT YOU DOWN?!
YEAH.
ISN'T IT WONNNNNDERFUL...?
GAZETTE
9
GET DOWN HERE!
HEY!
IT MUST BE A TRICK. OR SHE'S AN ENEMY AGENT REPLACEMENT, OR HYPNOTIZED...
WHAT, YOU CAN'T CONCEIVE THAT SHE MIGHT RECONSIDER AND SAY, "Y'KNOW, HE'S CUTE AND FUN AND BRAVE AND MAYBE WORTH MY TIME"?
WELL... NO, ACTUALLY.
I REALLY CAN'T.
OH, YEAH? WELL...
...I COULDN'T EITHER, REALLY.
BUT HEY, Y'KNOW WHAT?!

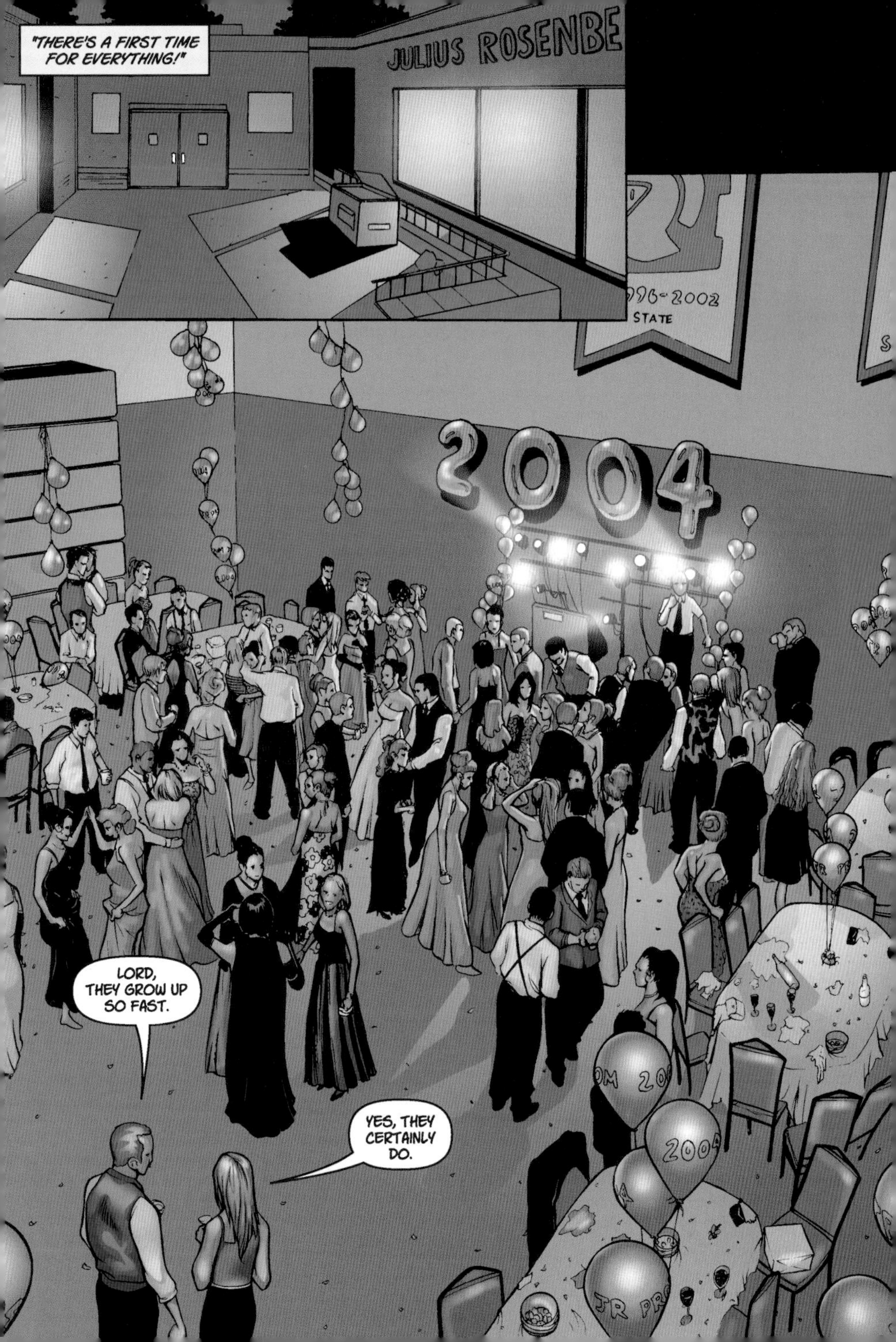
"THERE'S A FIRST TIME FOR EVERYTHING!"
JULIUS ROSENBE
2004
LORD, THEY GROW UP SO FAST.
YES, THEY CERTAINLY DO.

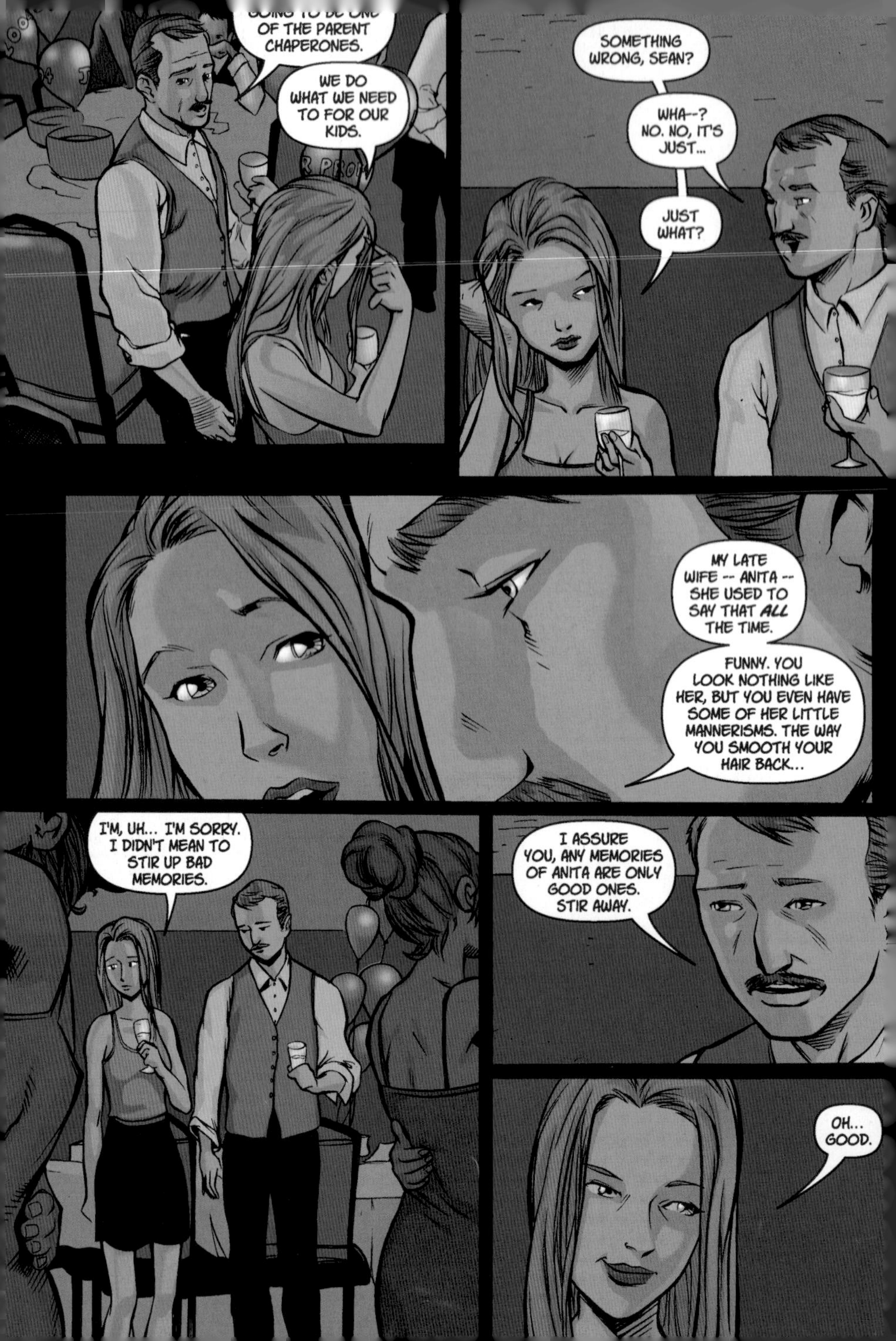
OF THE PARENT CHAPERONES.
WE DO WHAT WE NEED TO FOR OUR KIDS.
SOMETHING WRONG, SEAN?
WHA--? NO. NO, IT'S JUST...
JUST WHAT?
MY LATE WIFE -- ANITA -- SHE USED TO SAY THAT *ALL* THE TIME.
FUNNY. YOU LOOK NOTHING LIKE HER, BUT YOU EVEN HAVE SOME OF HER LITTLE MANNERISMS. THE WAY YOU SMOOTH YOUR HAIR BACK...
I'M, UH... I'M SORRY. I DIDN'T MEAN TO STIR UP BAD MEMORIES.
I ASSURE YOU, ANY MEMORIES OF ANITA ARE ONLY GOOD ONES. STIR AWAY.
OH... GOOD.

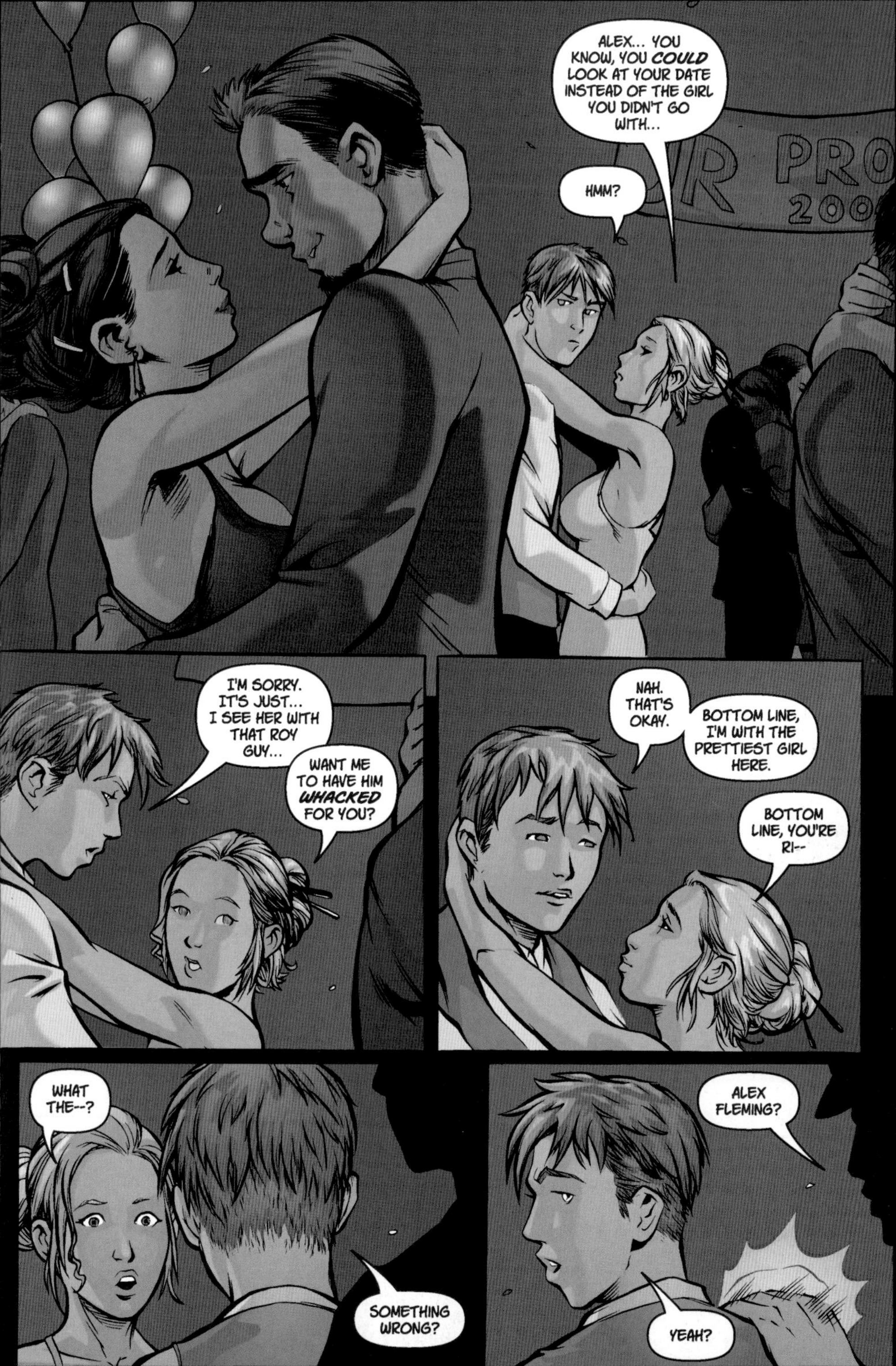
ALEX... YOU KNOW, YOU **COULD** LOOK AT YOUR DATE INSTEAD OF THE GIRL YOU DIDN'T GO WITH...
HMM?
JR PRO
200
I'M SORRY. IT'S JUST... I SEE HER WITH THAT ROY GUY...
WANT ME TO HAVE HIM ***WHACKED*** FOR YOU?
NAH. THAT'S OKAY.
BOTTOM LINE, I'M WITH THE PRETTIEST GIRL HERE.
BOTTOM LINE, YOU'RE RI--
WHAT THE--?
SOMETHING WRONG?
ALEX FLEMING?
YEAH?

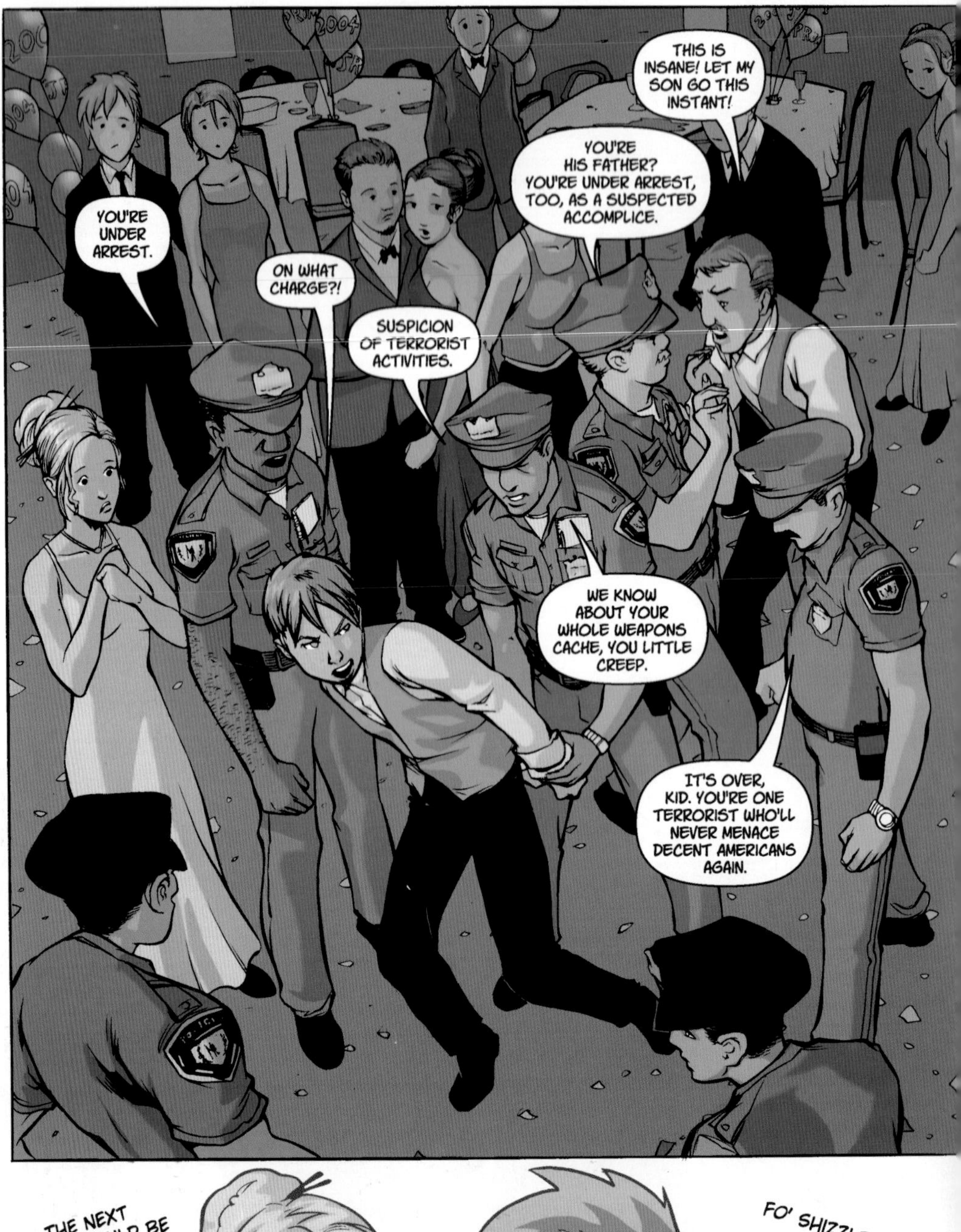
YOU'RE UNDER ARREST.
ON WHAT CHARGE?!
SUSPICION OF TERRORIST ACTIVITIES.
THIS IS INSANE! LET MY SON GO THIS INSTANT!
YOU'RE HIS FATHER? YOU'RE UNDER ARREST, TOO, AS A SUSPECTED ACCOMPLICE.
WE KNOW ABOUT YOUR WHOLE WEAPONS CACHE, YOU LITTLE CREEP.
IT'S OVER, KID. YOU'RE ONE TERRORIST WHO'LL NEVER MENACE DECENT AMERICANS AGAIN.

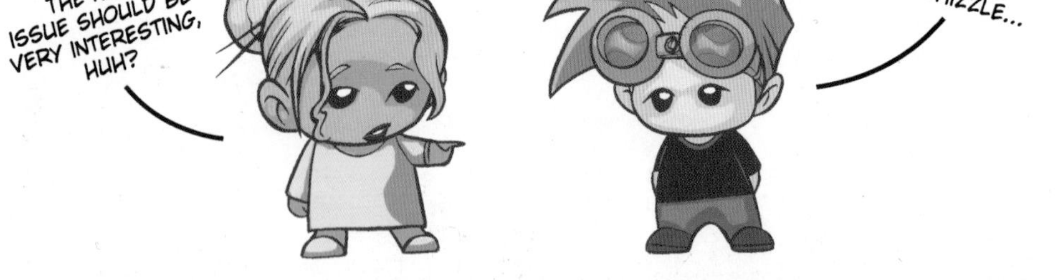
THE NEXT ISSUE SHOULD BE VERY INTERESTING, HUH?
FO' SHIZZLE...

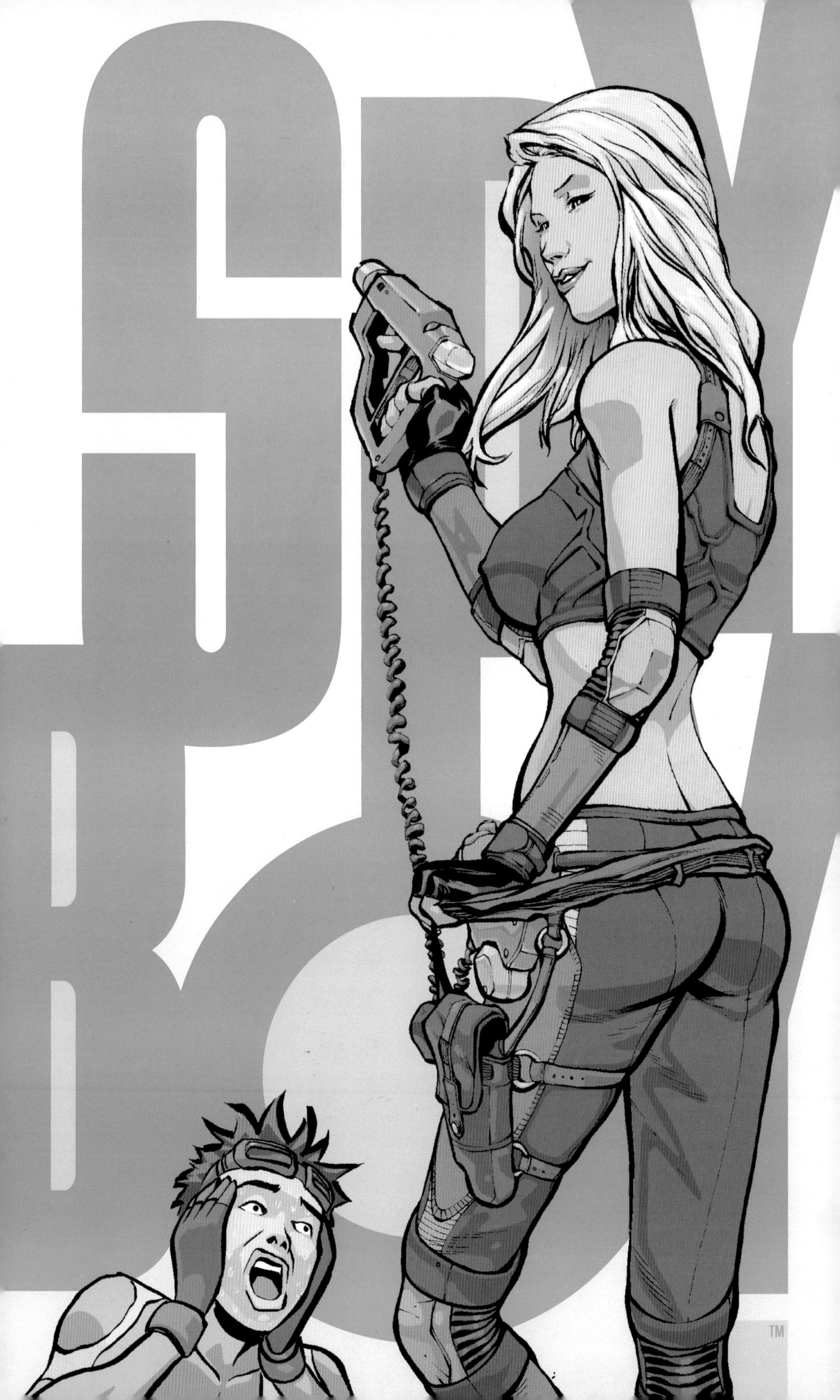
SPY
BOY
TM

SPY BOY™

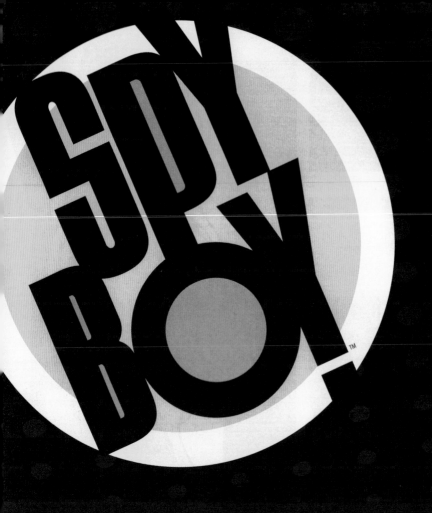

Part 3

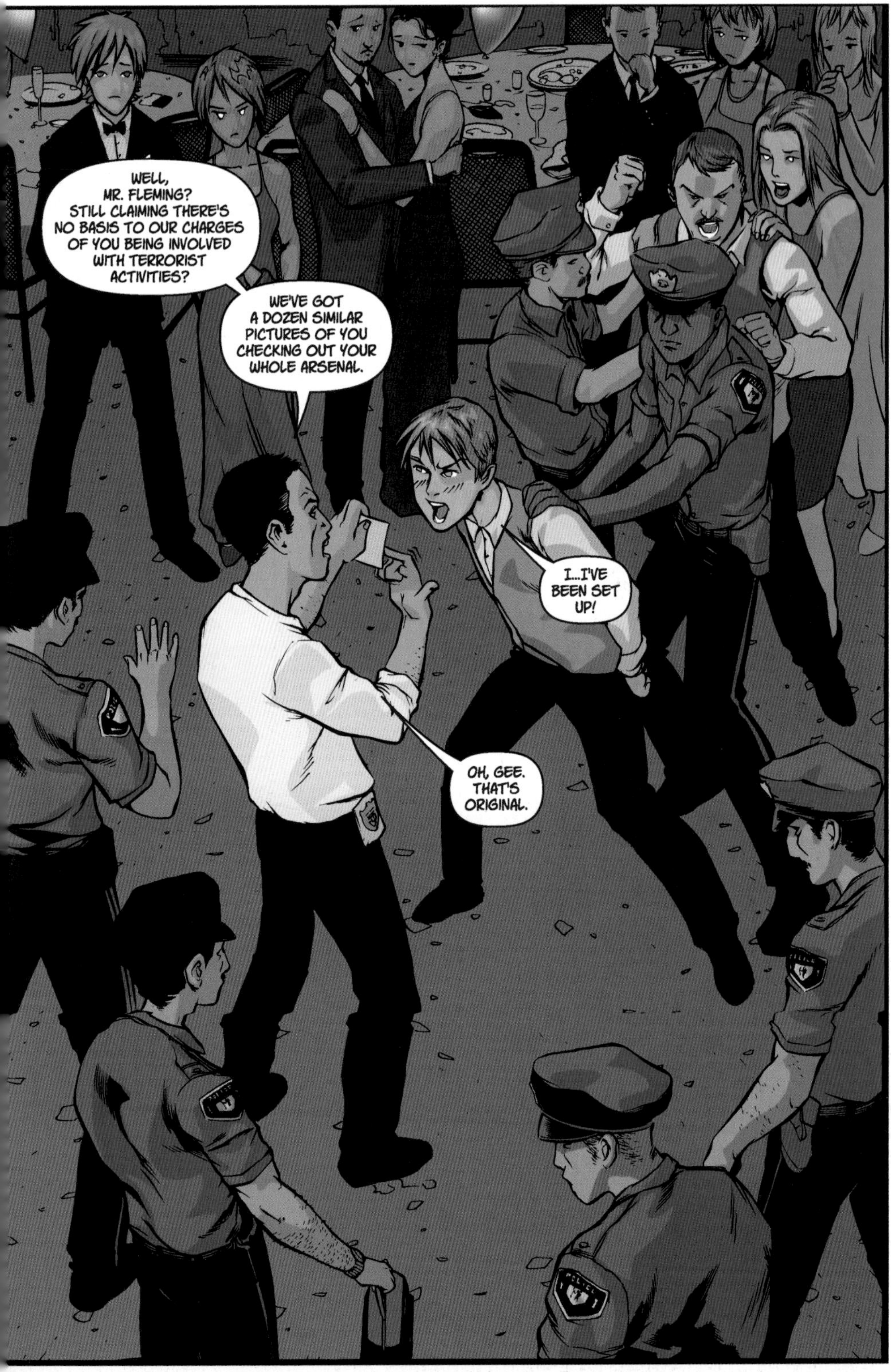
WELL, MR. FLEMING? STILL CLAIMING THERE'S NO BASIS TO OUR CHARGES OF YOU BEING INVOLVED WITH TERRORIST ACTIVITIES?
WE'VE GOT A DOZEN SIMILAR PICTURES OF YOU CHECKING OUT YOUR WHOLE ARSENAL.
I...I'VE BEEN SET UP!
OH, GEE. THAT'S ORIGINAL.

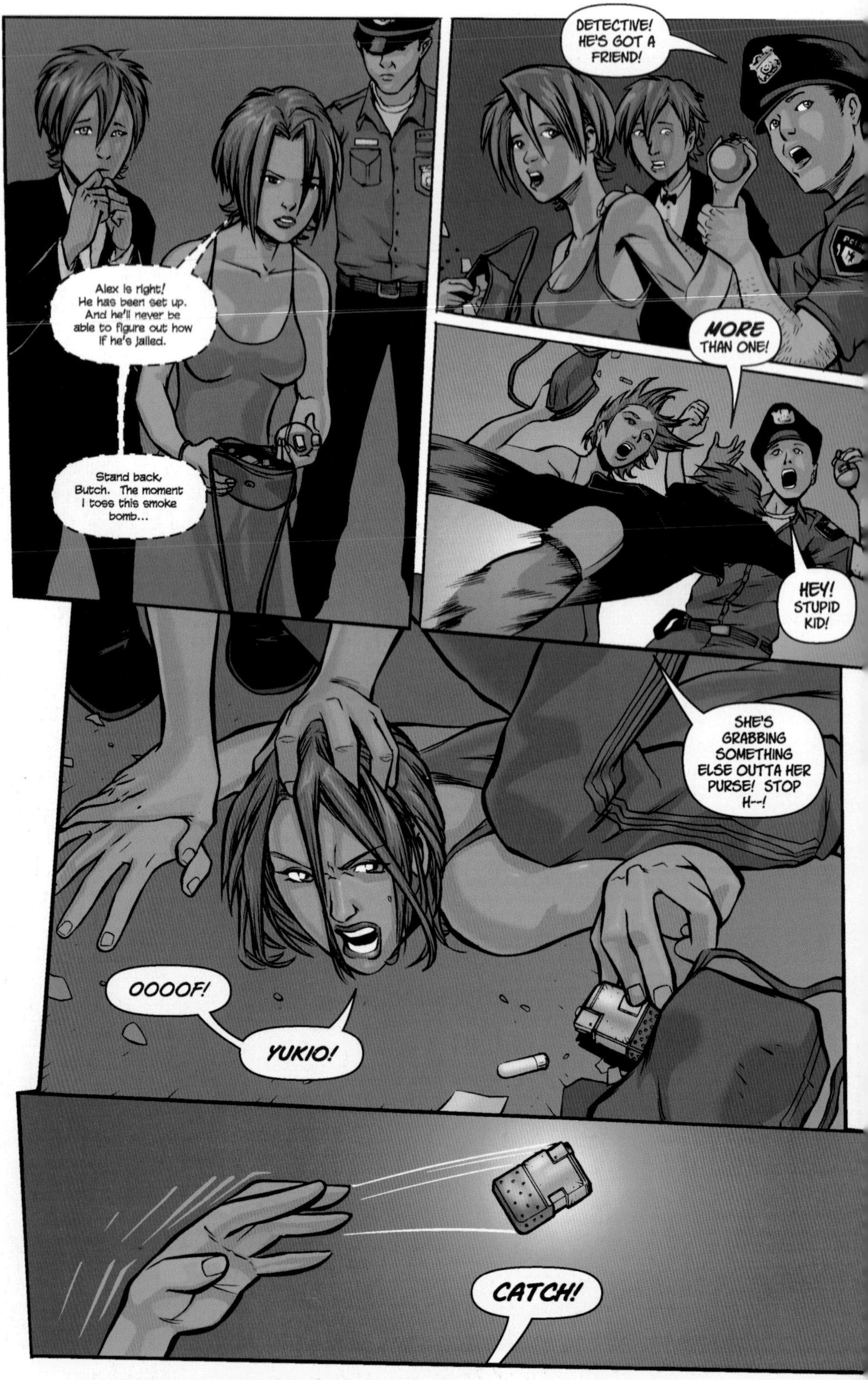

Alex is right! He has been set up. And he'll never be able to figure out how if he's jailed.
Stand back, Butch. The moment I toss this smoke bomb...
DETECTIVE! HE'S GOT A FRIEND!
MORE THAN ONE!
HEY! STUPID KID!
SHE'S GRABBING SOMETHING ELSE OUTTA HER PURSE! STOP H--!
OOOOF!
YUKIO!
CATCH!

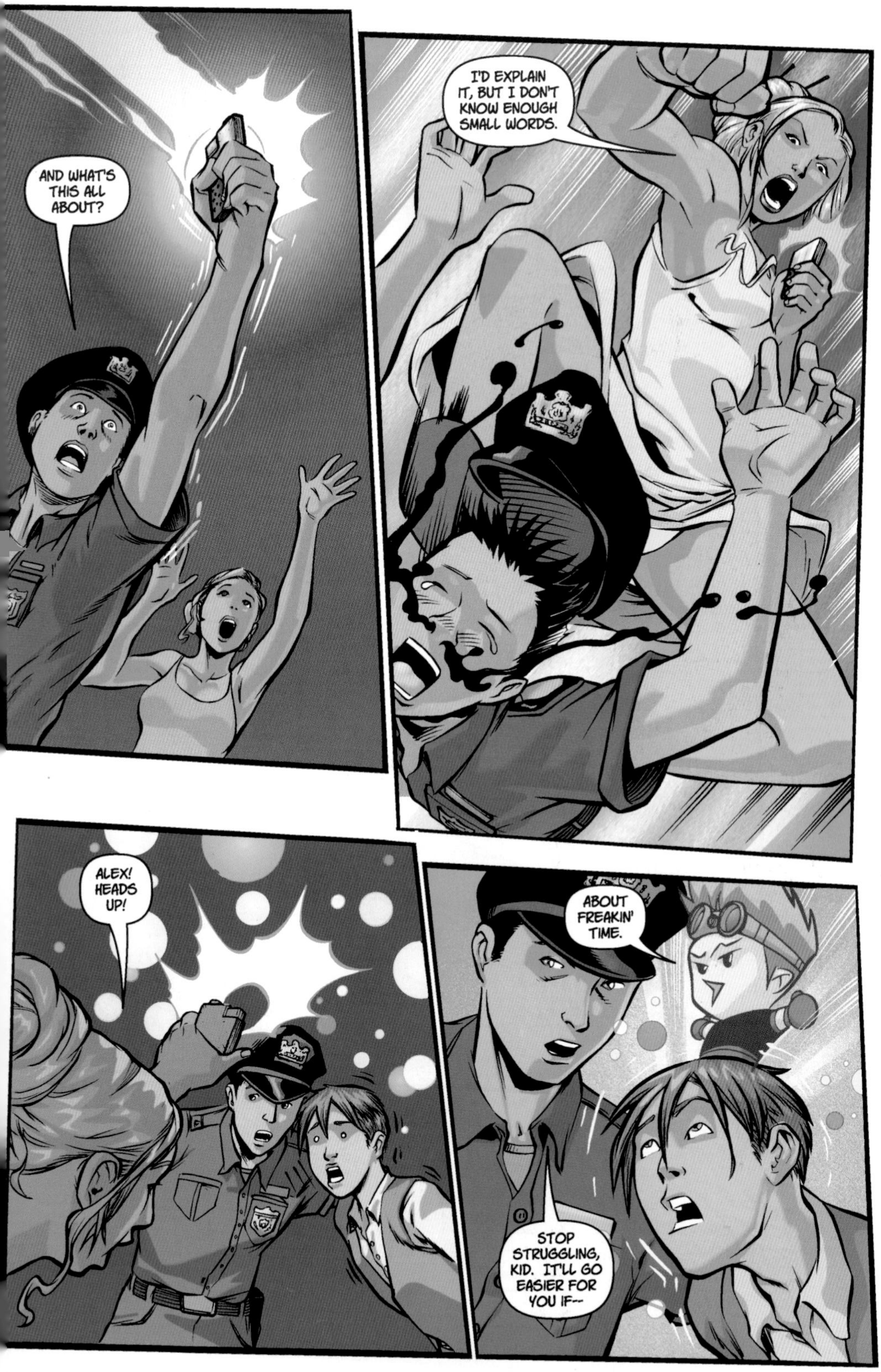
AND WHAT'S THIS ALL ABOUT?
I'D EXPLAIN IT, BUT I DON'T KNOW ENOUGH SMALL WORDS.
ALEX! HEADS UP!
ABOUT FREAKIN' TIME.
STOP STRUGGLING, KID. IT'LL GO EASIER FOR YOU IF--

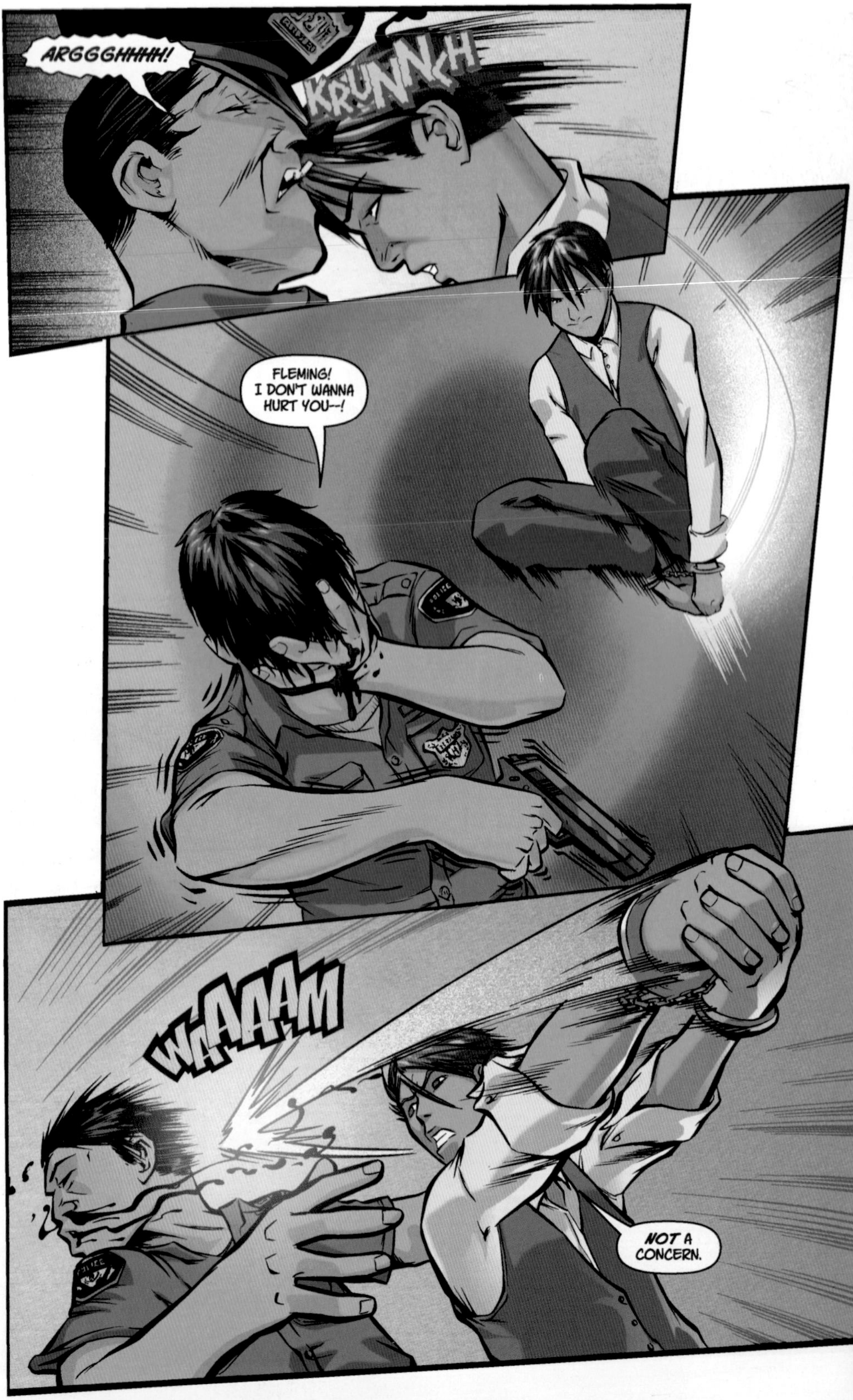
ARGGGHHHH!
KRUNNCH
FLEMING! I DON'T WANNA HURT YOU--!
WAAAAM
NOT A CONCERN.

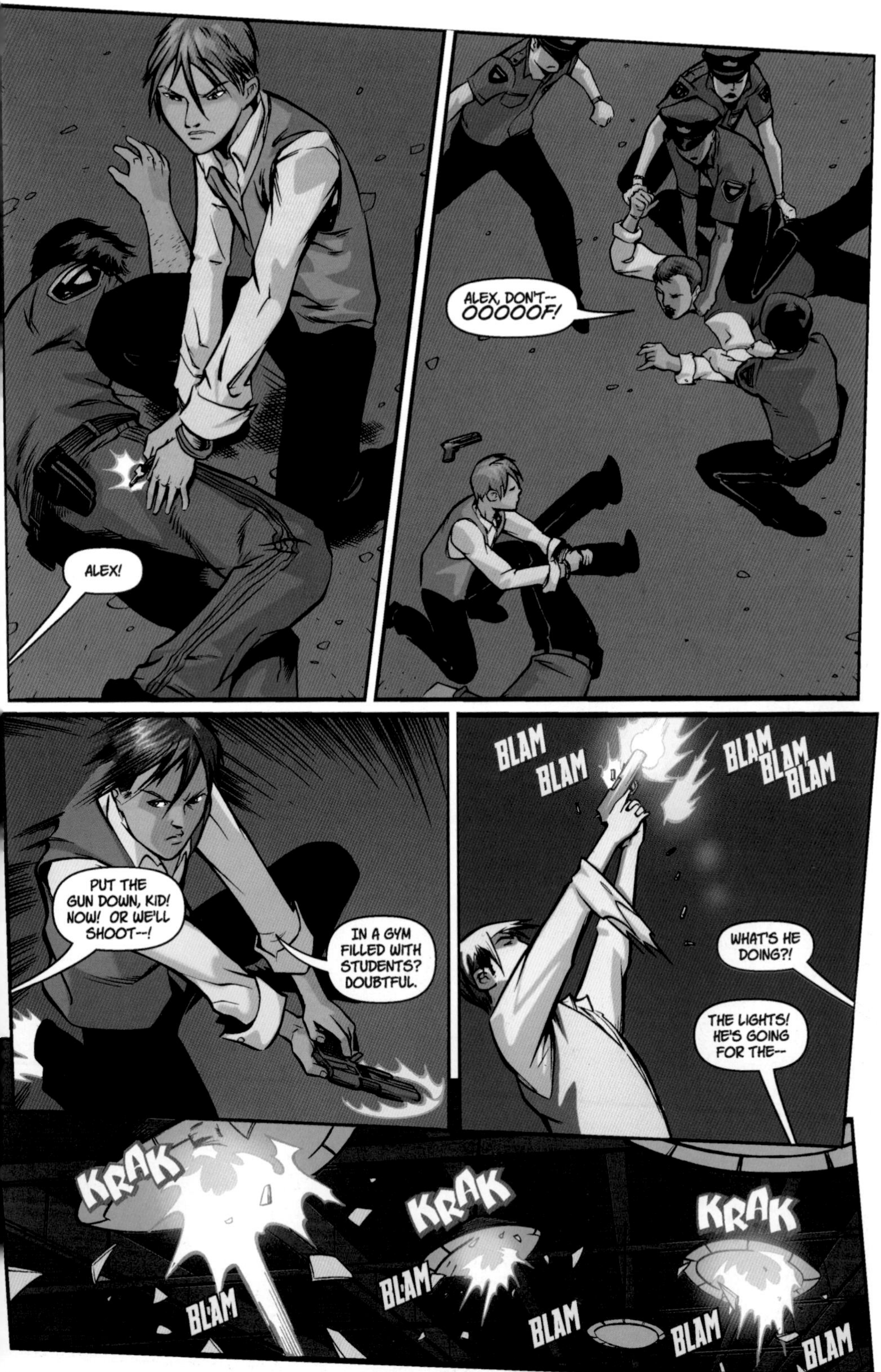
ALEX!
ALEX, DON'T-- OOOOOF!
PUT THE GUN DOWN, KID! NOW! OR WE'LL SHOOT--!
IN A GYM FILLED WITH STUDENTS? DOUBTFUL.
BLAM
BLAM
BLAM
BLAM
BLAM
WHAT'S HE DOING?!
THE LIGHTS! HE'S GOING FOR THE--
KRAK
KRAK
KRAK
BLAM
BLAM
BLAM
BLAM
BLAM

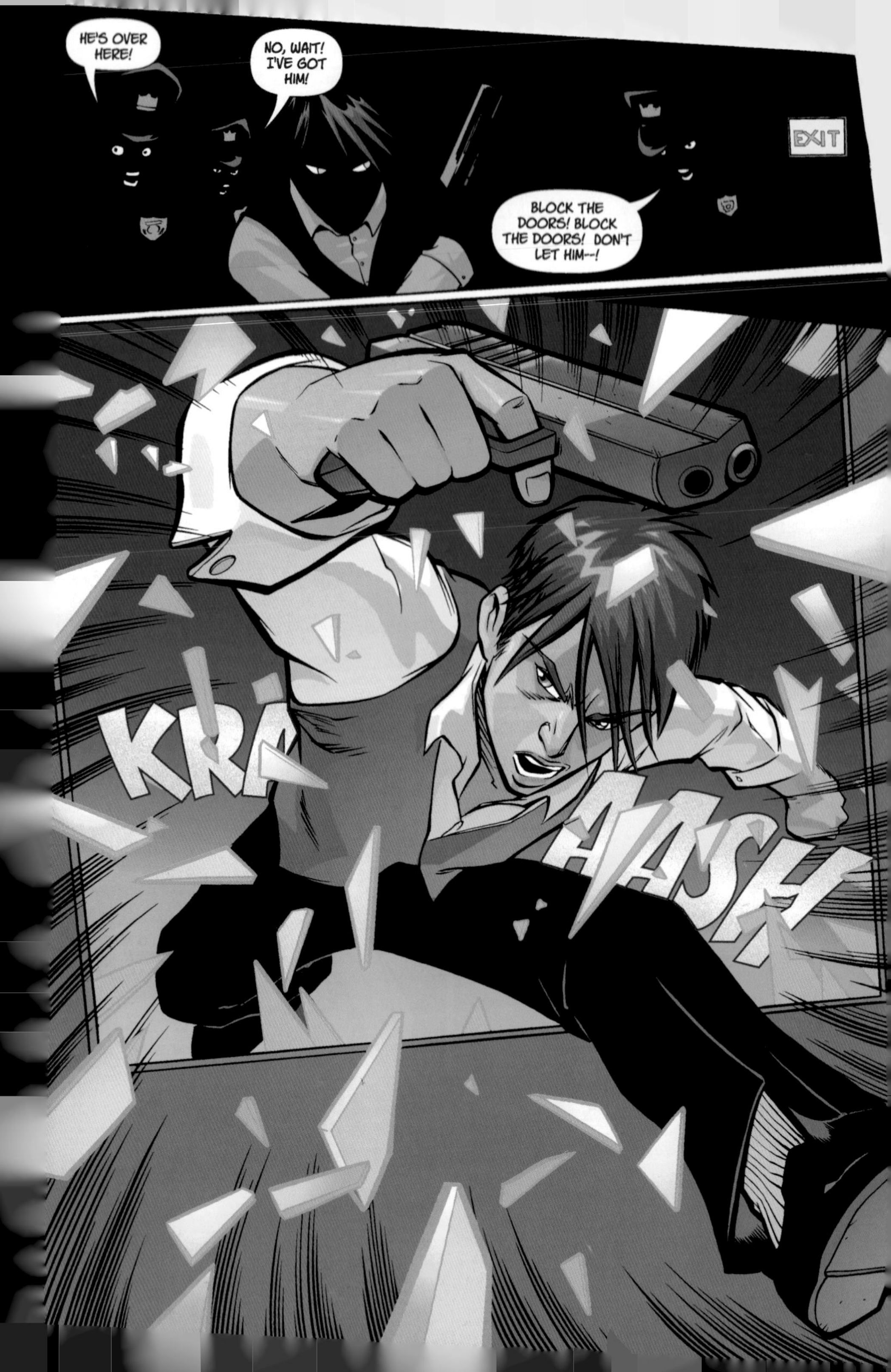
HE'S OVER HERE!
NO, WAIT! I'VE GOT HIM!
EXIT
BLOCK THE DOORS! BLOCK THE DOORS! DON'T LET HIM--!
KRAAASH

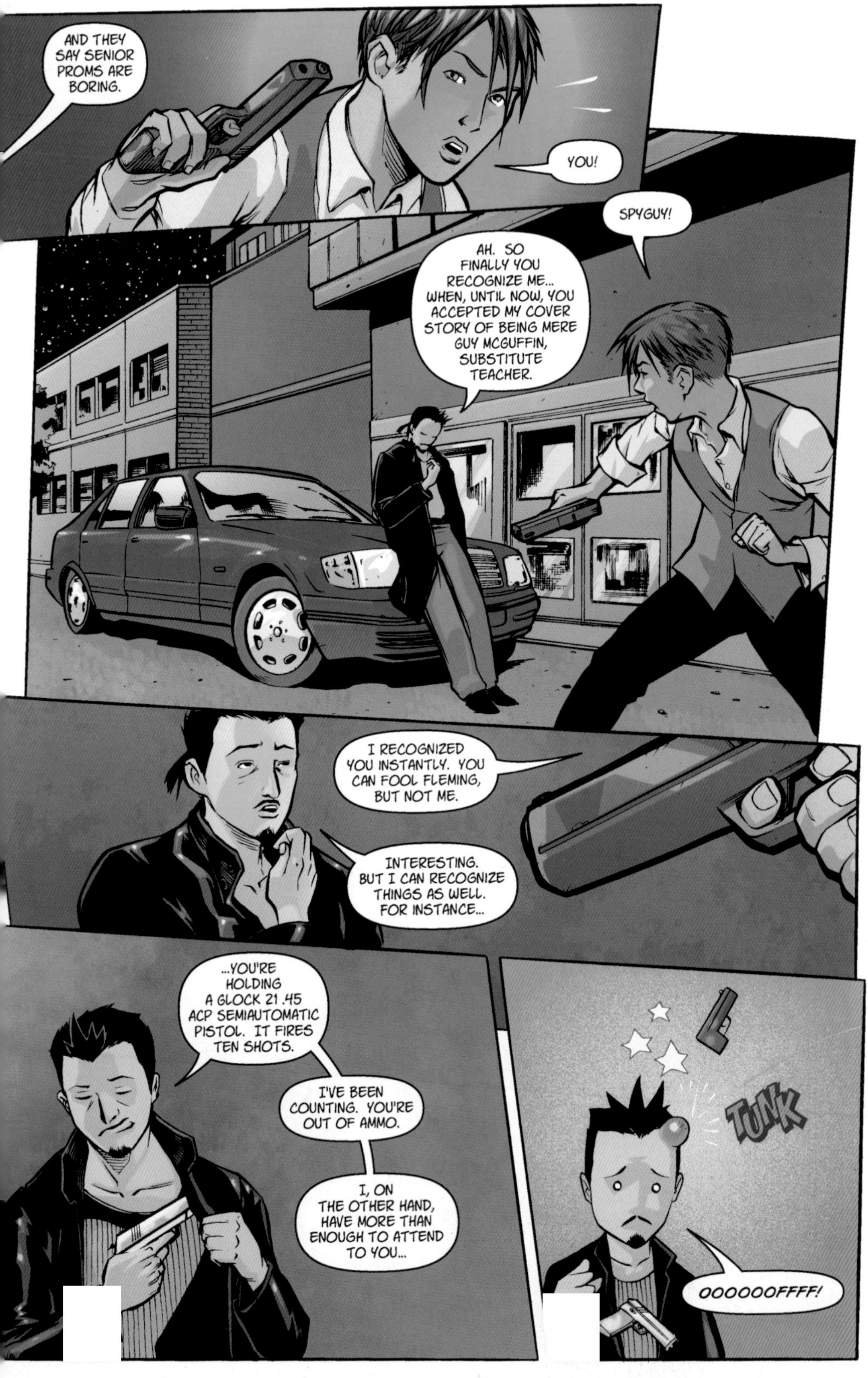
AND THEY SAY SENIOR PROMS ARE BORING.
YOU!
SPYGUY!
AH. SO FINALLY YOU RECOGNIZE ME... WHEN, UNTIL NOW, YOU ACCEPTED MY COVER STORY OF BEING MERE GUY MCGUFFIN, SUBSTITUTE TEACHER.
I RECOGNIZED YOU INSTANTLY. YOU CAN FOOL FLEMING, BUT NOT ME.
INTERESTING. BUT I CAN RECOGNIZE THINGS AS WELL. FOR INSTANCE...
...YOU'RE HOLDING A GLOCK 21 .45 ACP SEMIAUTOMATIC PISTOL. IT FIRES TEN SHOTS.
I'VE BEEN COUNTING. YOU'RE OUT OF AMMO.
I, ON THE OTHER HAND, HAVE MORE THAN ENOUGH TO ATTEND TO YOU...
TUNK
OOOOOOFFFF!

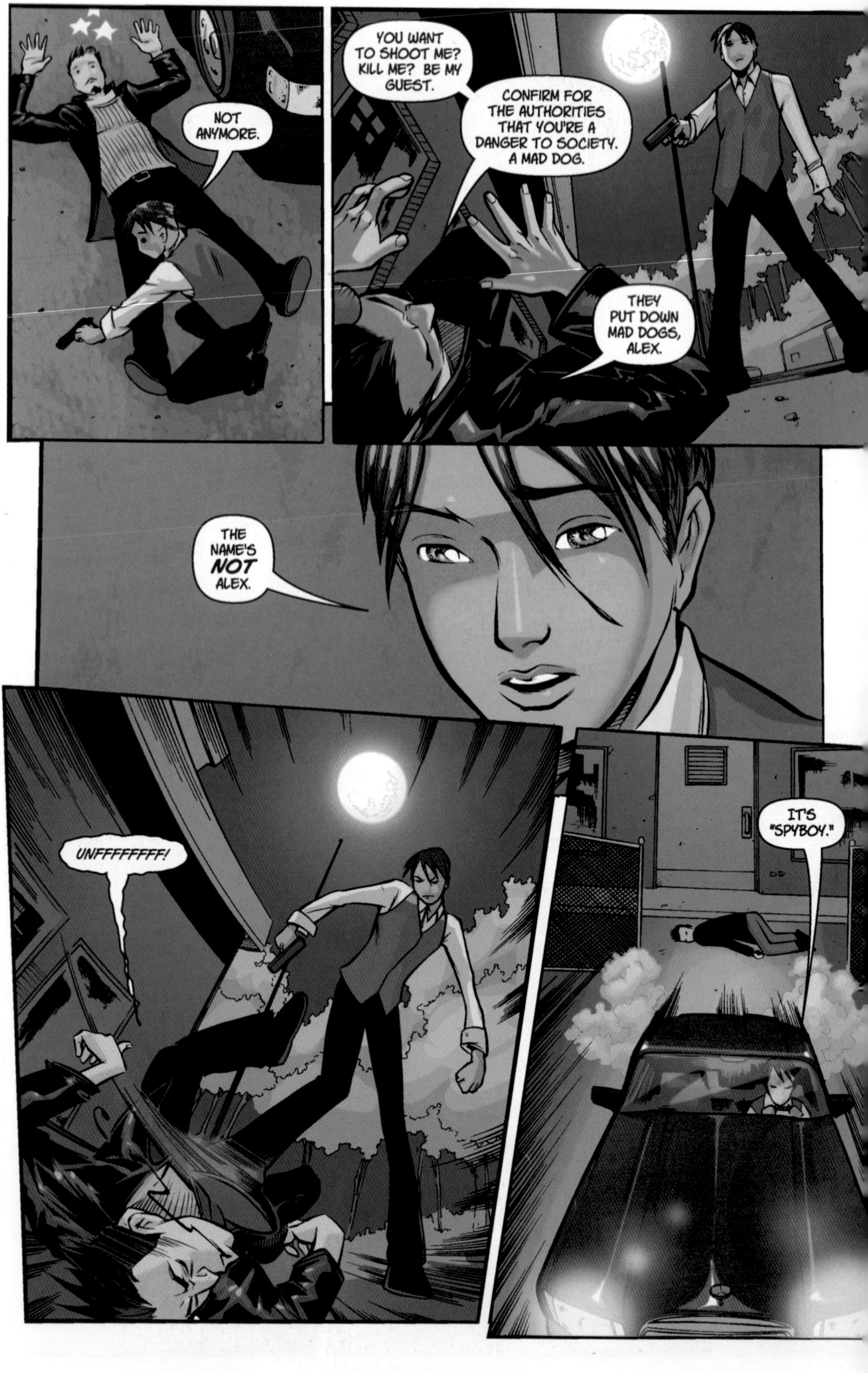
NOT ANYMORE.
YOU WANT TO SHOOT ME? KILL ME? BE MY GUEST.
CONFIRM FOR THE AUTHORITIES THAT YOU'RE A DANGER TO SOCIETY. A MAD DOG.
THEY PUT DOWN MAD DOGS, ALEX.
THE NAME'S ***NOT*** ALEX.
UNFFFFFFFF!
IT'S "SPYBOY."

PRIME NUMBER!

I THINK YOU'D BETTER SEE THIS.

SCANDAL!!
REPORTER WITH POLITICAL MOTIVE

BREAKING NEWS

THE MONITOR DEPARTMENT FLAGGED THIS OFF THE LOCAL NEWS FEEDS IN NORTH JERSEY.

IS THIS A JOKE?

NO, SIR.

IS *THIS* A JOKE?

TEEN TERROR

I WISH IT WERE, SIR.

TEEN TERRORIST!

GET ME THE FLEMING HOUSE, NOW.

NOW!

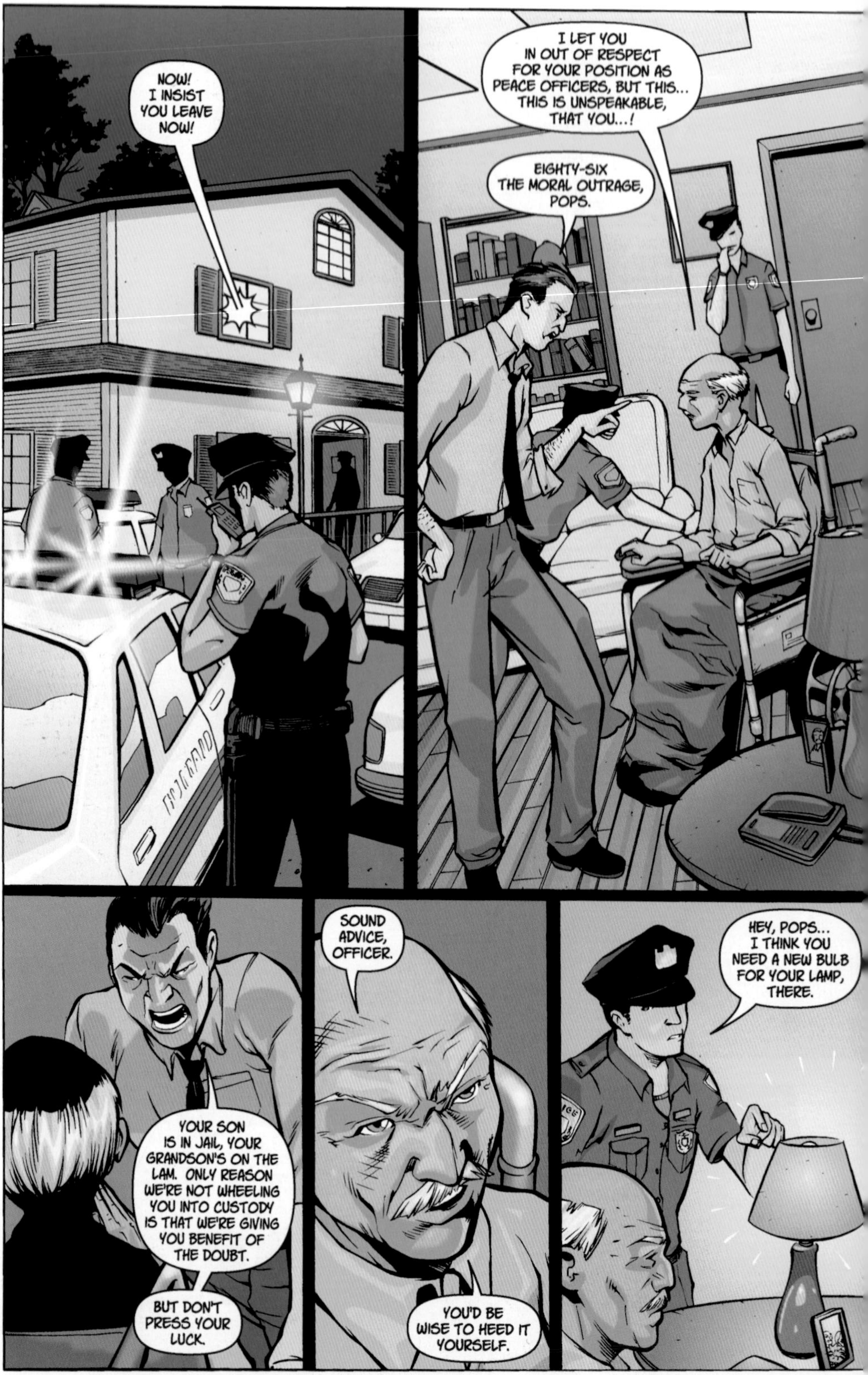
NOW! I INSIST YOU LEAVE NOW!
I LET YOU IN OUT OF RESPECT FOR YOUR POSITION AS PEACE OFFICERS, BUT THIS... THIS IS UNSPEAKABLE, THAT YOU...!
EIGHTY-SIX THE MORAL OUTRAGE, POPS.
YOUR SON IS IN JAIL, YOUR GRANDSON'S ON THE LAM. ONLY REASON WE'RE NOT WHEELING YOU INTO CUSTODY IS THAT WE'RE GIVING YOU BENEFIT OF THE DOUBT.
BUT DON'T PRESS YOUR LUCK.
SOUND ADVICE, OFFICER.
YOU'D BE WISE TO HEED IT YOURSELF.
HEY, POPS... I THINK YOU NEED A NEW BULB FOR YOUR LAMP, THERE.

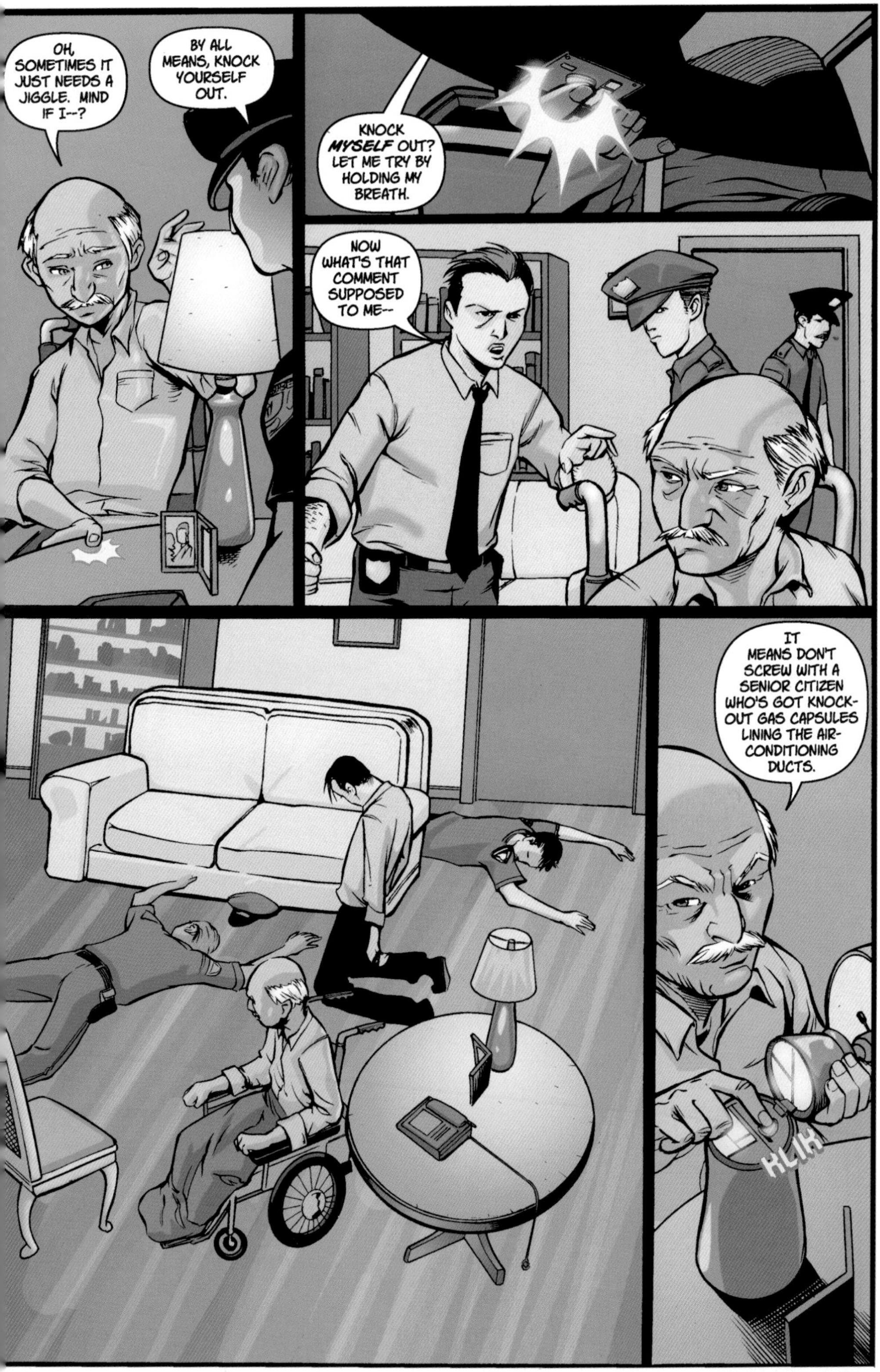
OH, SOMETIMES IT JUST NEEDS A JIGGLE. MIND IF I--?
BY ALL MEANS, KNOCK YOURSELF OUT.
KNOCK *MYSELF* OUT? LET ME TRY BY HOLDING MY BREATH.
NOW WHAT'S THAT COMMENT SUPPOSED TO ME--
IT MEANS DON'T SCREW WITH A SENIOR CITIZEN WHO'S GOT KNOCK-OUT GAS CAPSULES LINING THE AIR-CONDITIONING DUCTS.
KLIK

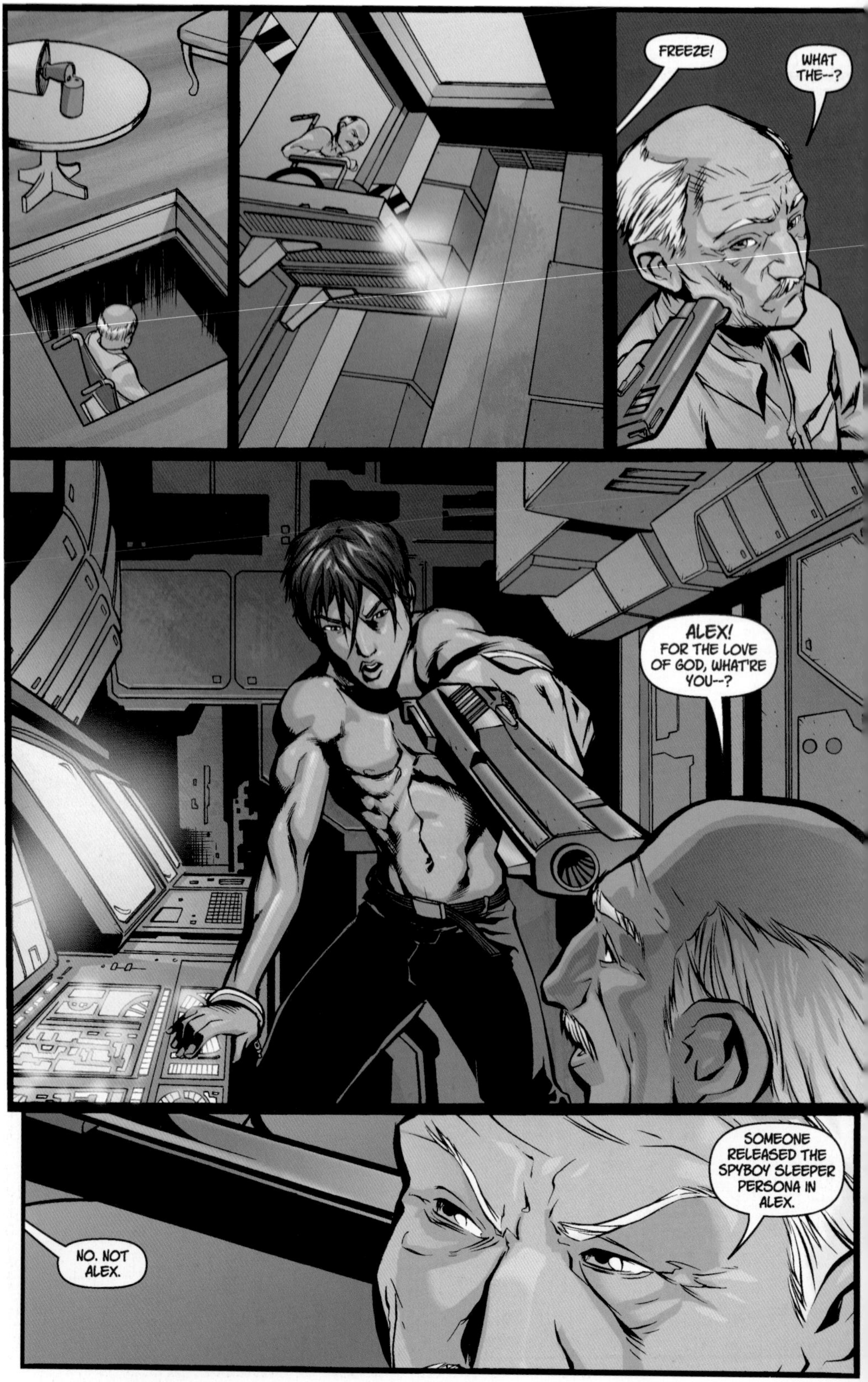
FREEZE!
WHAT THE--?
ALEX! FOR THE LOVE OF GOD, WHAT'RE YOU--?
SOMEONE RELEASED THE SPYBOY SLEEPER PERSONA IN ALEX.
NO. NOT ALEX.

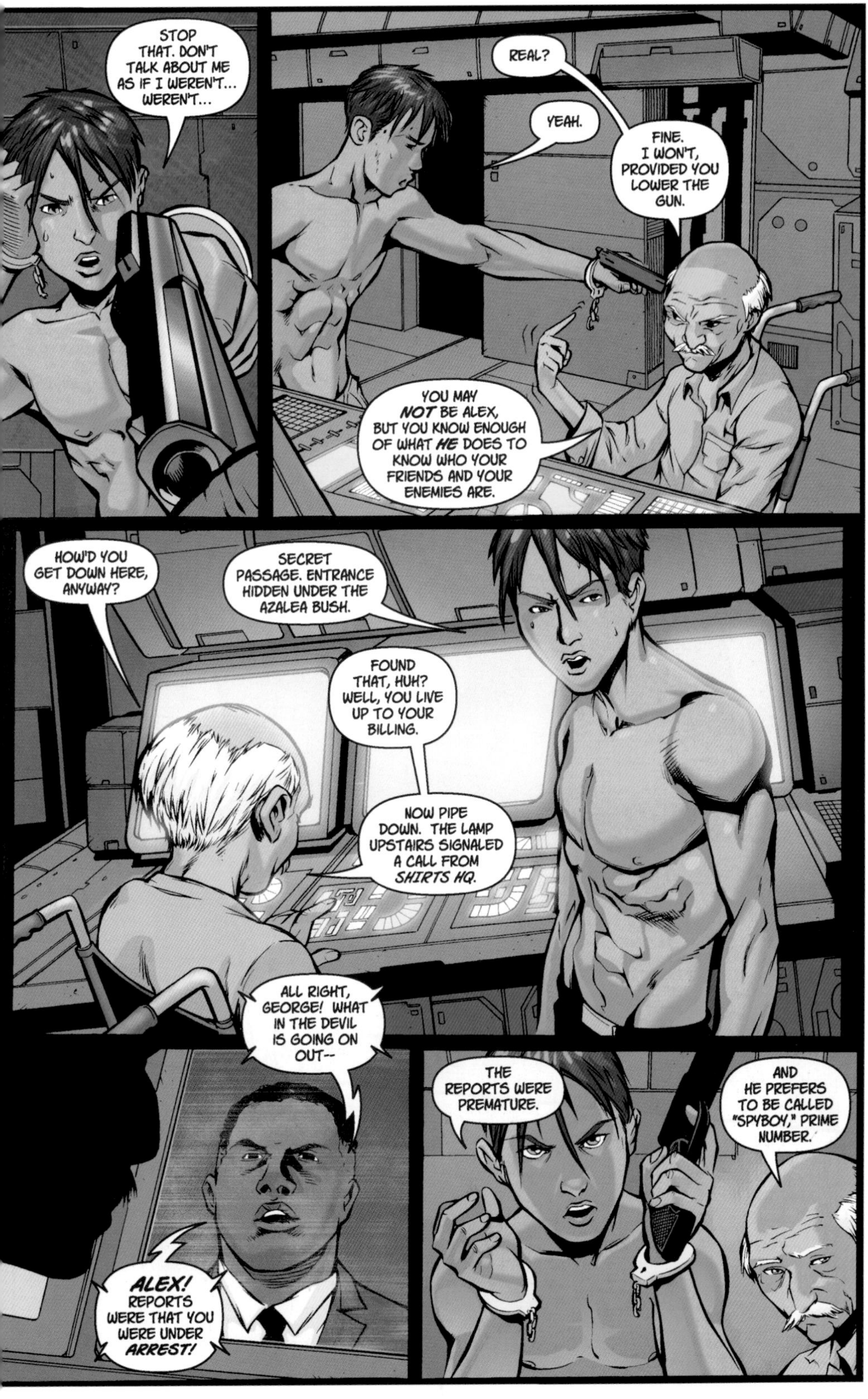
STOP THAT. DON'T TALK ABOUT ME AS IF I WEREN'T... WEREN'T...
REAL?
YEAH.
FINE. I WON'T, PROVIDED YOU LOWER THE GUN.
YOU MAY NOT BE ALEX, BUT YOU KNOW ENOUGH OF WHAT HE DOES TO KNOW WHO YOUR FRIENDS AND YOUR ENEMIES ARE.
HOW'D YOU GET DOWN HERE, ANYWAY?
SECRET PASSAGE. ENTRANCE HIDDEN UNDER THE AZALEA BUSH.
FOUND THAT, HUH? WELL, YOU LIVE UP TO YOUR BILLING.
NOW PIPE DOWN. THE LAMP UPSTAIRS SIGNALED A CALL FROM SHIRTS HQ.
ALL RIGHT, GEORGE! WHAT IN THE DEVIL IS GOING ON OUT--
ALEX! REPORTS WERE THAT YOU WERE UNDER ARREST!
THE REPORTS WERE PREMATURE.
AND HE PREFERS TO BE CALLED "SPYBOY," PRIME NUMBER.

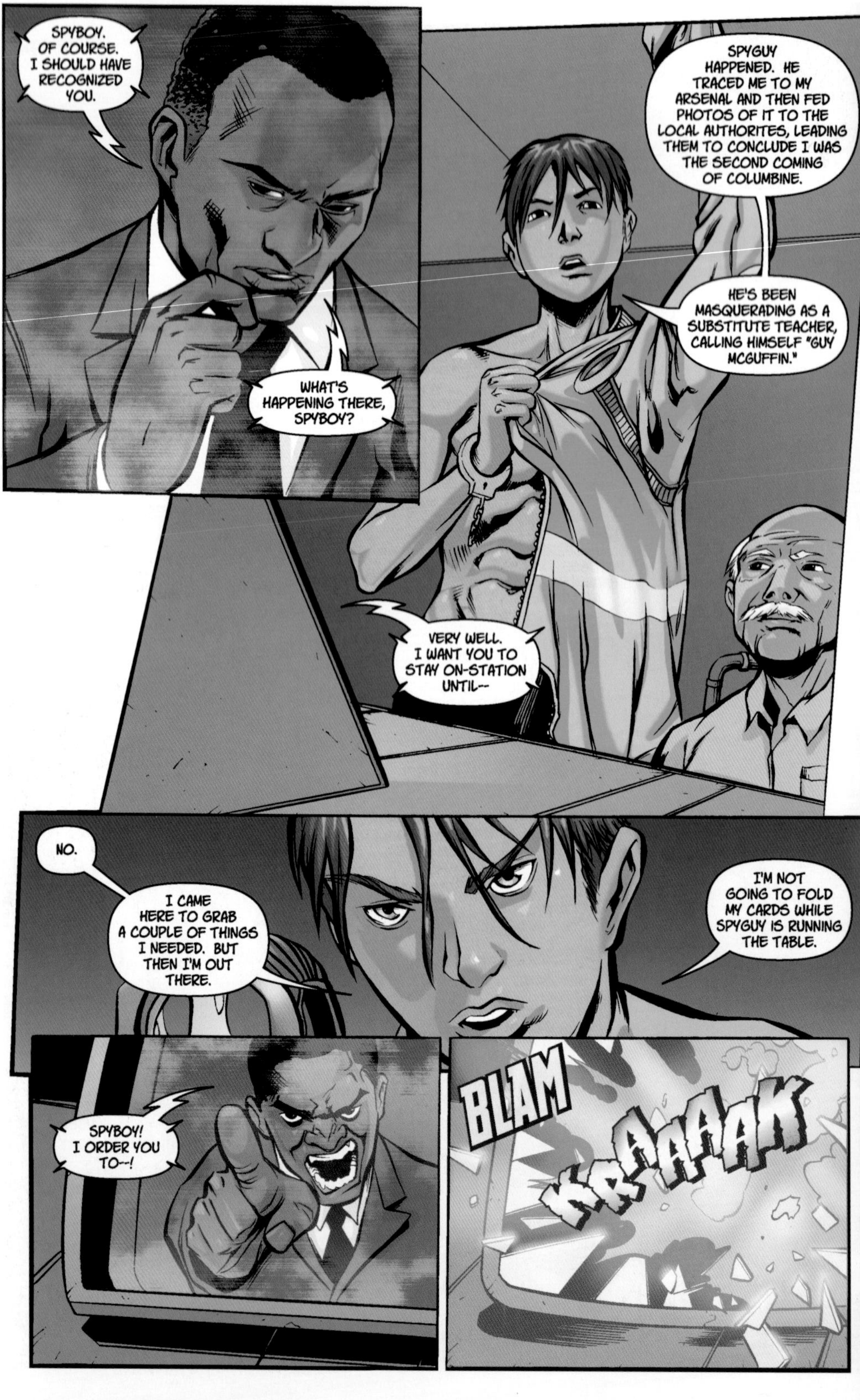
SPYBOY. OF COURSE. I SHOULD HAVE RECOGNIZED YOU.
SPYGUY HAPPENED. HE TRACED ME TO MY ARSENAL AND THEN FED PHOTOS OF IT TO THE LOCAL AUTHORITES, LEADING THEM TO CONCLUDE I WAS THE SECOND COMING OF COLUMBINE.
HE'S BEEN MASQUERADING AS A SUBSTITUTE TEACHER, CALLING HIMSELF "GUY MCGUFFIN."
WHAT'S HAPPENING THERE, SPYBOY?
VERY WELL. I WANT YOU TO STAY ON-STATION UNTIL--
NO.
I CAME HERE TO GRAB A COUPLE OF THINGS I NEEDED. BUT THEN I'M OUT THERE.
I'M NOT GOING TO FOLD MY CARDS WHILE SPYGUY IS RUNNING THE TABLE.
SPYBOY! I ORDER YOU TO--!
BLAM
KRAAAAK

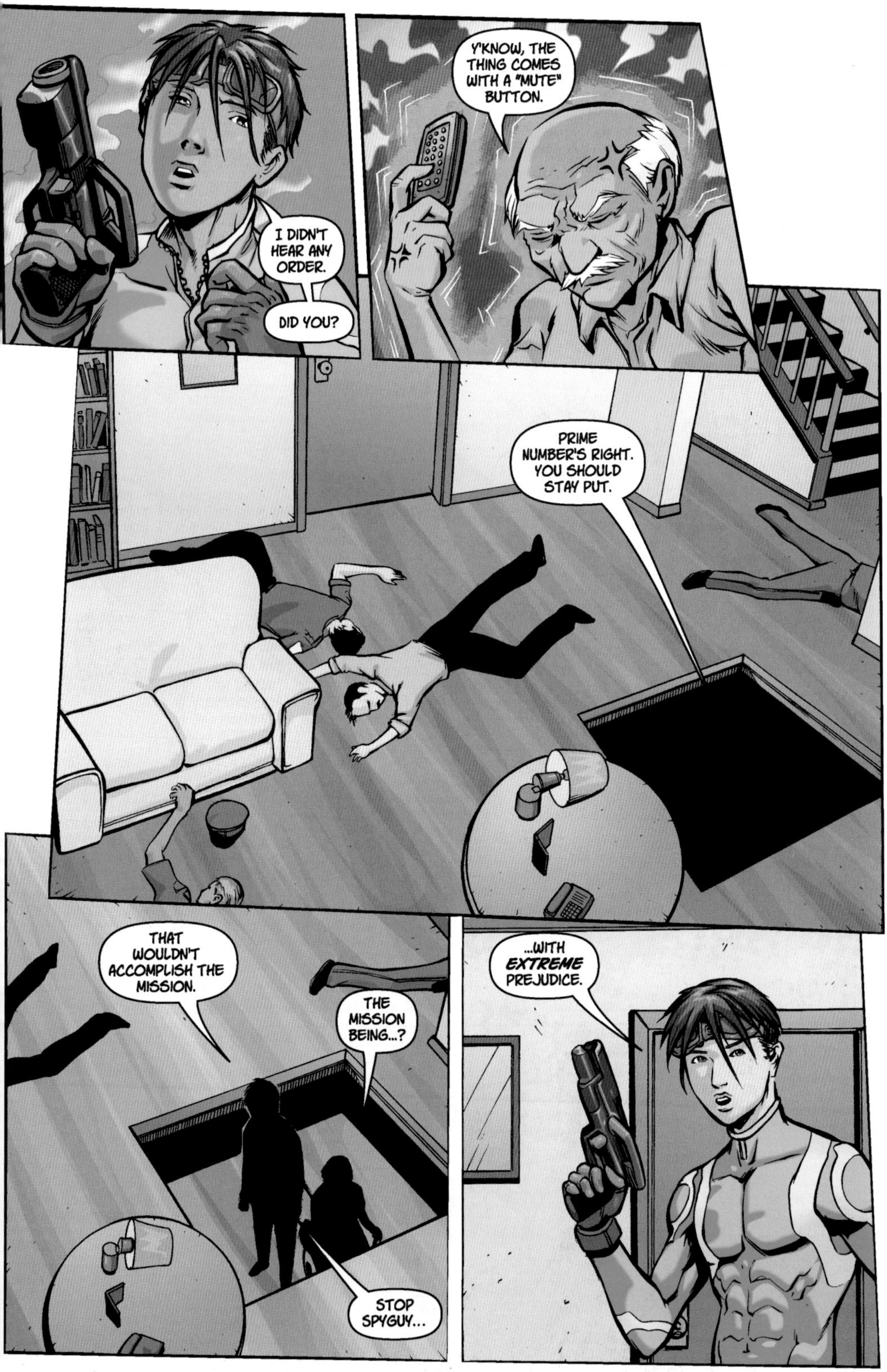
I DIDN'T HEAR ANY ORDER.
DID YOU?
Y'KNOW, THE THING COMES WITH A "MUTE" BUTTON.
PRIME NUMBER'S RIGHT. YOU SHOULD STAY PUT.
THAT WOULDN'T ACCOMPLISH THE MISSION.
THE MISSION BEING...?
STOP SPYGUY...
...WITH *EXTREME* PREJUDICE.

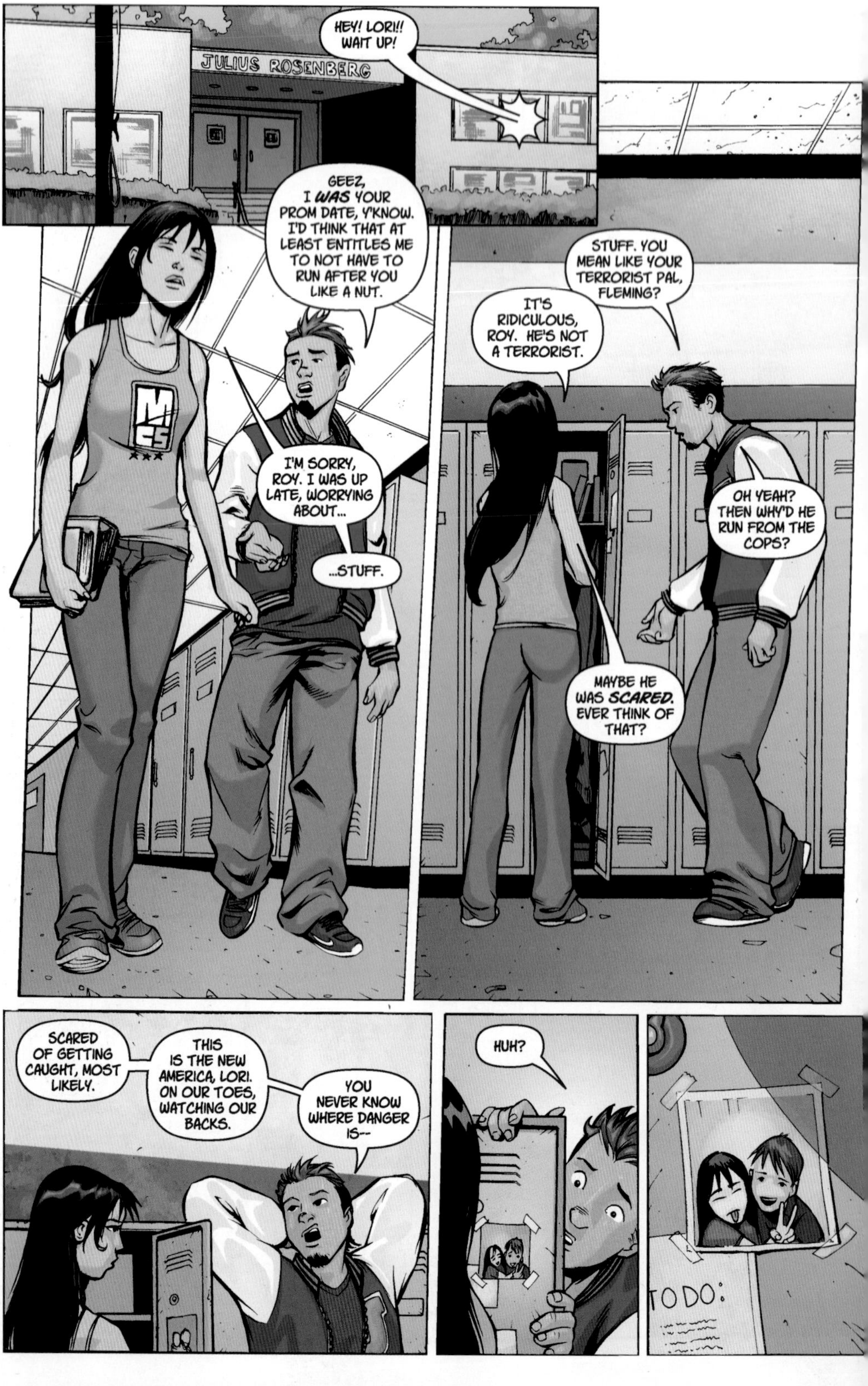
HEY! LORI!!
WAIT UP!
JULIUS ROSENBERG
GEEZ, I *WAS* YOUR PROM DATE, Y'KNOW. I'D THINK THAT AT LEAST ENTITLES ME TO NOT HAVE TO RUN AFTER YOU LIKE A NUT.
I'M SORRY, ROY. I WAS UP LATE, WORRYING ABOUT...
...STUFF.
STUFF. YOU MEAN LIKE YOUR TERRORIST PAL, FLEMING?
IT'S RIDICULOUS, ROY. HE'S NOT A TERRORIST.
OH YEAH? THEN WHY'D HE RUN FROM THE COPS?
MAYBE HE WAS *SCARED.* EVER THINK OF THAT?
SCARED OF GETTING CAUGHT, MOST LIKELY.
THIS IS THE NEW AMERICA, LORI. ON OUR TOES, WATCHING OUR BACKS.
YOU NEVER KNOW WHERE DANGER IS--
HUH?
TO DO:

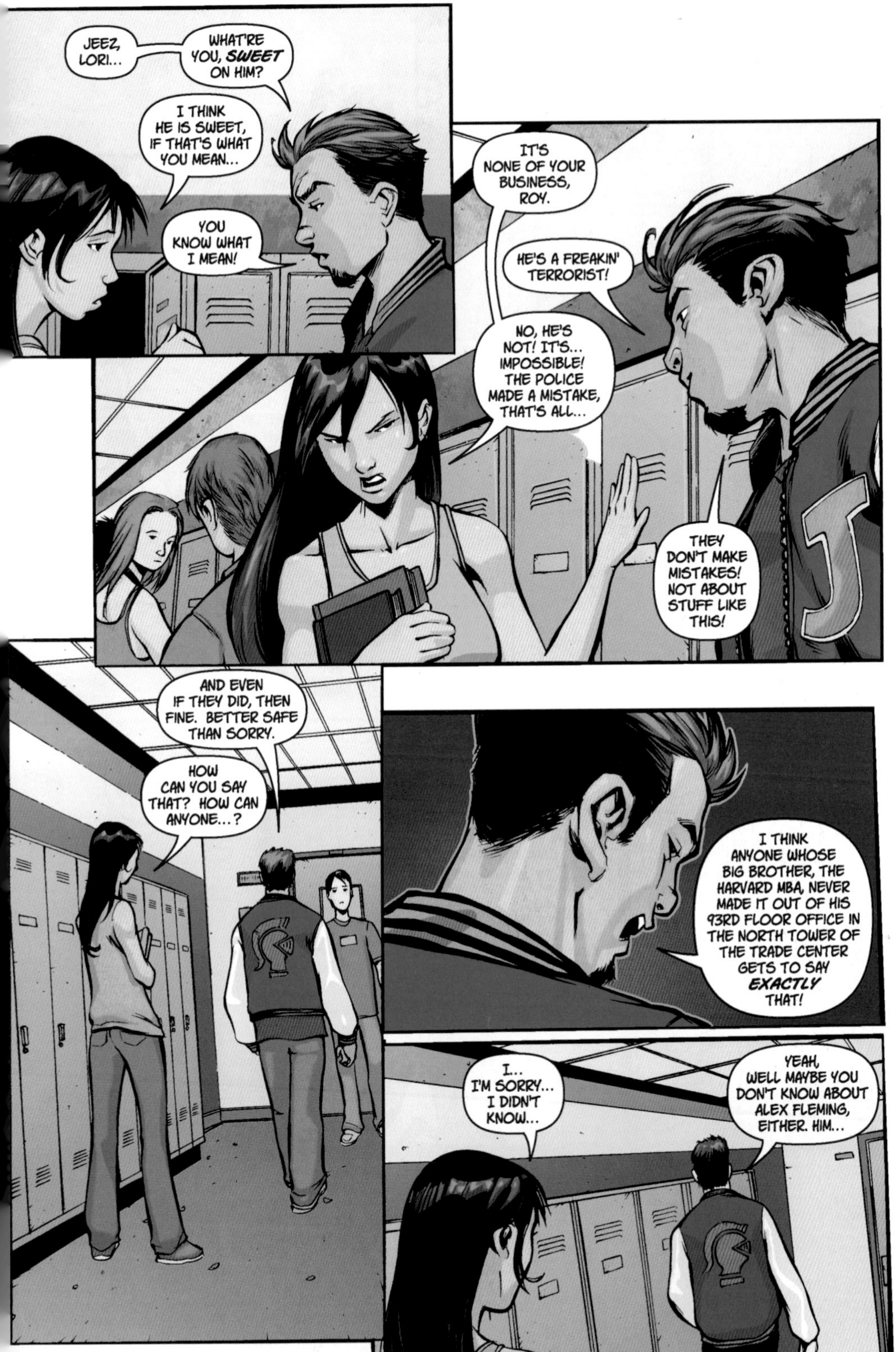
JEEZ, LORI...
WHAT'RE YOU, ***SWEET*** ON HIM?
I THINK HE IS SWEET, IF THAT'S WHAT YOU MEAN...
YOU KNOW WHAT I MEAN!
IT'S NONE OF YOUR BUSINESS, ROY.
HE'S A FREAKIN' TERRORIST!
NO, HE'S NOT! IT'S... IMPOSSIBLE! THE POLICE MADE A MISTAKE, THAT'S ALL...
THEY DON'T MAKE MISTAKES! NOT ABOUT STUFF LIKE THIS!
AND EVEN IF THEY DID, THEN FINE. BETTER SAFE THAN SORRY.
HOW CAN YOU SAY THAT? HOW CAN ANYONE...?
I THINK ANYONE WHOSE BIG BROTHER, THE HARVARD MBA, NEVER MADE IT OUT OF HIS 93RD FLOOR OFFICE IN THE NORTH TOWER OF THE TRADE CENTER GETS TO SAY ***EXACTLY*** THAT!
I... I'M SORRY... I DIDN'T KNOW...
YEAH, WELL MAYBE YOU DON'T KNOW ABOUT ALEX FLEMING, EITHER. HIM...

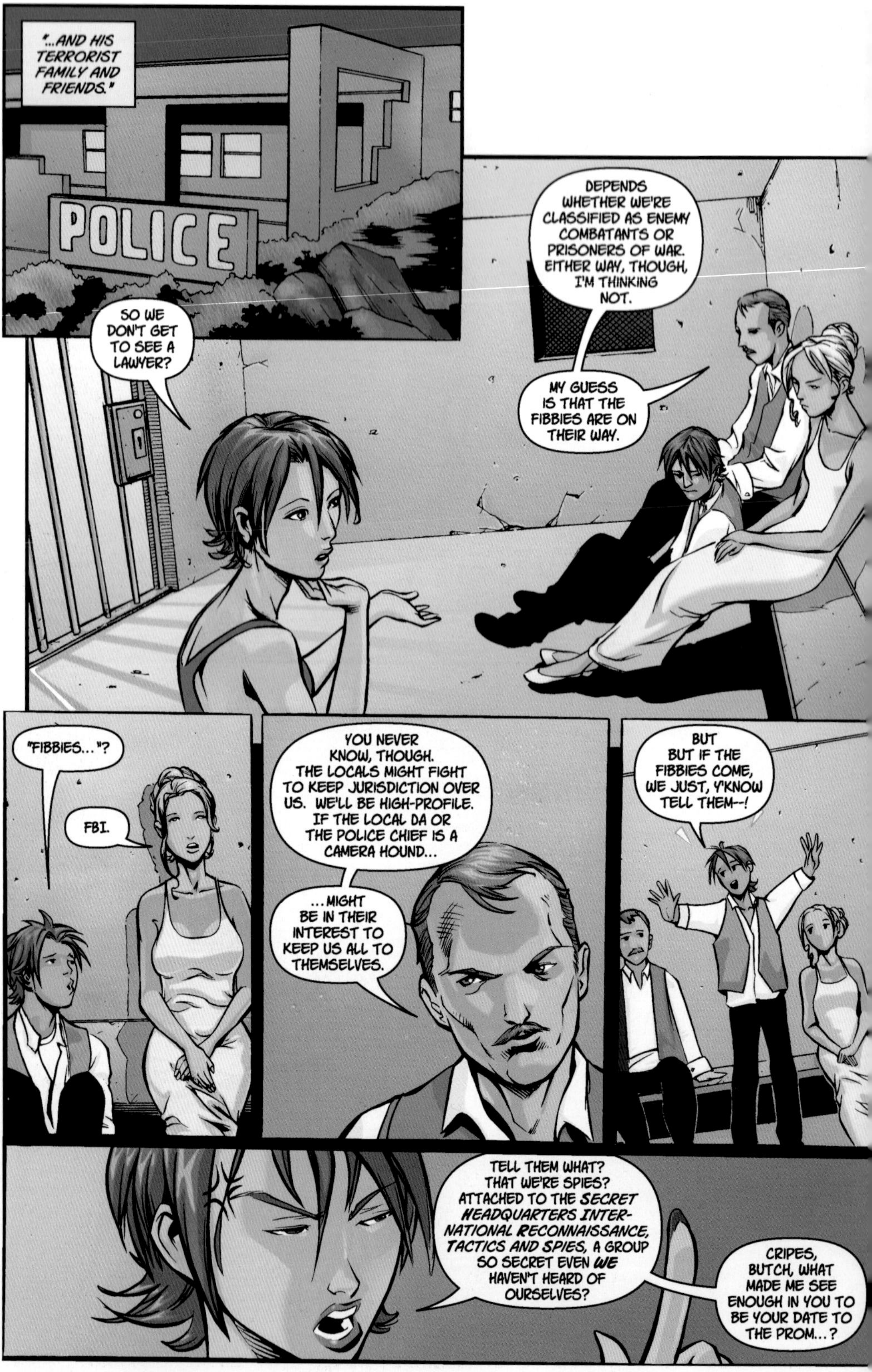
"...AND HIS TERRORIST FAMILY AND FRIENDS."
POLICE
SO WE DON'T GET TO SEE A LAWYER?
DEPENDS WHETHER WE'RE CLASSIFIED AS ENEMY COMBATANTS OR PRISONERS OF WAR. EITHER WAY, THOUGH, I'M THINKING NOT.
MY GUESS IS THAT THE FIBBIES ARE ON THEIR WAY.
"FIBBIES..."?
FBI.
YOU NEVER KNOW, THOUGH. THE LOCALS MIGHT FIGHT TO KEEP JURISDICTION OVER US. WE'LL BE HIGH-PROFILE. IF THE LOCAL DA OR THE POLICE CHIEF IS A CAMERA HOUND...
...MIGHT BE IN THEIR INTEREST TO KEEP US ALL TO THEMSELVES.
BUT BUT IF THE FIBBIES COME, WE JUST, Y'KNOW TELL THEM--!
TELL THEM WHAT? THAT WE'RE SPIES? ATTACHED TO THE SECRET HEADQUARTERS INTER-NATIONAL RECONNAISSANCE, TACTICS AND SPIES, A GROUP SO SECRET EVEN WE HAVEN'T HEARD OF OURSELVES?
CRIPES, BUTCH, WHAT MADE ME SEE ENOUGH IN YOU TO BE YOUR DATE TO THE PROM...?

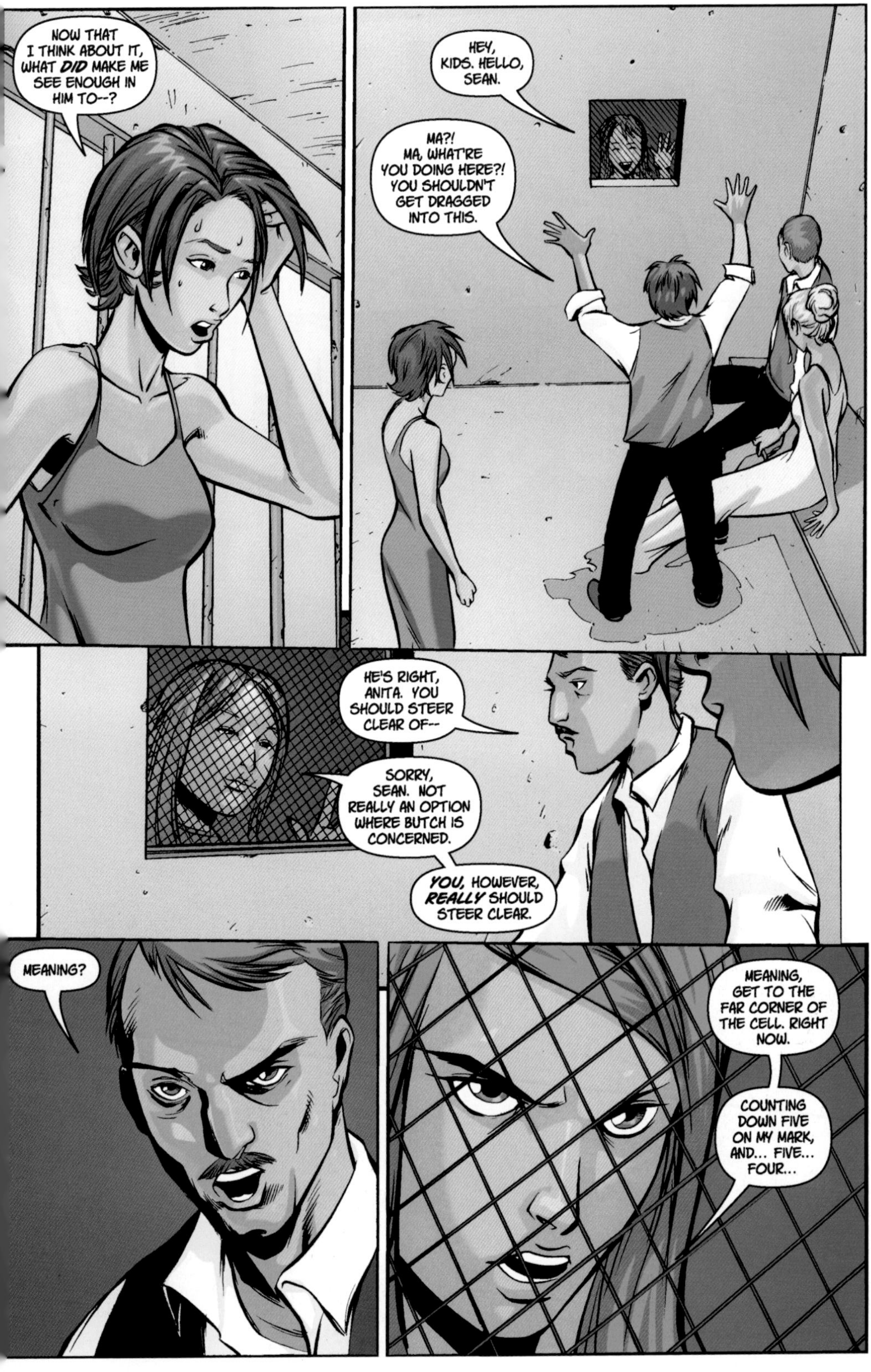
NOW THAT I THINK ABOUT IT, WHAT *DID* MAKE ME SEE ENOUGH IN HIM TO--?
HEY, KIDS. HELLO, SEAN.
MA?! MA, WHAT'RE YOU DOING HERE?! YOU SHOULDN'T GET DRAGGED INTO THIS.
HE'S RIGHT, ANITA. YOU SHOULD STEER CLEAR OF--
SORRY, SEAN. NOT REALLY AN OPTION WHERE BUTCH IS CONCERNED.
YOU, HOWEVER, *REALLY* SHOULD STEER CLEAR.
MEANING?
MEANING, GET TO THE FAR CORNER OF THE CELL. RIGHT NOW.
COUNTING DOWN FIVE ON MY MARK, AND... FIVE... FOUR...

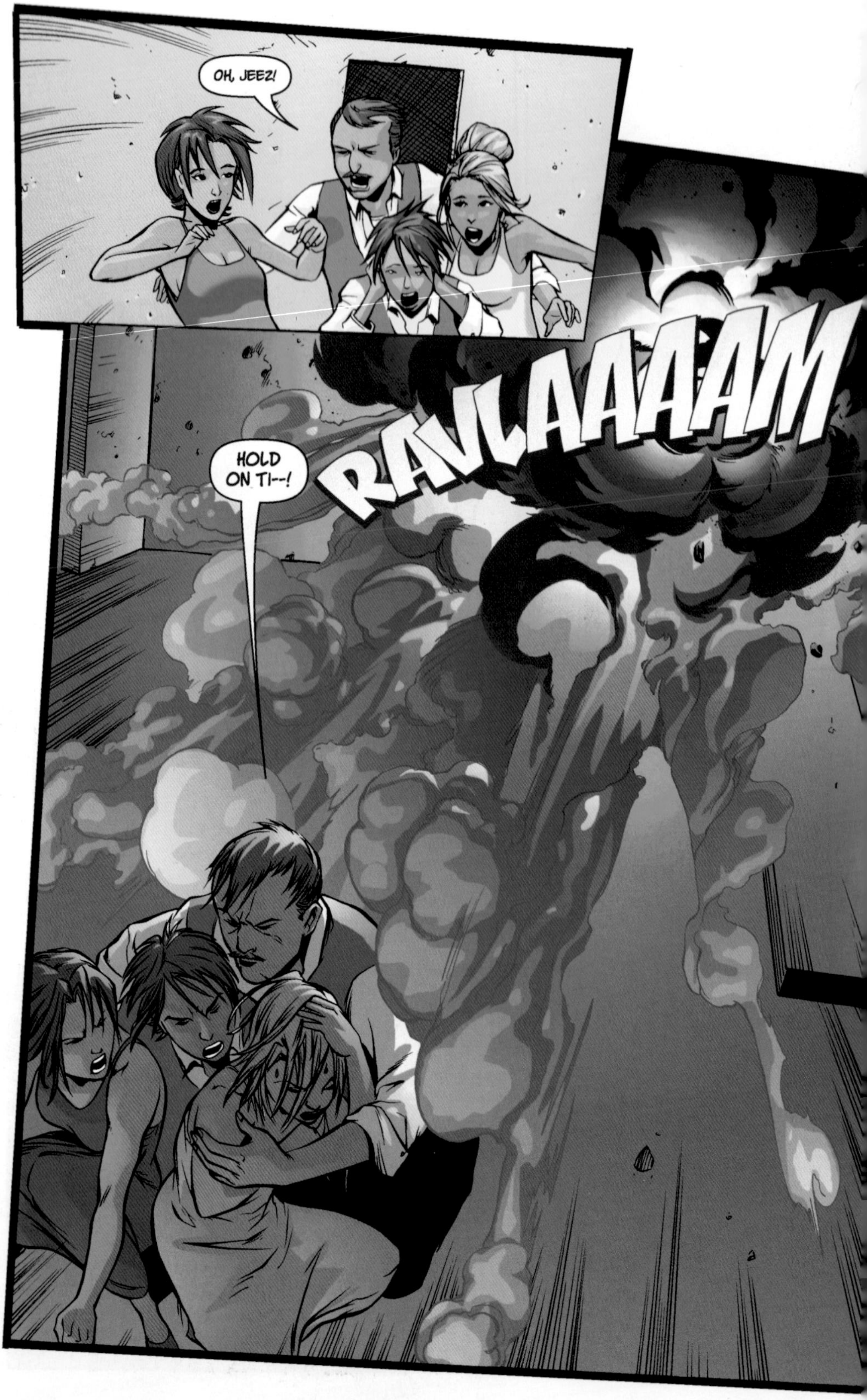
OH, JEEZ!
HOLD ON TI--!
RAVLAAAAM

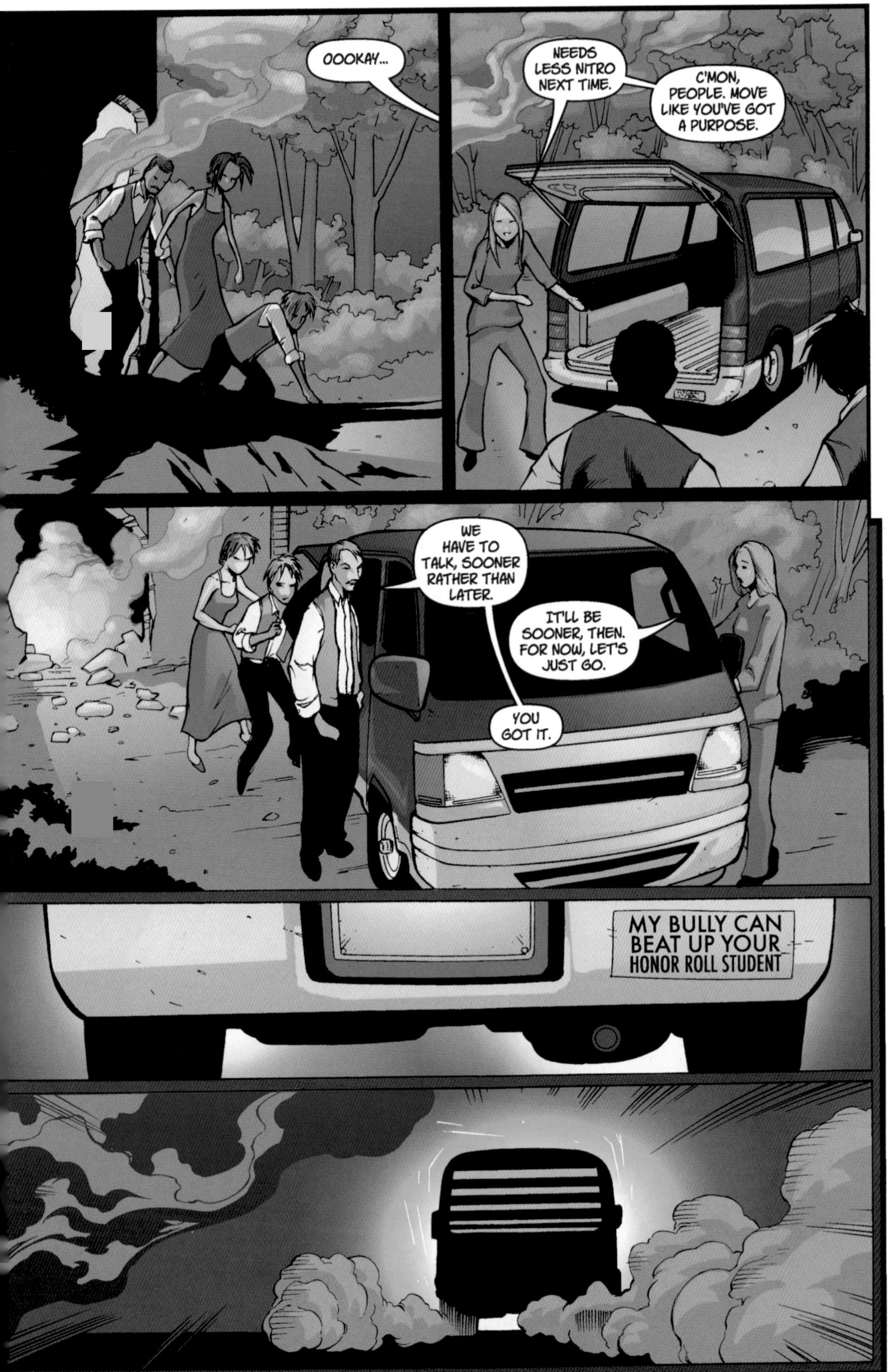
OOOKAY...
NEEDS LESS NITRO NEXT TIME.
C'MON, PEOPLE. MOVE LIKE YOU'VE GOT A PURPOSE.
WE HAVE TO TALK, SOONER RATHER THAN LATER.
IT'LL BE SOONER, THEN. FOR NOW, LET'S JUST GO.
YOU GOT IT.
MY BULLY CAN BEAT UP YOUR HONOR ROLL STUDENT

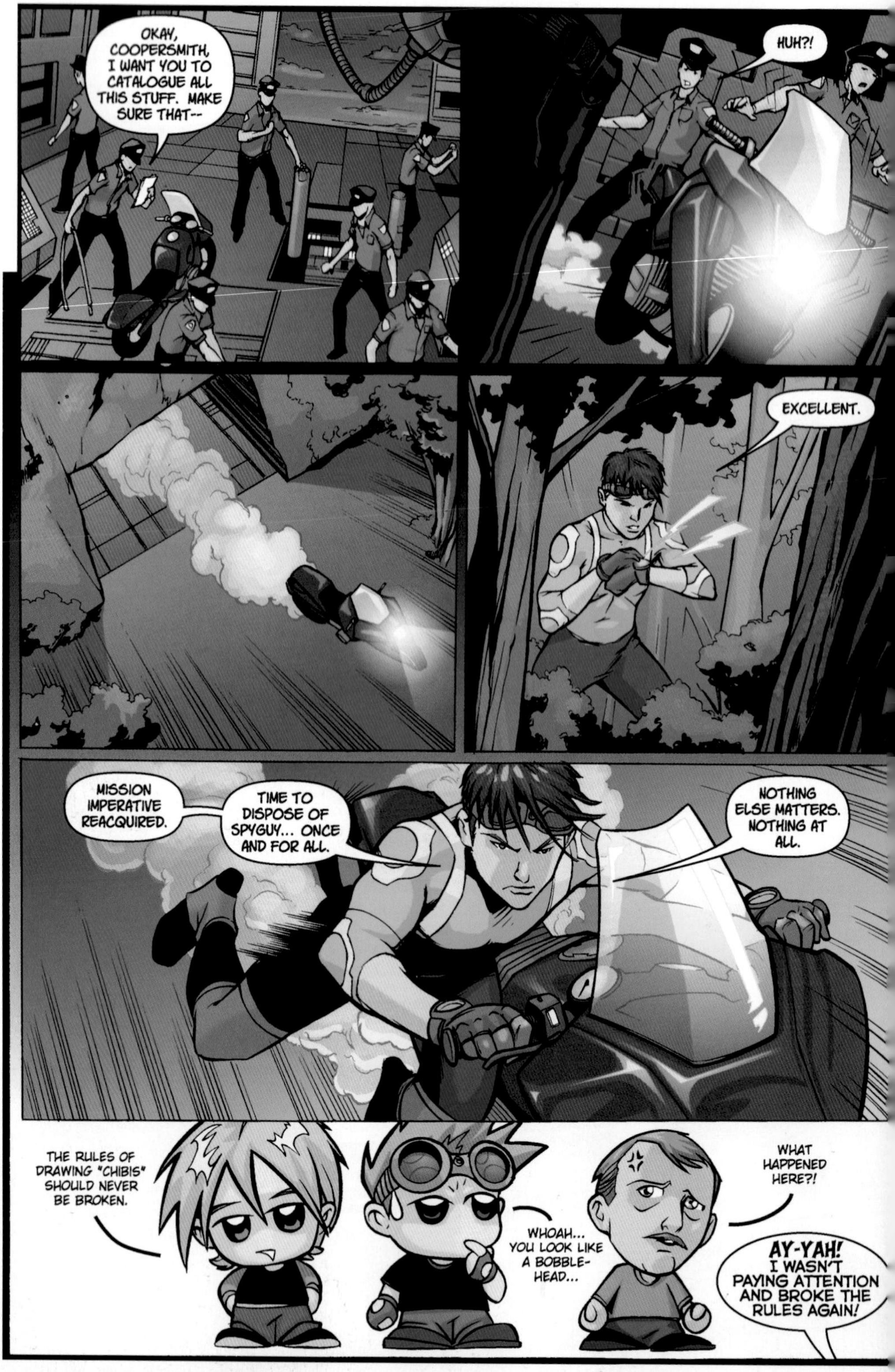
OKAY, COOPERSMITH, I WANT YOU TO CATALOGUE ALL THIS STUFF. MAKE SURE THAT--
HUH?!
EXCELLENT.
MISSION IMPERATIVE REACQUIRED.
TIME TO DISPOSE OF SPYGUY... ONCE AND FOR ALL.
NOTHING ELSE MATTERS. NOTHING AT ALL.
THE RULES OF DRAWING "CHIBIS" SHOULD NEVER BE BROKEN.
WHOAH... YOU LOOK LIKE A BOBBLE-HEAD...
WHAT HAPPENED HERE?!
AY-YAH! I WASN'T PAYING ATTENTION AND BROKE THE RULES AGAIN!

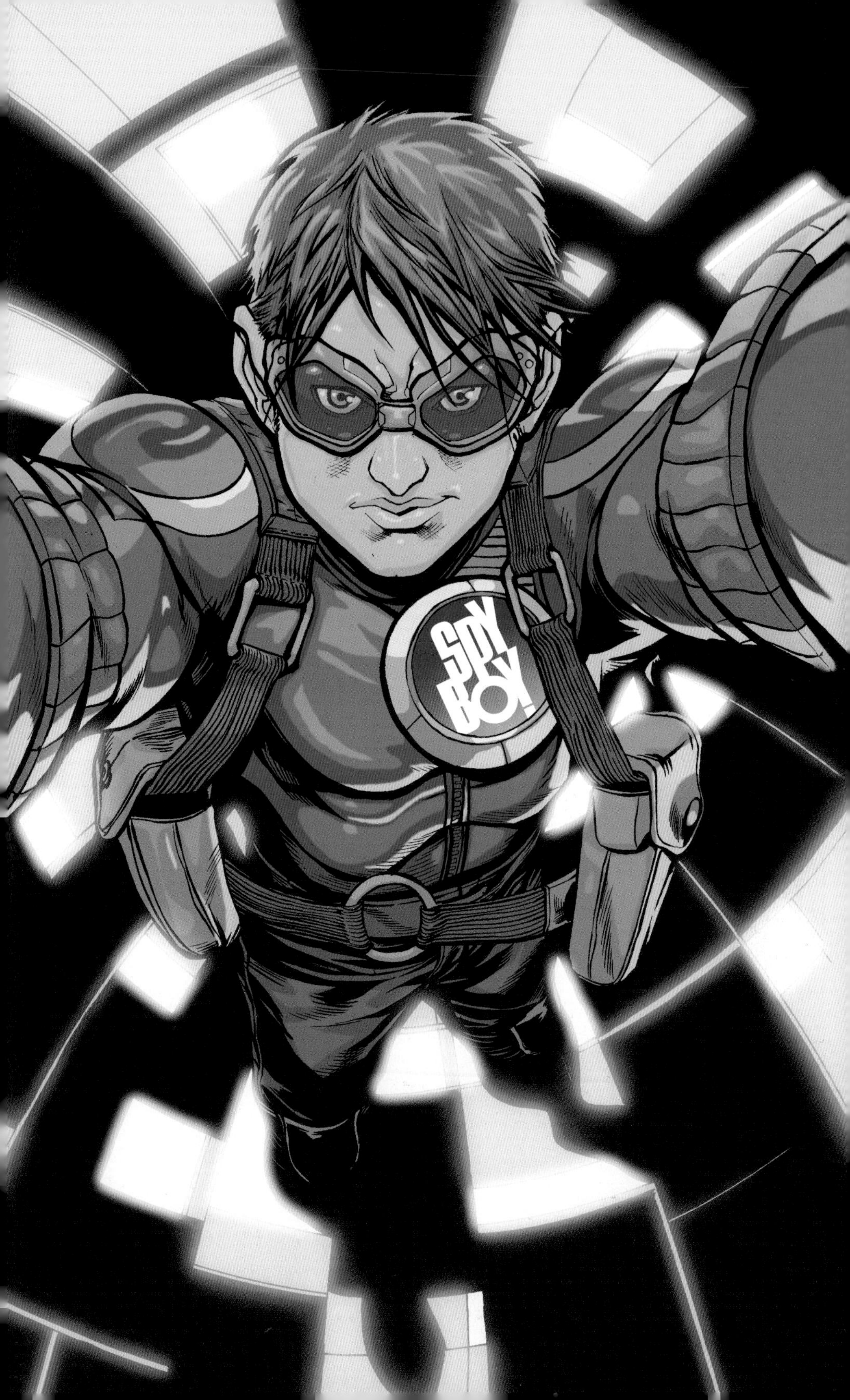
SPY BOY!

SPY BOY™

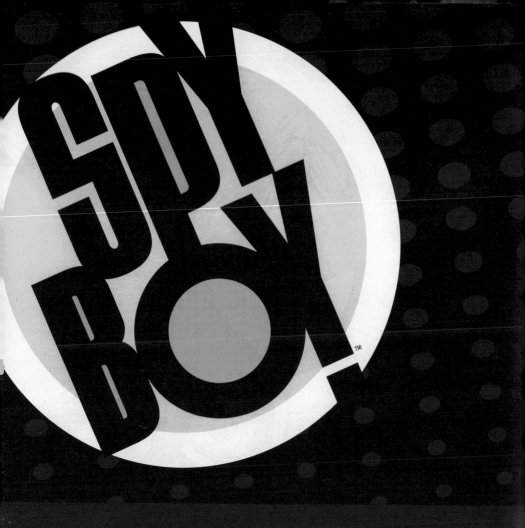

Part 4

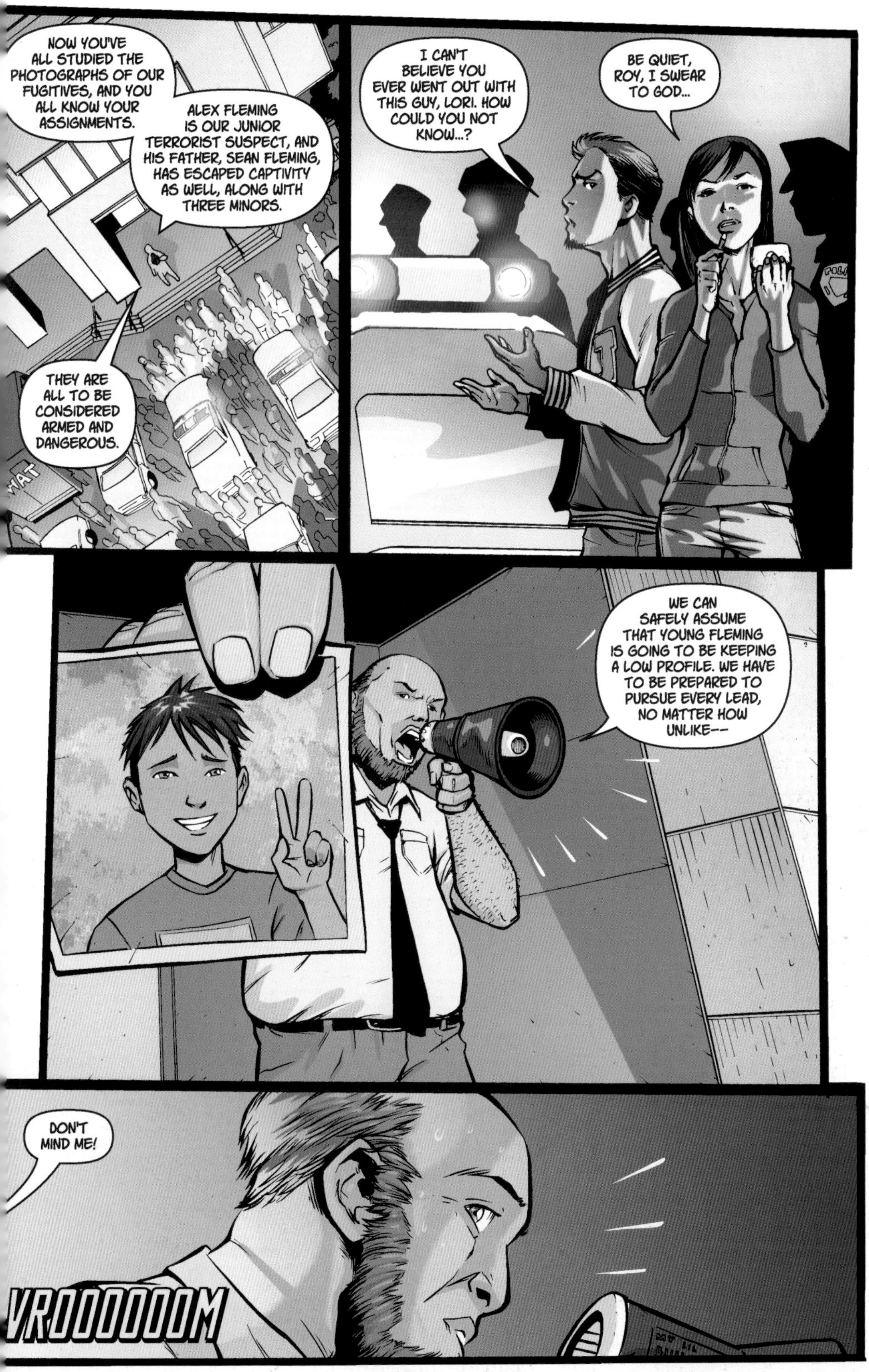

NOW YOU'VE ALL STUDIED THE PHOTOGRAPHS OF OUR FUGITIVES, AND YOU ALL KNOW YOUR ASSIGNMENTS.
ALEX FLEMING IS OUR JUNIOR TERRORIST SUSPECT, AND HIS FATHER, SEAN FLEMING, HAS ESCAPED CAPTIVITY AS WELL, ALONG WITH THREE MINORS.
THEY ARE ALL TO BE CONSIDERED ARMED AND DANGEROUS.
I CAN'T BELIEVE YOU EVER WENT OUT WITH THIS GUY, LORI. HOW COULD YOU NOT KNOW...?
BE QUIET, ROY, I SWEAR TO GOD...
WE CAN SAFELY ASSUME THAT YOUNG FLEMING IS GOING TO BE KEEPING A LOW PROFILE. WE HAVE TO BE PREPARED TO PURSUE EVERY LEAD, NO MATTER HOW UNLIKE--
DON'T MIND ME!
VROOOOOOM

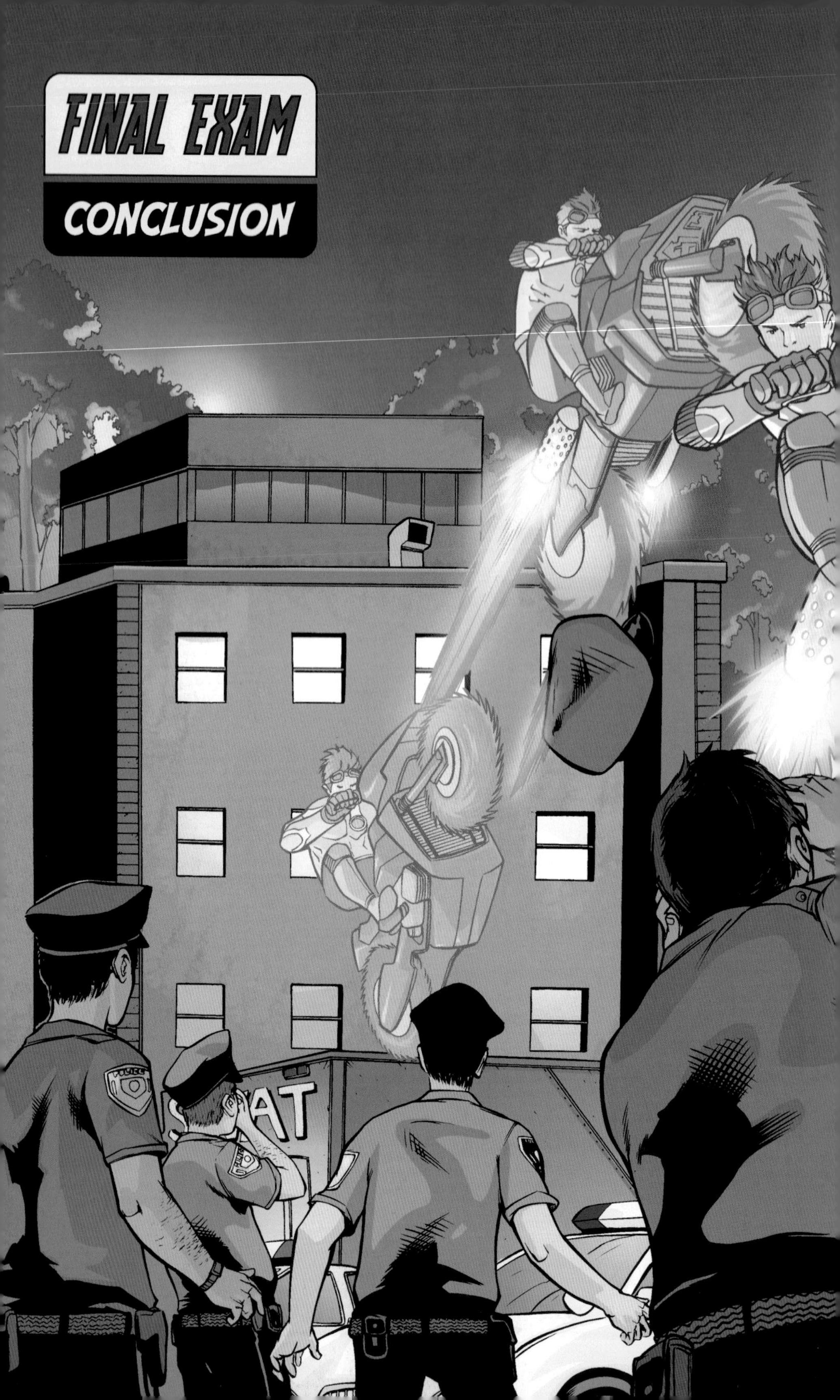
FINAL EXAM
CONCLUSION
POLICE
SWAT

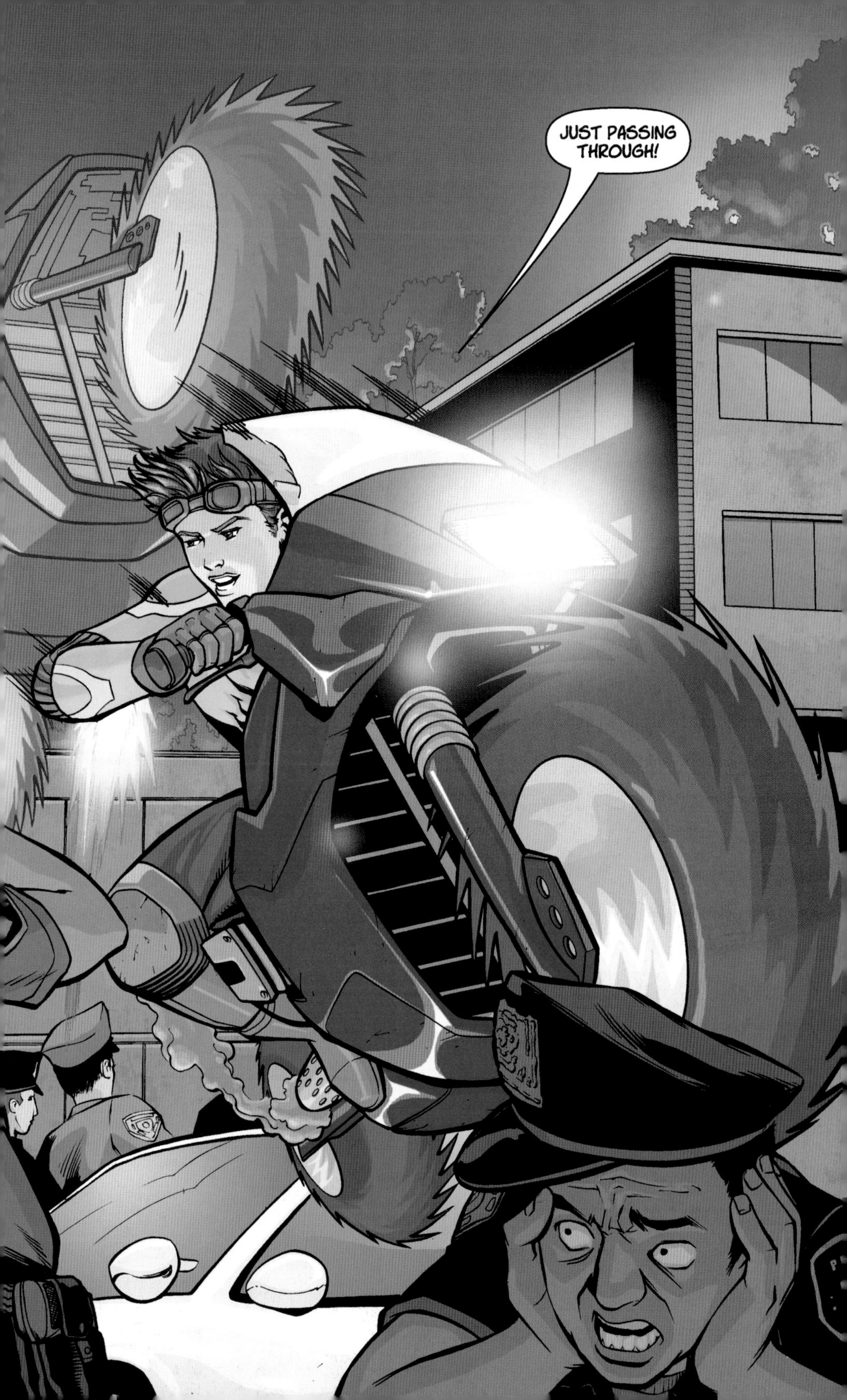
JUST PASSING THROUGH!

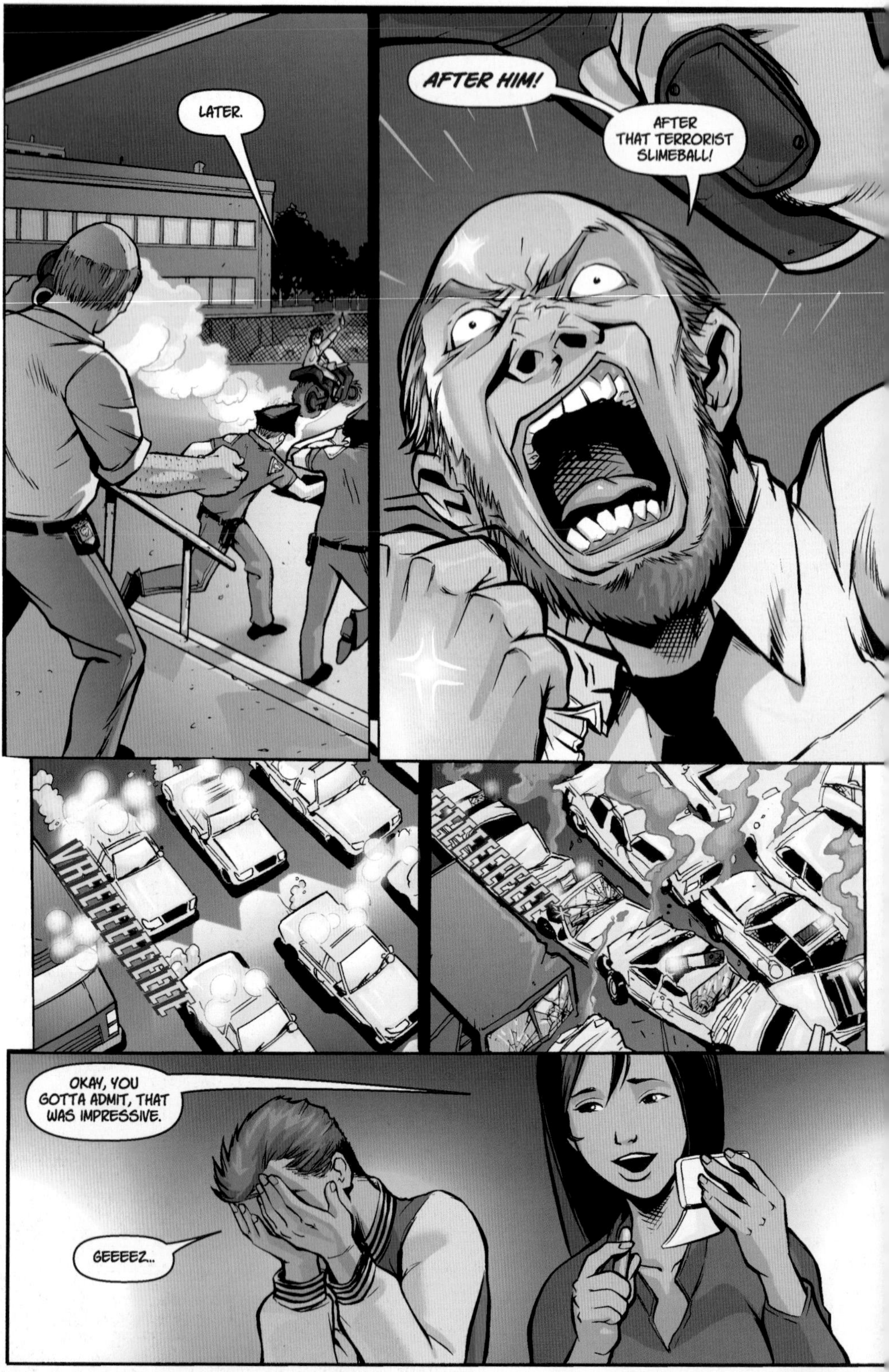
LATER.
AFTER HIM!
AFTER THAT TERRORIST SLIMEBALL!
VREEEEEEEEEEEEEEEEEEEEEEEL
OKAY, YOU GOTTA ADMIT, THAT WAS IMPRESSIVE.
GEEEEZ...

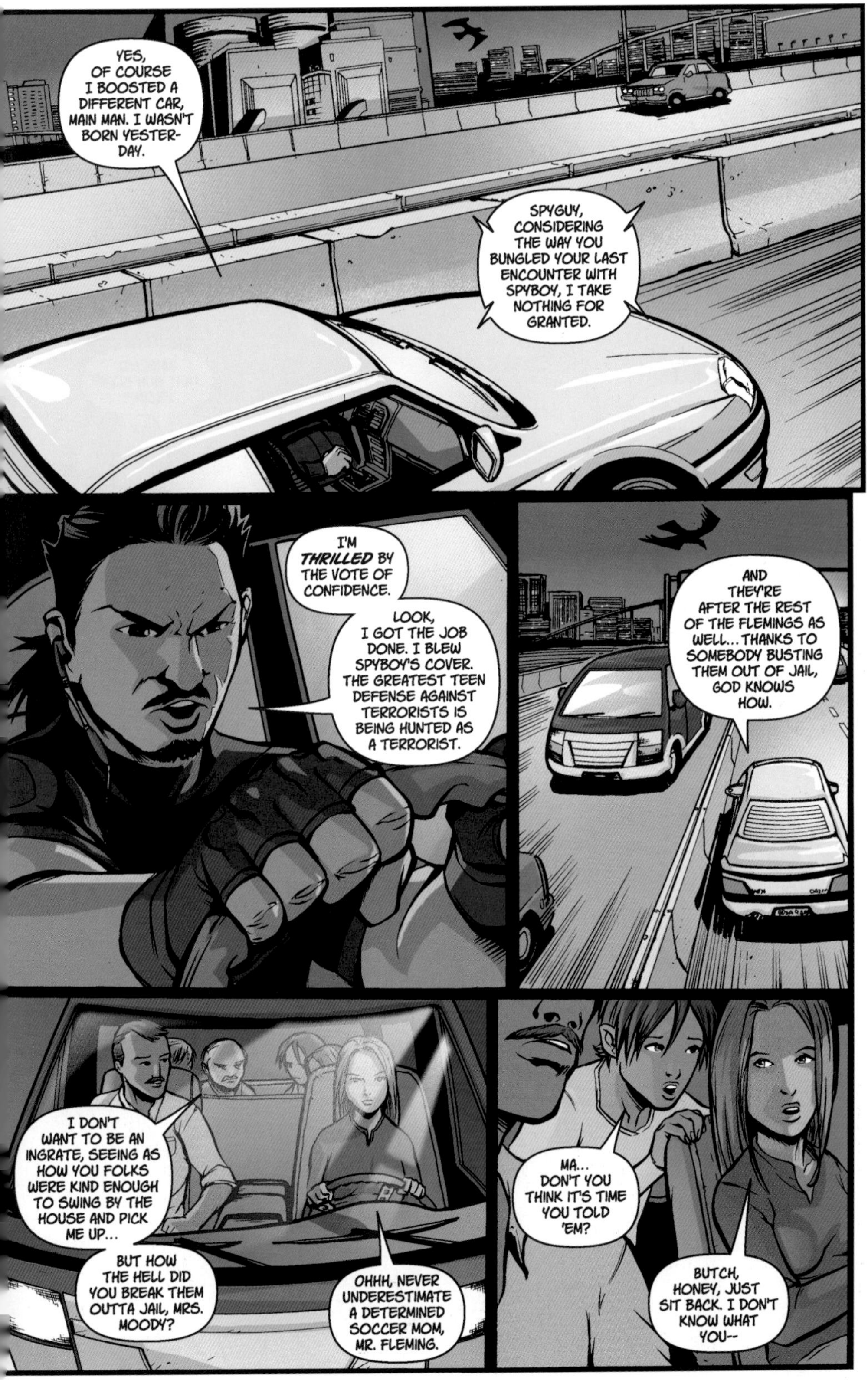
YES, OF COURSE I BOOSTED A DIFFERENT CAR, MAIN MAN. I WASN'T BORN YESTER-DAY.
SPYGUY, CONSIDERING THE WAY YOU BUNGLED YOUR LAST ENCOUNTER WITH SPYBOY, I TAKE NOTHING FOR GRANTED.
I'M *THRILLED* BY THE VOTE OF CONFIDENCE.
LOOK, I GOT THE JOB DONE. I BLEW SPYBOY'S COVER. THE GREATEST TEEN DEFENSE AGAINST TERRORISTS IS BEING HUNTED AS A TERRORIST.
AND THEY'RE AFTER THE REST OF THE FLEMINGS AS WELL... THANKS TO SOMEBODY BUSTING THEM OUT OF JAIL, GOD KNOWS HOW.
I DON'T WANT TO BE AN INGRATE, SEEING AS HOW YOU FOLKS WERE KIND ENOUGH TO SWING BY THE HOUSE AND PICK ME UP...
BUT HOW THE HELL DID YOU BREAK THEM OUTTA JAIL, MRS. MOODY?
OHHH, NEVER UNDERESTIMATE A DETERMINED SOCCER MOM, MR. FLEMING.
MA... DON'T YOU THINK IT'S TIME YOU TOLD 'EM?
BUTCH, HONEY, JUST SIT BACK. I DON'T KNOW WHAT YOU--

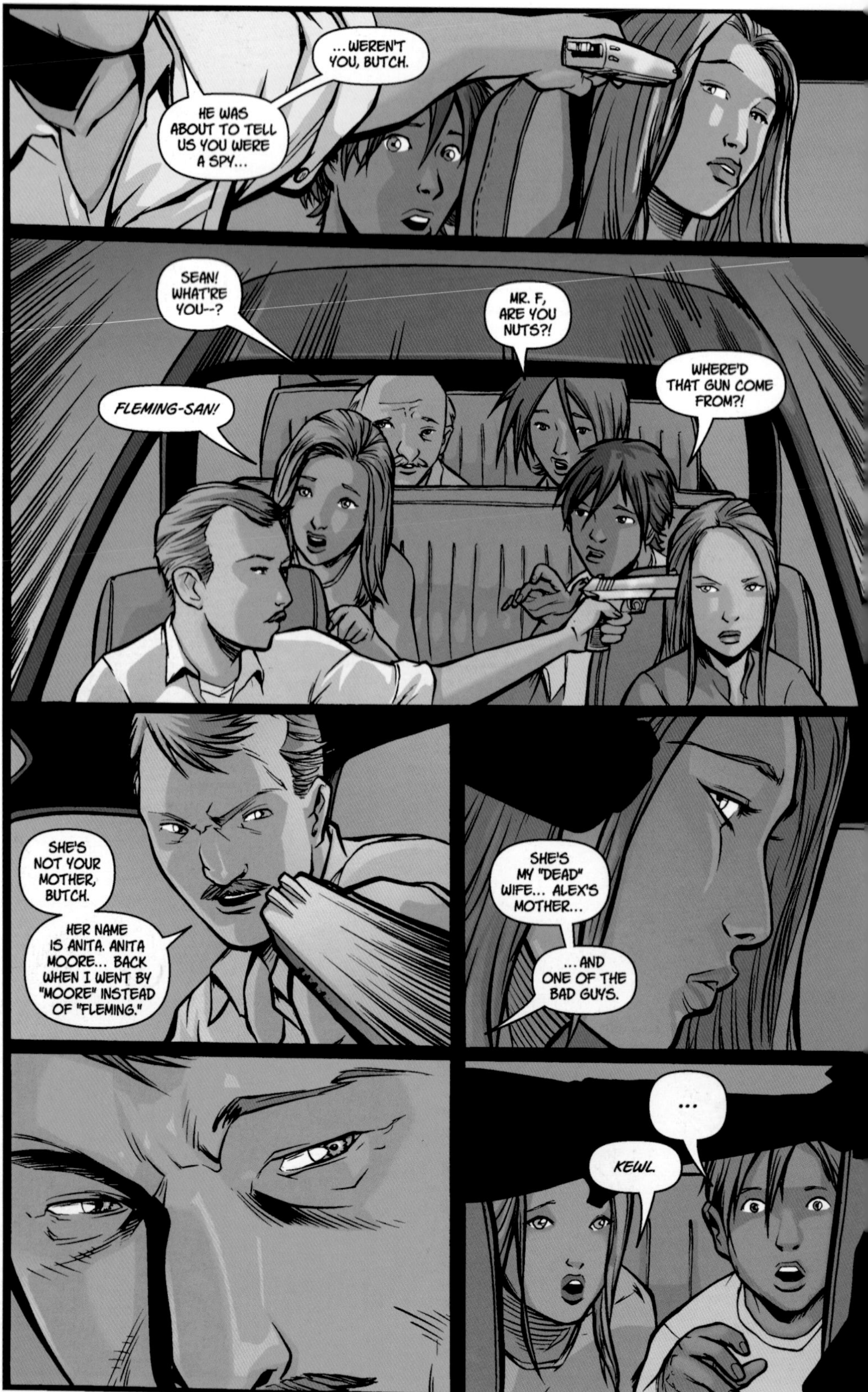
HE WAS ABOUT TO TELL US YOU WERE A SPY...
...WEREN'T YOU, BUTCH.
SEAN! WHAT'RE YOU--?
MR. F, ARE YOU NUTS?!
FLEMING-SAN!
WHERE'D THAT GUN COME FROM?!
SHE'S NOT YOUR MOTHER, BUTCH.
HER NAME IS ANITA. ANITA MOORE... BACK WHEN I WENT BY "MOORE" INSTEAD OF "FLEMING."
SHE'S MY "DEAD" WIFE... ALEX'S MOTHER...
...AND ONE OF THE BAD GUYS.
...
KEWL.

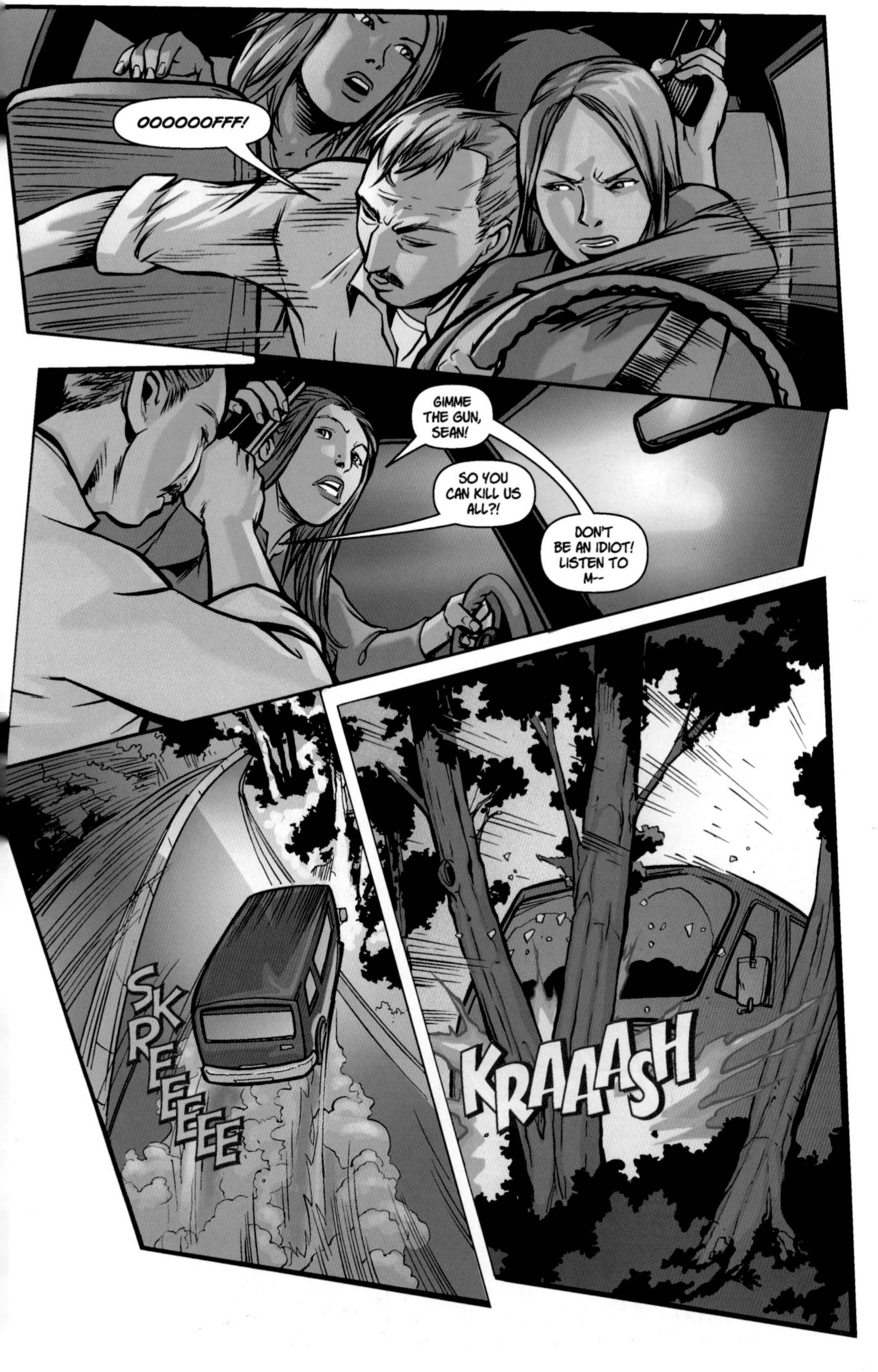
OOOOOOFFF!
GIMME THE GUN, SEAN!
SO YOU CAN KILL US ALL?!
DON'T BE AN IDIOT! LISTEN TO M--
SKREEEEEE
KRAAASH

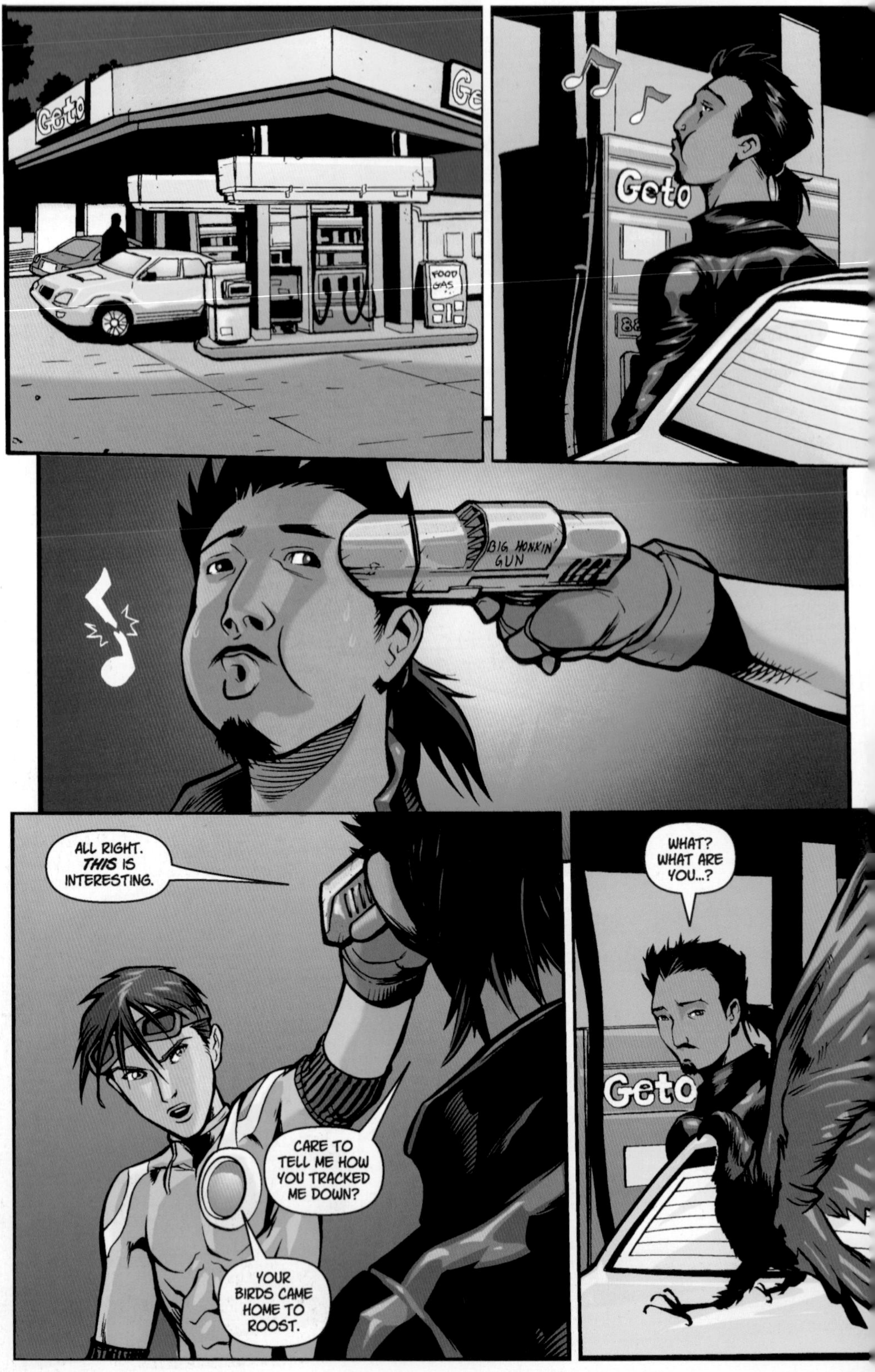
Geto
Geto
FOOD GAS
Geto
BIG HONKIN' GUN
ALL RIGHT. THIS IS INTERESTING.
WHAT? WHAT ARE YOU...?
CARE TO TELL ME HOW YOU TRACKED ME DOWN?
YOUR BIRDS CAME HOME TO ROOST.
Geto

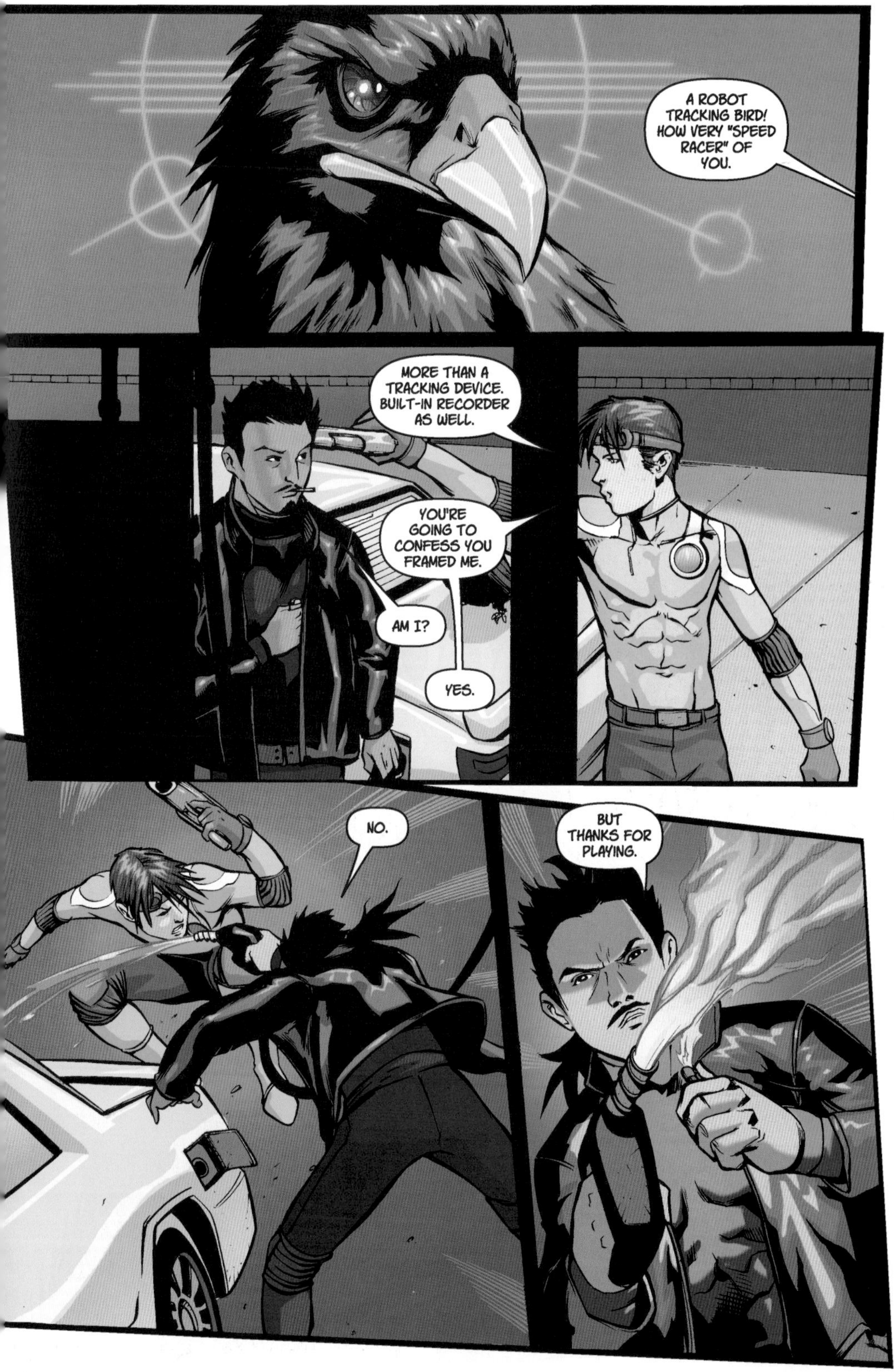
A ROBOT TRACKING BIRD! HOW VERY "SPEED RACER" OF YOU.
MORE THAN A TRACKING DEVICE. BUILT-IN RECORDER AS WELL.
YOU'RE GOING TO CONFESS YOU FRAMED ME.
AM I?
YES.
NO.
BUT THANKS FOR PLAYING.

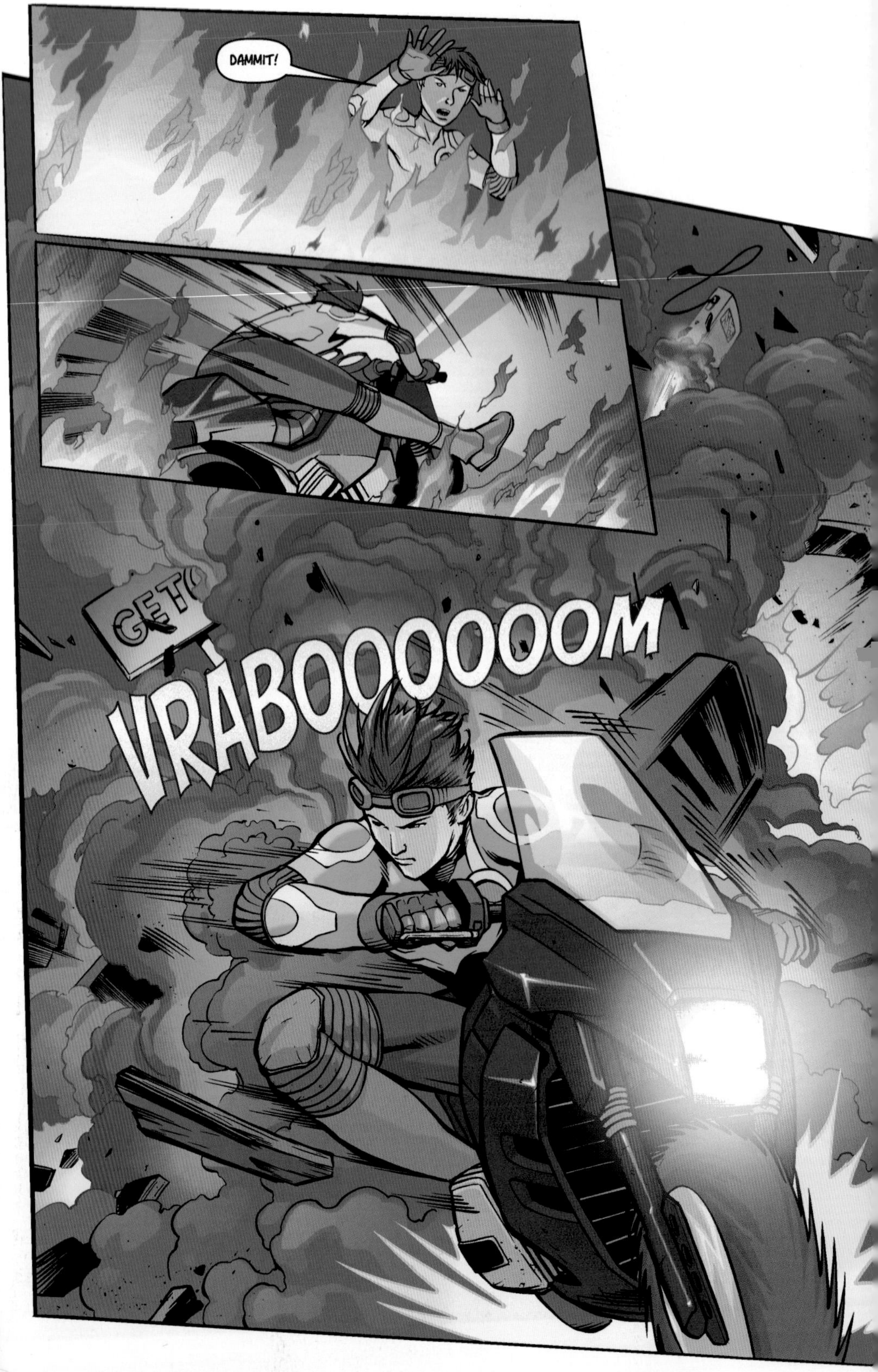
DAMMIT!
GET
VRABOOOOOOOM

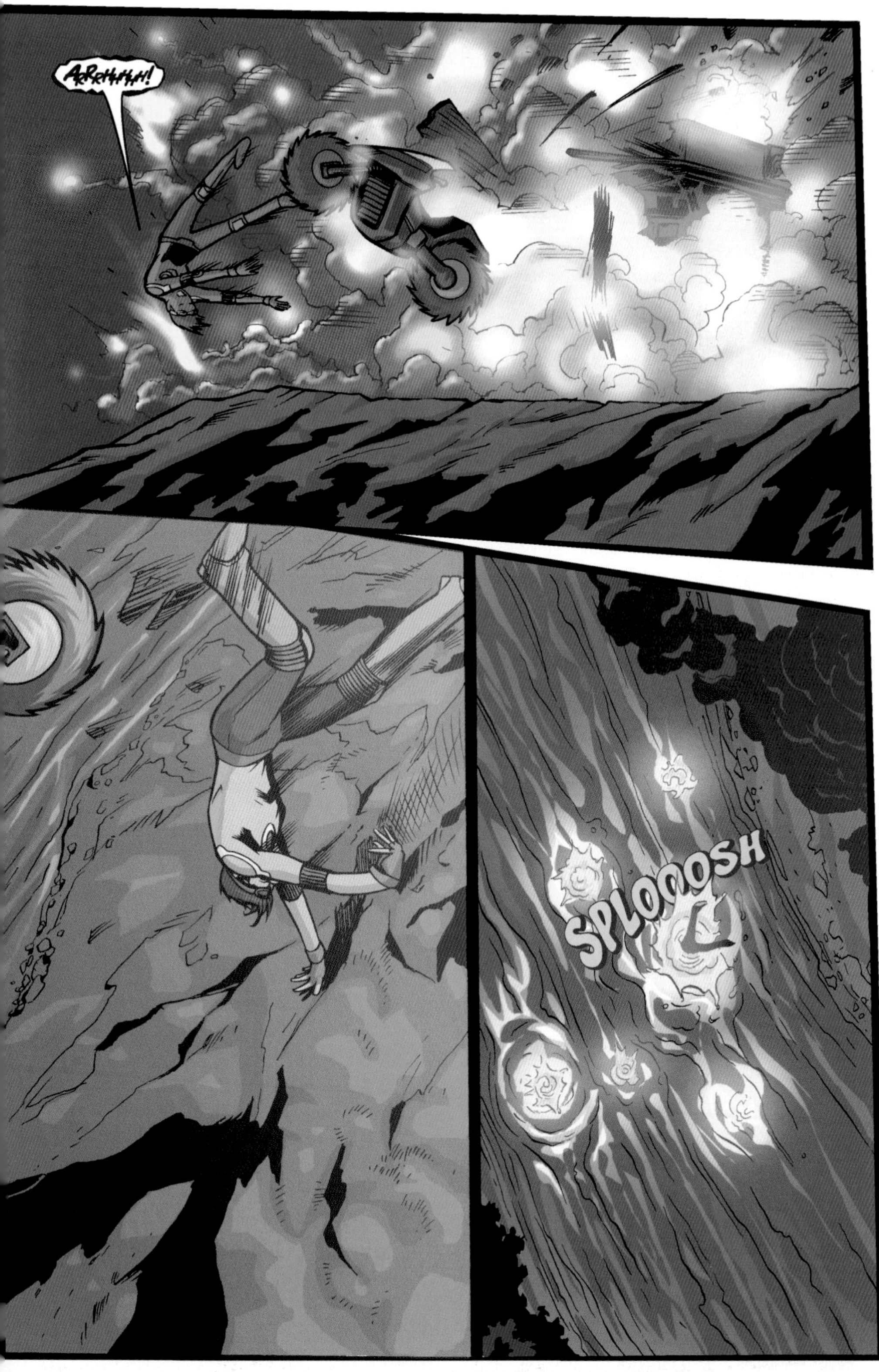
ARRHHHHH!
SPLOOOSH

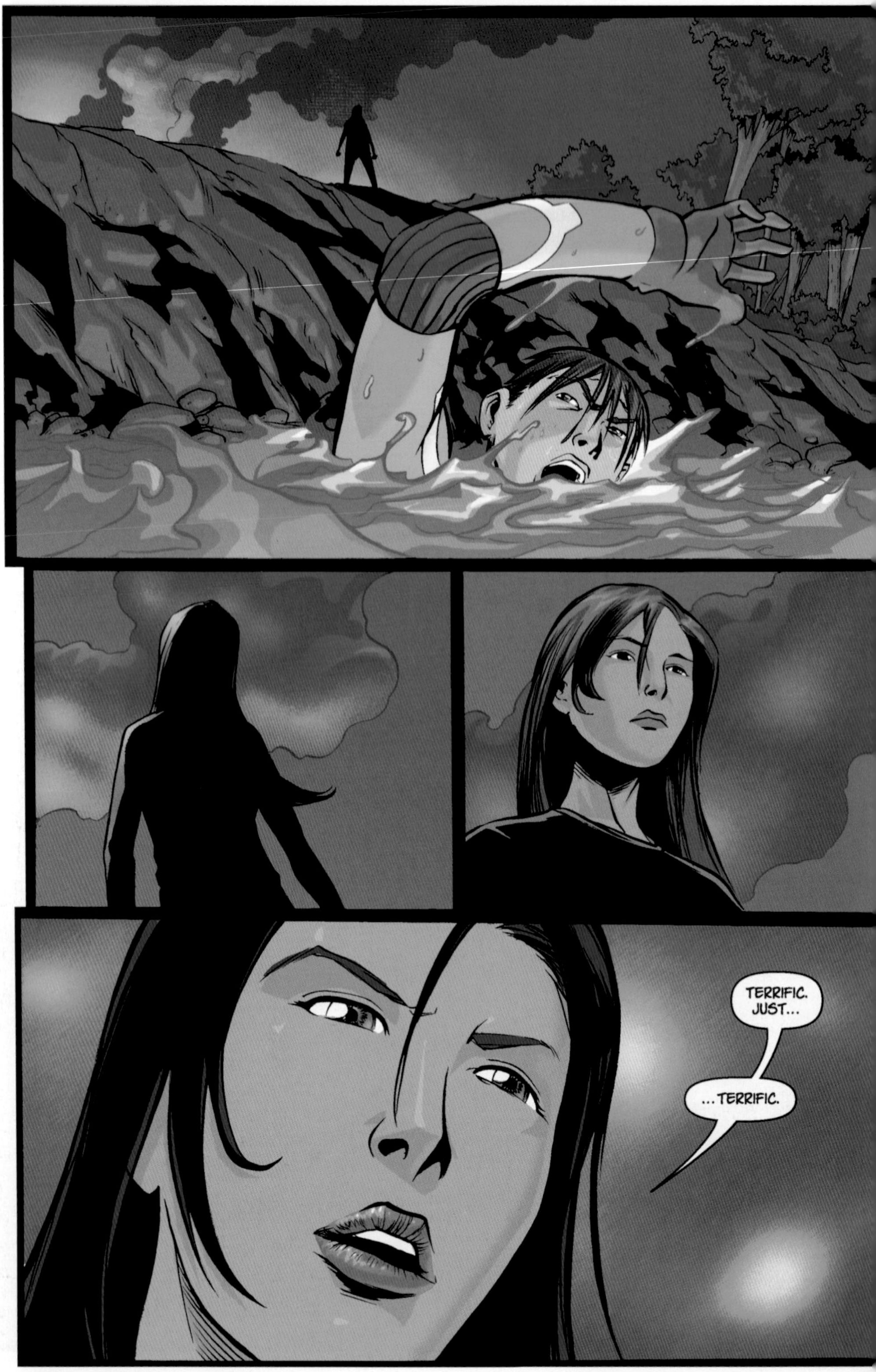
TERRIFIC. JUST...
...TERRIFIC.

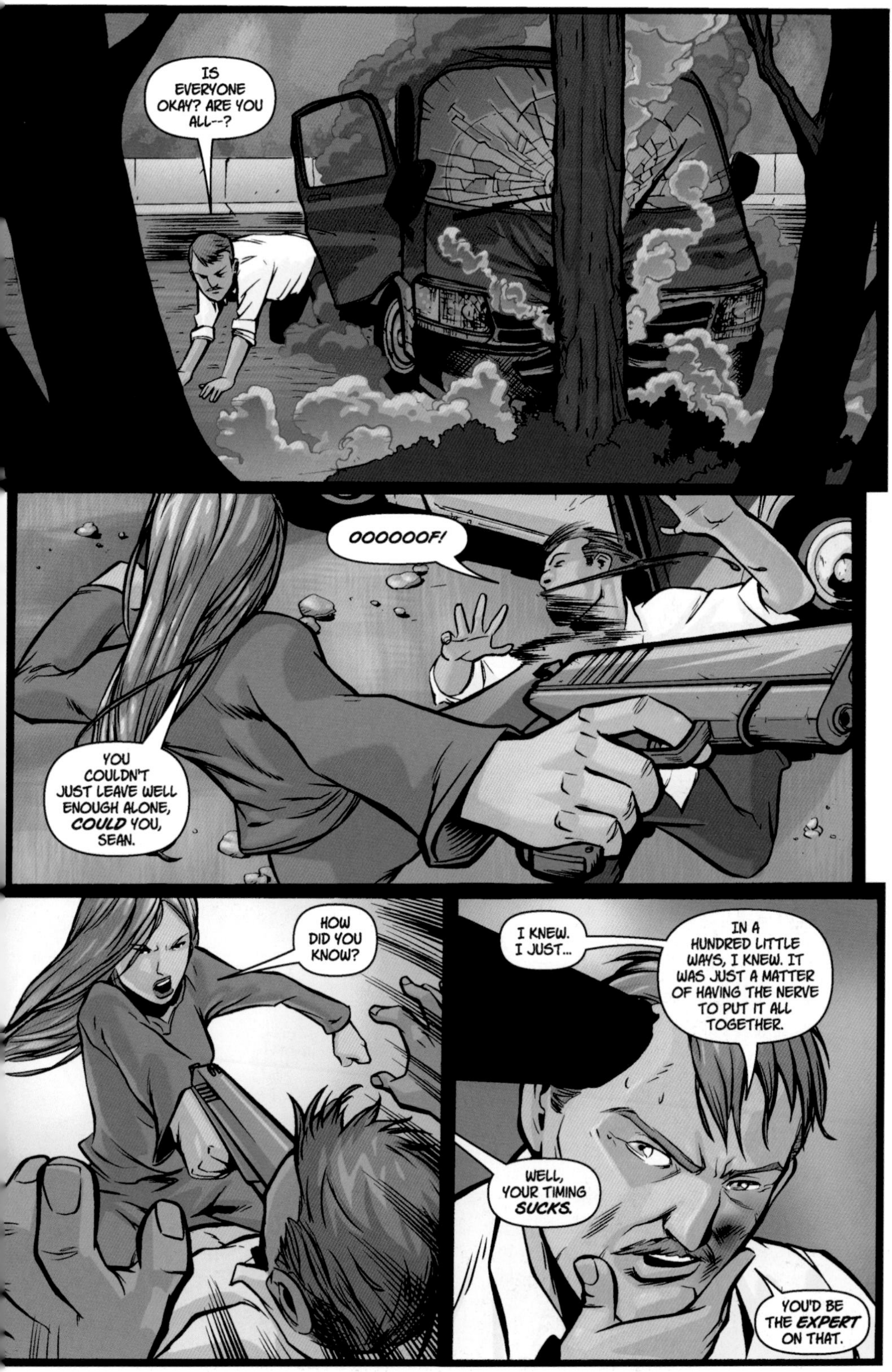
IS EVERYONE OKAY? ARE YOU ALL--?
OOOOOOF!
YOU COULDN'T JUST LEAVE WELL ENOUGH ALONE, *COULD* YOU, SEAN.
HOW DID YOU KNOW?
I KNEW. I JUST...
IN A HUNDRED LITTLE WAYS, I KNEW. IT WAS JUST A MATTER OF HAVING THE NERVE TO PUT IT ALL TOGETHER.
WELL, YOUR TIMING *SUCKS.*
YOU'D BE THE *EXPERT* ON THAT.

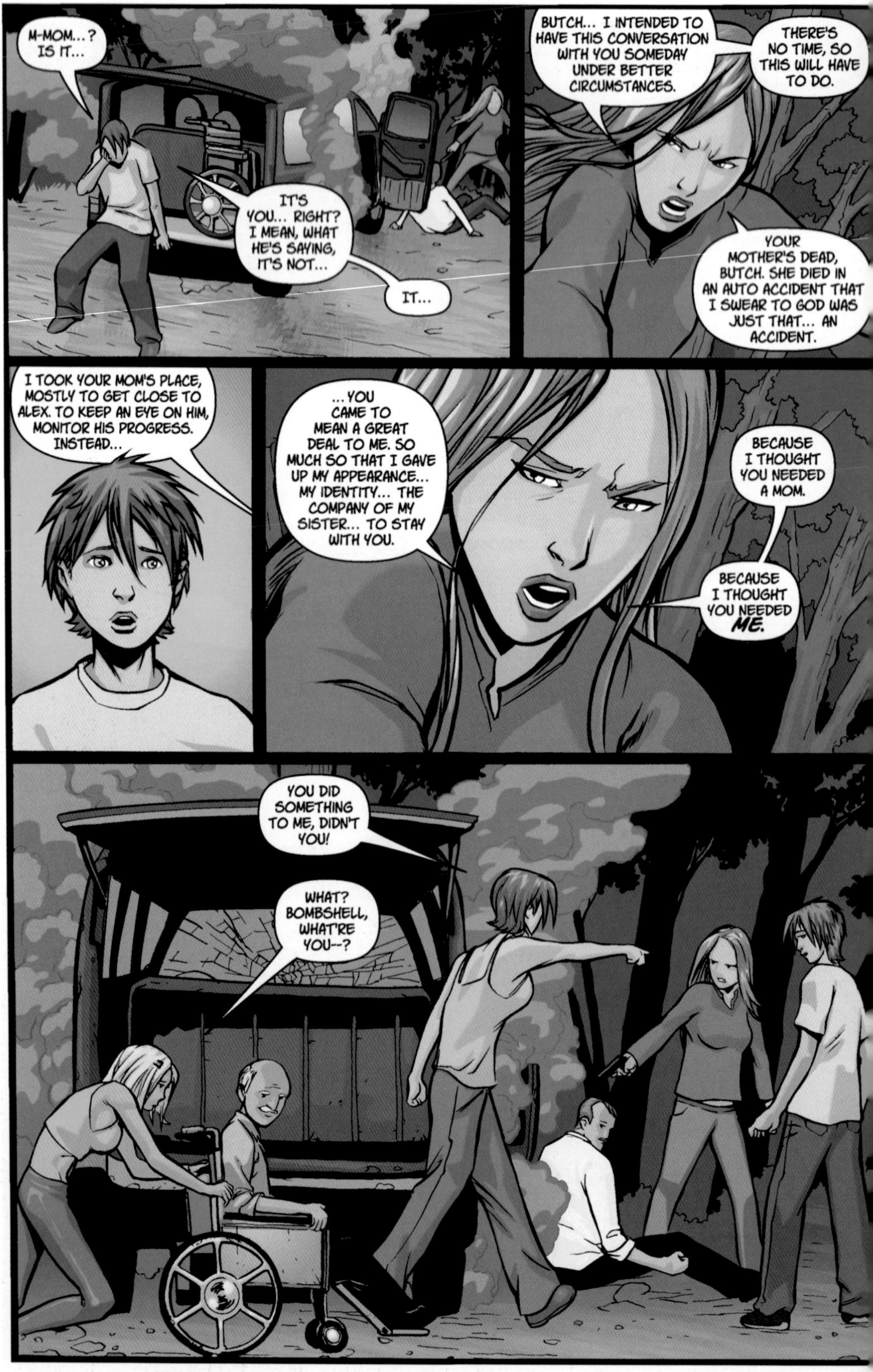
M-MOM...? IS IT...
IT'S YOU... RIGHT? I MEAN, WHAT HE'S SAYING, IT'S NOT...
IT...
BUTCH... I INTENDED TO HAVE THIS CONVERSATION WITH YOU SOMEDAY UNDER BETTER CIRCUMSTANCES.
THERE'S NO TIME, SO THIS WILL HAVE TO DO.
YOUR MOTHER'S DEAD, BUTCH. SHE DIED IN AN AUTO ACCIDENT THAT I SWEAR TO GOD WAS JUST THAT... AN ACCIDENT.
I TOOK YOUR MOM'S PLACE, MOSTLY TO GET CLOSE TO ALEX. TO KEEP AN EYE ON HIM, MONITOR HIS PROGRESS. INSTEAD...
...YOU CAME TO MEAN A GREAT DEAL TO ME. SO MUCH SO THAT I GAVE UP MY APPEARANCE... MY IDENTITY... THE COMPANY OF MY SISTER... TO STAY WITH YOU.
BECAUSE I THOUGHT YOU NEEDED A MOM.
BECAUSE I THOUGHT YOU NEEDED ME.
YOU DID SOMETHING TO ME, DIDN'T YOU!
WHAT? BOMBSHELL, WHAT'RE YOU--?

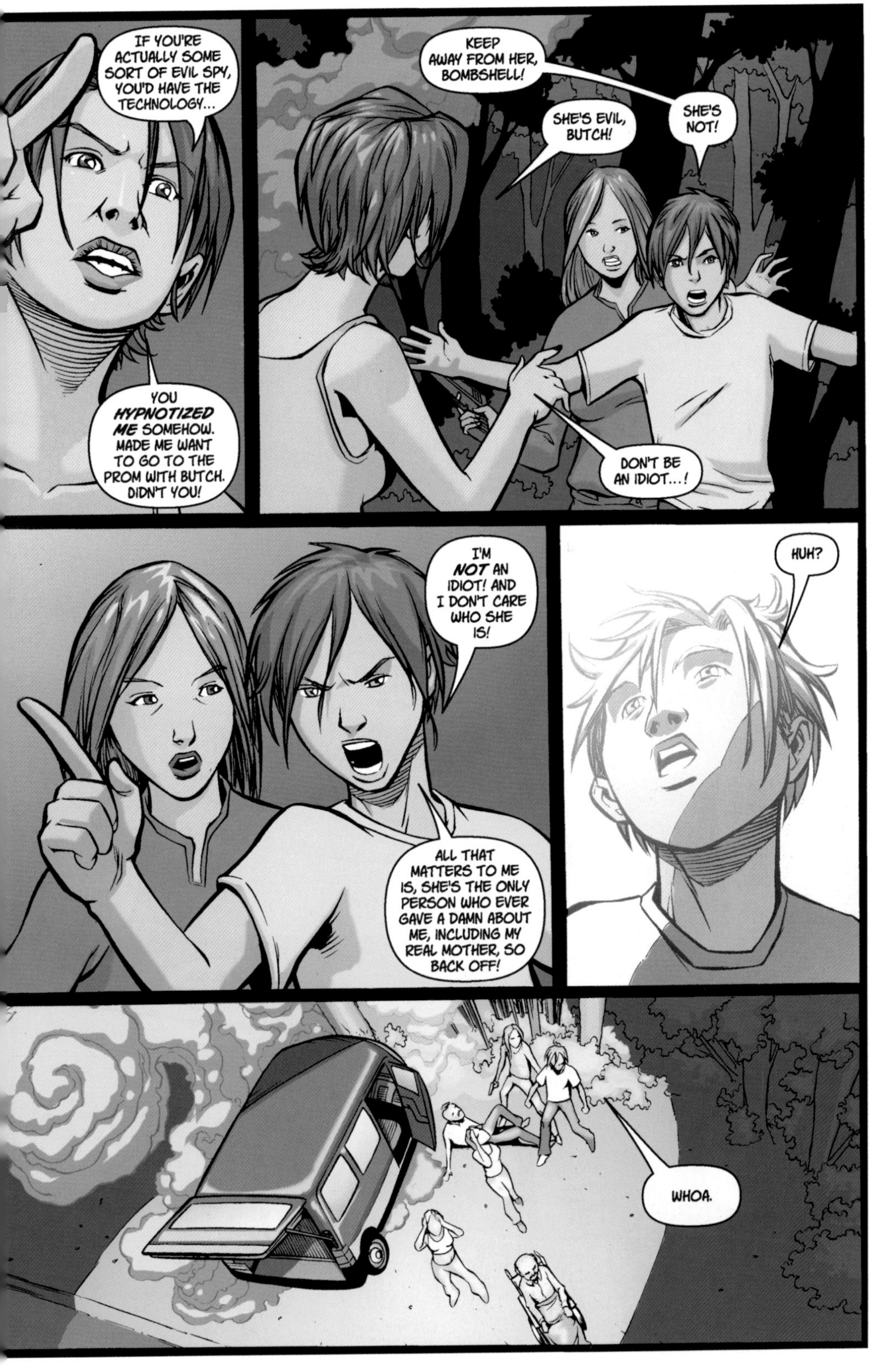
IF YOU'RE ACTUALLY SOME SORT OF EVIL SPY, YOU'D HAVE THE TECHNOLOGY...
YOU HYPNOTIZED ME SOMEHOW. MADE ME WANT TO GO TO THE PROM WITH BUTCH. DIDN'T YOU!
KEEP AWAY FROM HER, BOMBSHELL!
SHE'S EVIL, BUTCH!
SHE'S NOT!
DON'T BE AN IDIOT...!
I'M NOT AN IDIOT! AND I DON'T CARE WHO SHE IS!
ALL THAT MATTERS TO ME IS, SHE'S THE ONLY PERSON WHO EVER GAVE A DAMN ABOUT ME, INCLUDING MY REAL MOTHER, SO BACK OFF!
HUH?
WHOA.

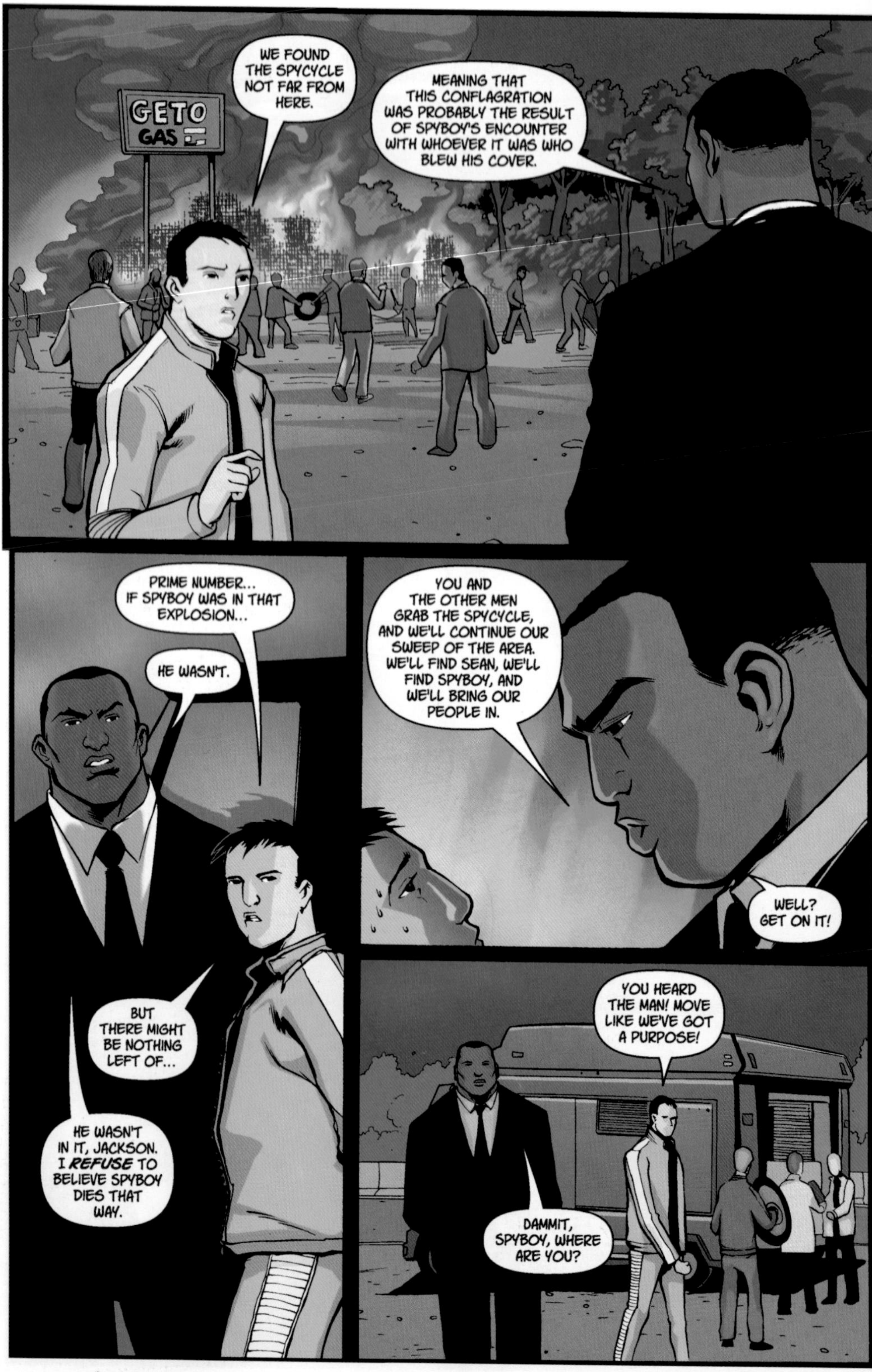
GETO GAS
WE FOUND THE SPYCYCLE NOT FAR FROM HERE.
MEANING THAT THIS CONFLAGRATION WAS PROBABLY THE RESULT OF SPYBOY'S ENCOUNTER WITH WHOEVER IT WAS WHO BLEW HIS COVER.
PRIME NUMBER... IF SPYBOY WAS IN THAT EXPLOSION...
HE WASN'T.
BUT THERE MIGHT BE NOTHING LEFT OF...
HE WASN'T IN IT, JACKSON. I *REFUSE* TO BELIEVE SPYBOY DIES THAT WAY.
YOU AND THE OTHER MEN GRAB THE SPYCYCLE, AND WE'LL CONTINUE OUR SWEEP OF THE AREA. WE'LL FIND SEAN, WE'LL FIND SPYBOY, AND WE'LL BRING OUR PEOPLE IN.
WELL? GET ON IT!
YOU HEARD THE MAN! MOVE LIKE WE'VE GOT A PURPOSE!
DAMMIT, SPYBOY, WHERE ARE YOU?

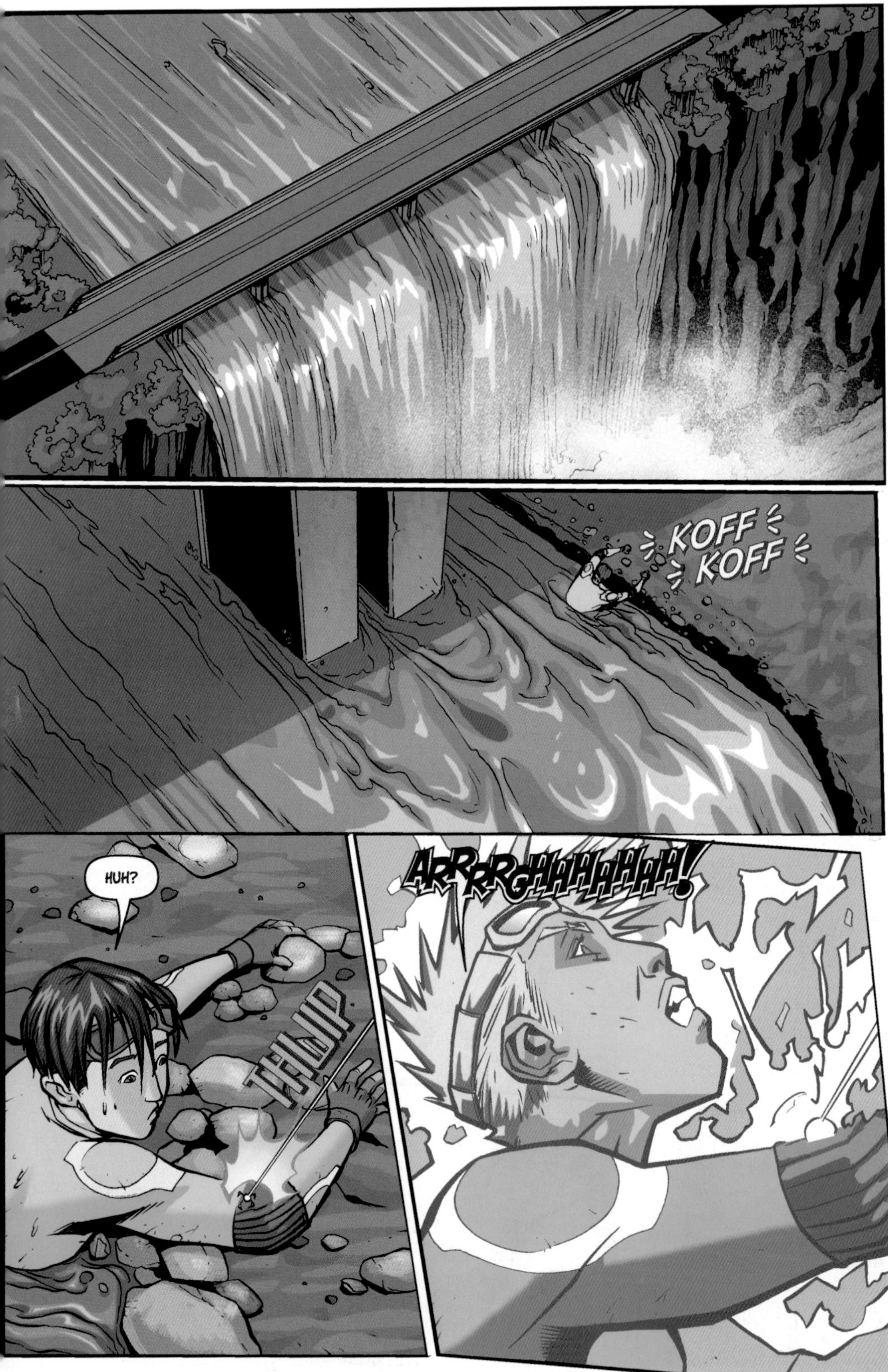
KOFF KOFF
HUH?
THUMP
ARRRRGHAAAAAAH!

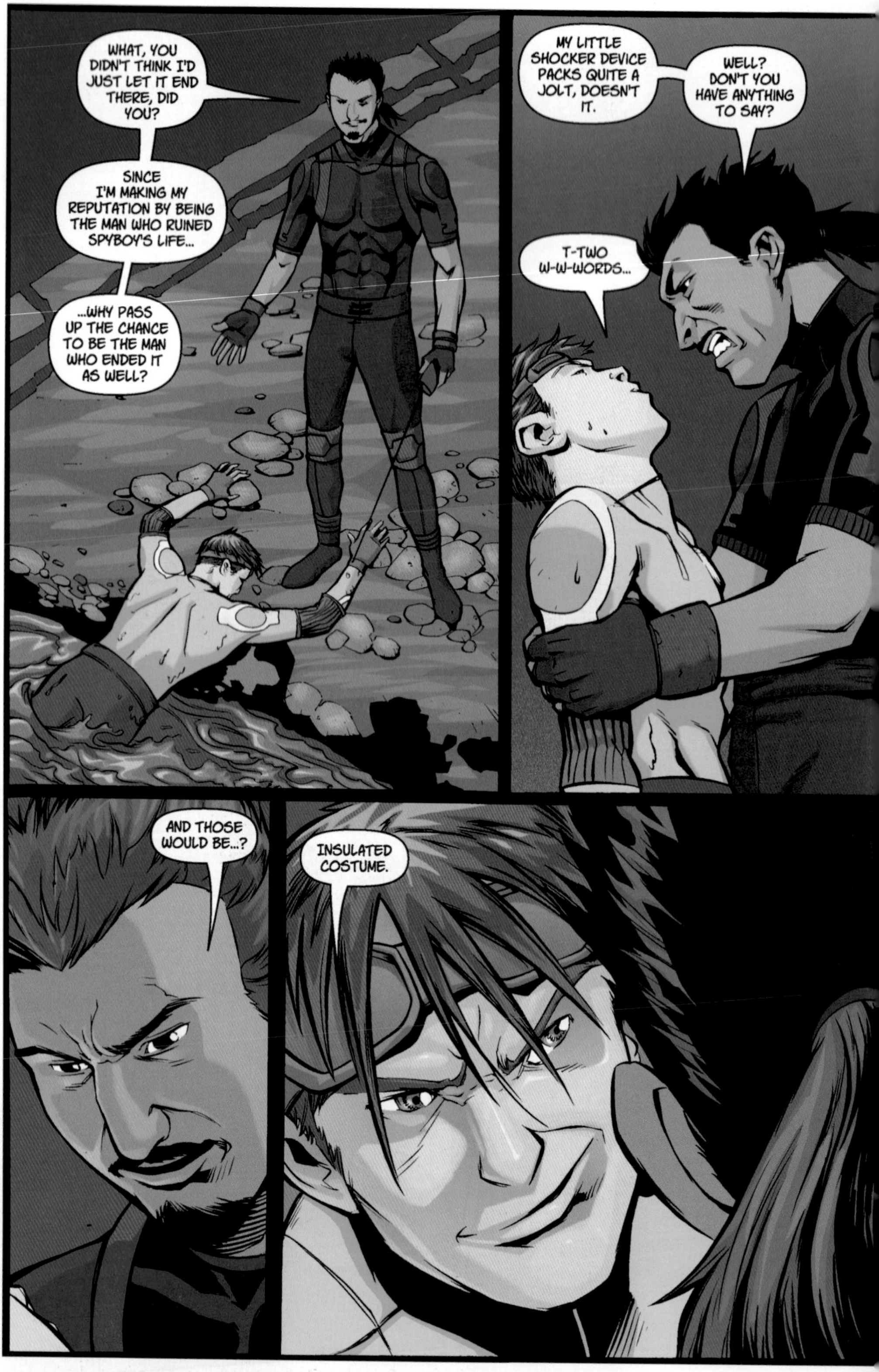
WHAT, YOU DIDN'T THINK I'D JUST LET IT END THERE, DID YOU?
SINCE I'M MAKING MY REPUTATION BY BEING THE MAN WHO RUINED SPYBOY'S LIFE...
...WHY PASS UP THE CHANCE TO BE THE MAN WHO ENDED IT AS WELL?
MY LITTLE SHOCKER DEVICE PACKS QUITE A JOLT, DOESN'T IT.
WELL? DON'T YOU HAVE ANYTHING TO SAY?
T-TWO W-W-WORDS...
AND THOSE WOULD BE...?
INSULATED COSTUME.

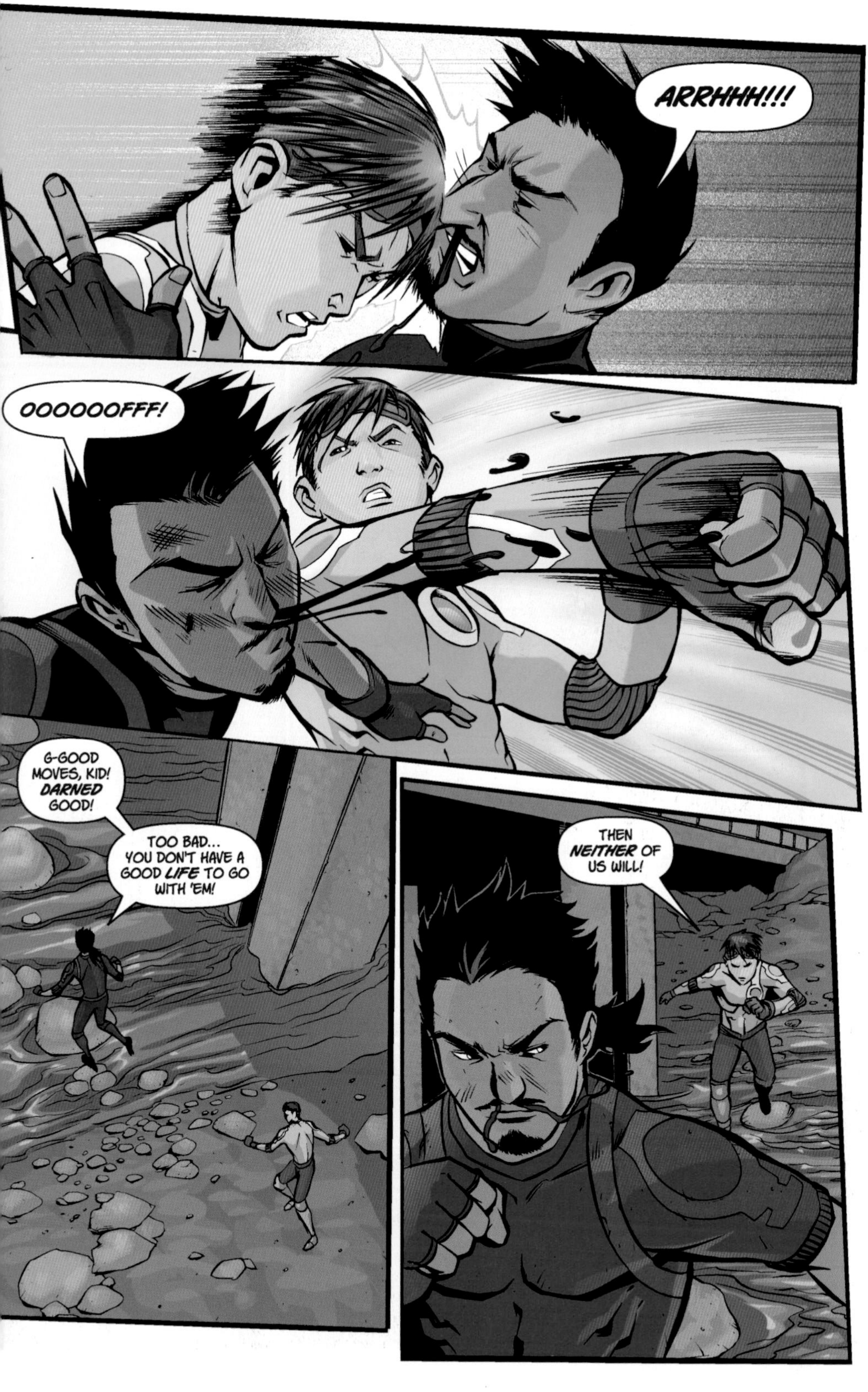
ARRHHH!!!
OOOOOOFFF!
G-GOOD MOVES, KID! DARNED GOOD!
TOO BAD... YOU DON'T HAVE A GOOD LIFE TO GO WITH 'EM!
THEN NEITHER OF US WILL!

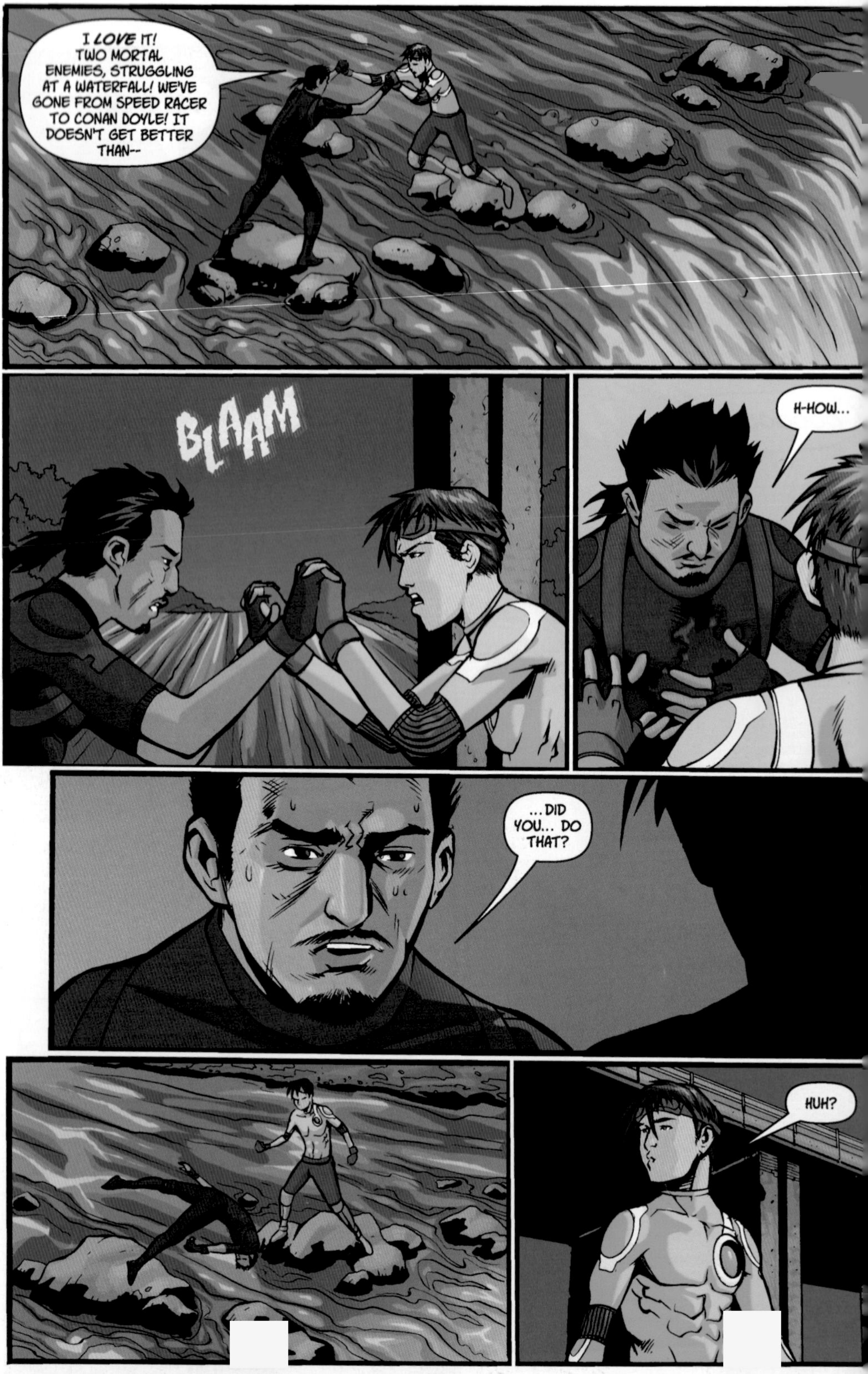
I LOVE IT! TWO MORTAL ENEMIES, STRUGGLING AT A WATERFALL! WE'VE GONE FROM SPEED RACER TO CONAN DOYLE! IT DOESN'T GET BETTER THAN--
BLAAM
H-HOW...
...DID YOU... DO THAT?
HUH?

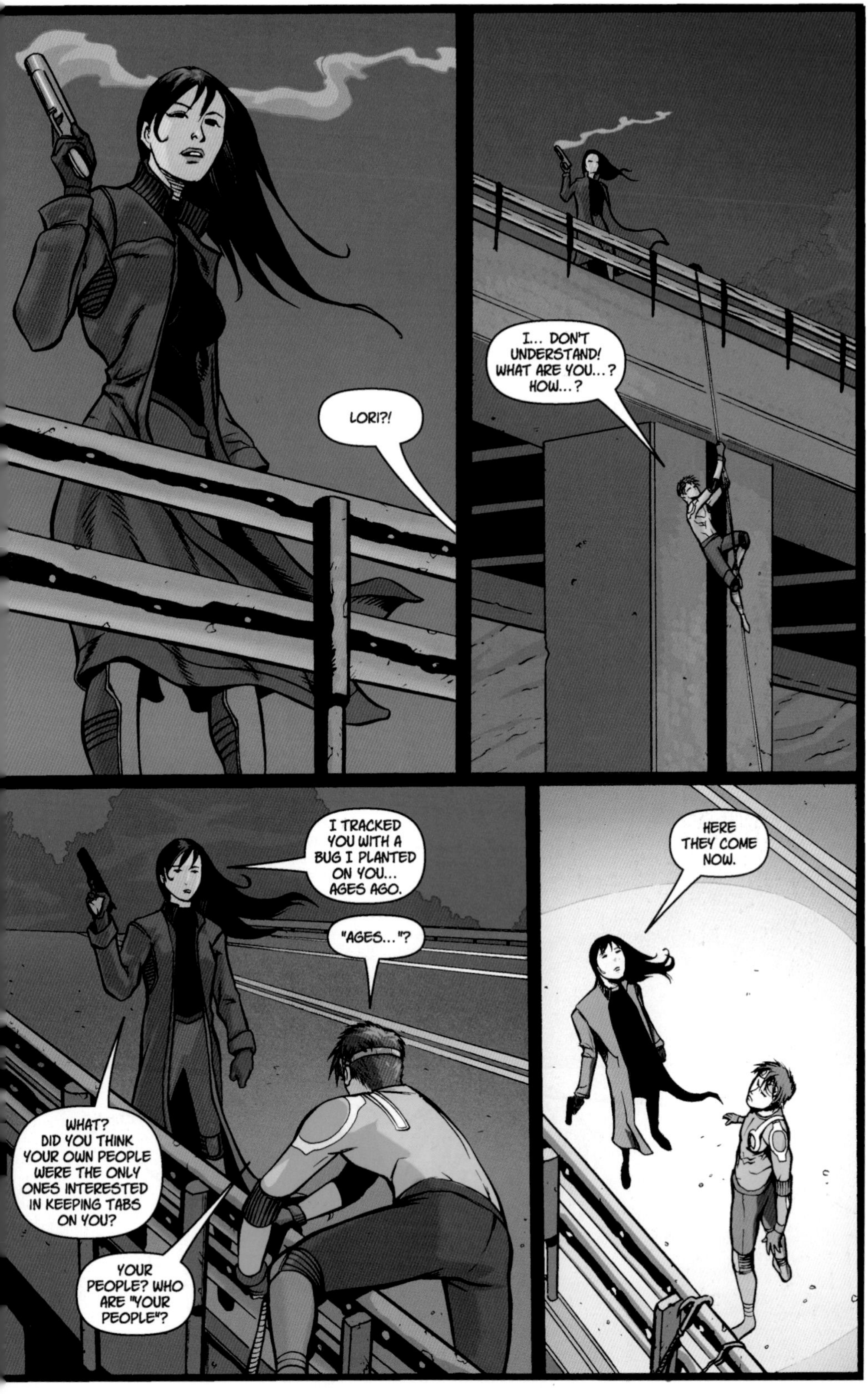
LORI?!
I... DON'T UNDERSTAND! WHAT ARE YOU...? HOW...?
I TRACKED YOU WITH A BUG I PLANTED ON YOU... AGES AGO.
"AGES..."?
WHAT? DID YOU THINK YOUR OWN PEOPLE WERE THE ONLY ONES INTERESTED IN KEEPING TABS ON YOU?
YOUR PEOPLE? WHO ARE "YOUR PEOPLE"?
HERE THEY COME NOW.

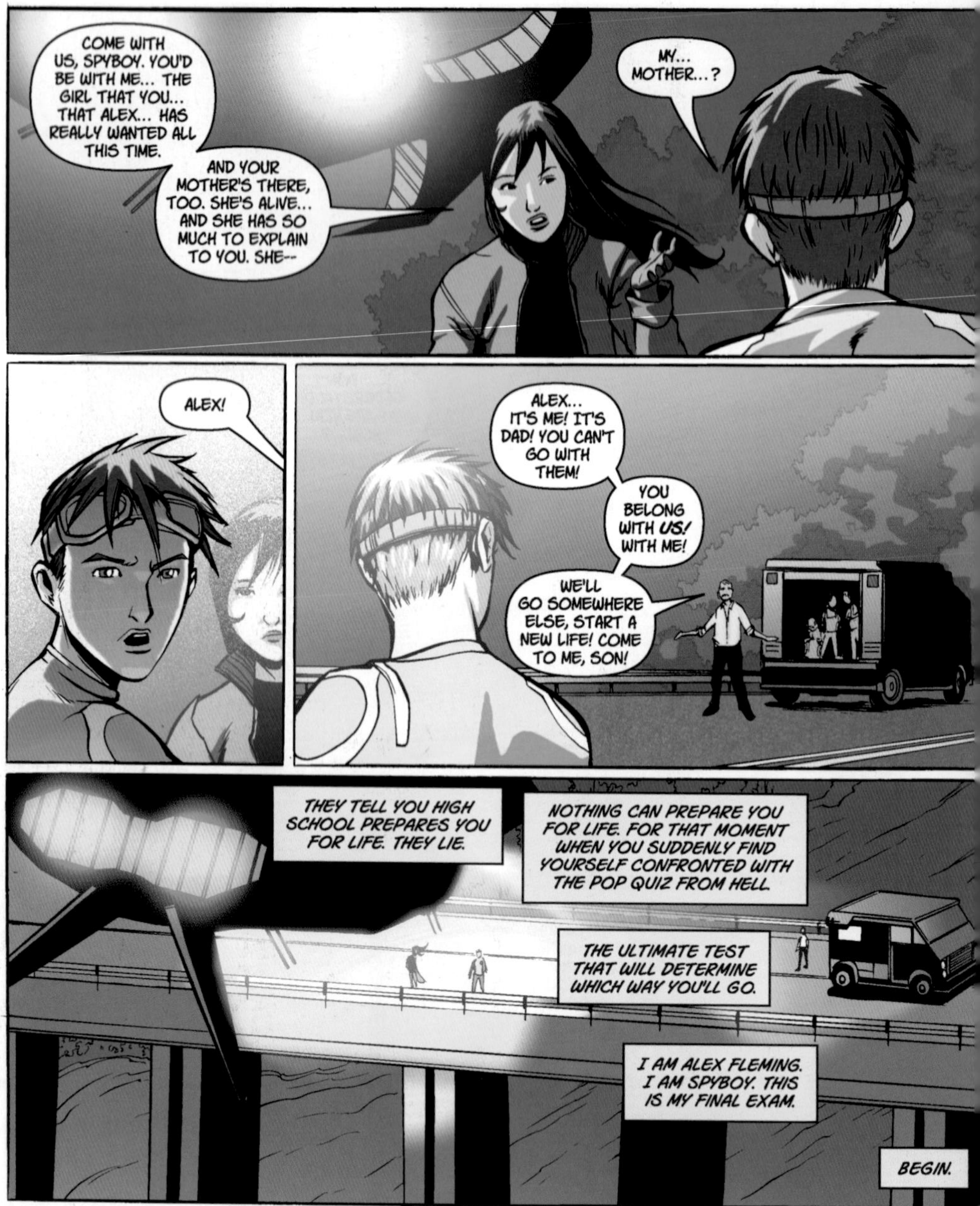
COME WITH US, SPYBOY. YOU'D BE WITH ME... THE GIRL THAT YOU... THAT ALEX... HAS REALLY WANTED ALL THIS TIME.
AND YOUR MOTHER'S THERE, TOO. SHE'S ALIVE... AND SHE HAS SO MUCH TO EXPLAIN TO YOU. SHE--
MY... MOTHER...?
ALEX!
ALEX... IT'S ME! IT'S DAD! YOU CAN'T GO WITH THEM!
YOU BELONG WITH US! WITH ME!
WE'LL GO SOMEWHERE ELSE, START A NEW LIFE! COME TO ME, SON!
THEY TELL YOU HIGH SCHOOL PREPARES YOU FOR LIFE. THEY LIE.
NOTHING CAN PREPARE YOU FOR LIFE. FOR THAT MOMENT WHEN YOU SUDDENLY FIND YOURSELF CONFRONTED WITH THE POP QUIZ FROM HELL.
THE ULTIMATE TEST THAT WILL DETERMINE WHICH WAY YOU'LL GO.
I AM ALEX FLEMING. I AM SPYBOY. THIS IS MY FINAL EXAM.
BEGIN.

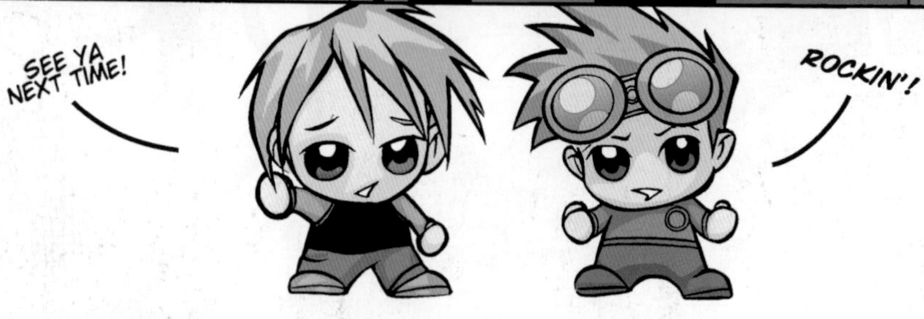
SEE YA NEXT TIME!
ROCKIN'!

Sketch page

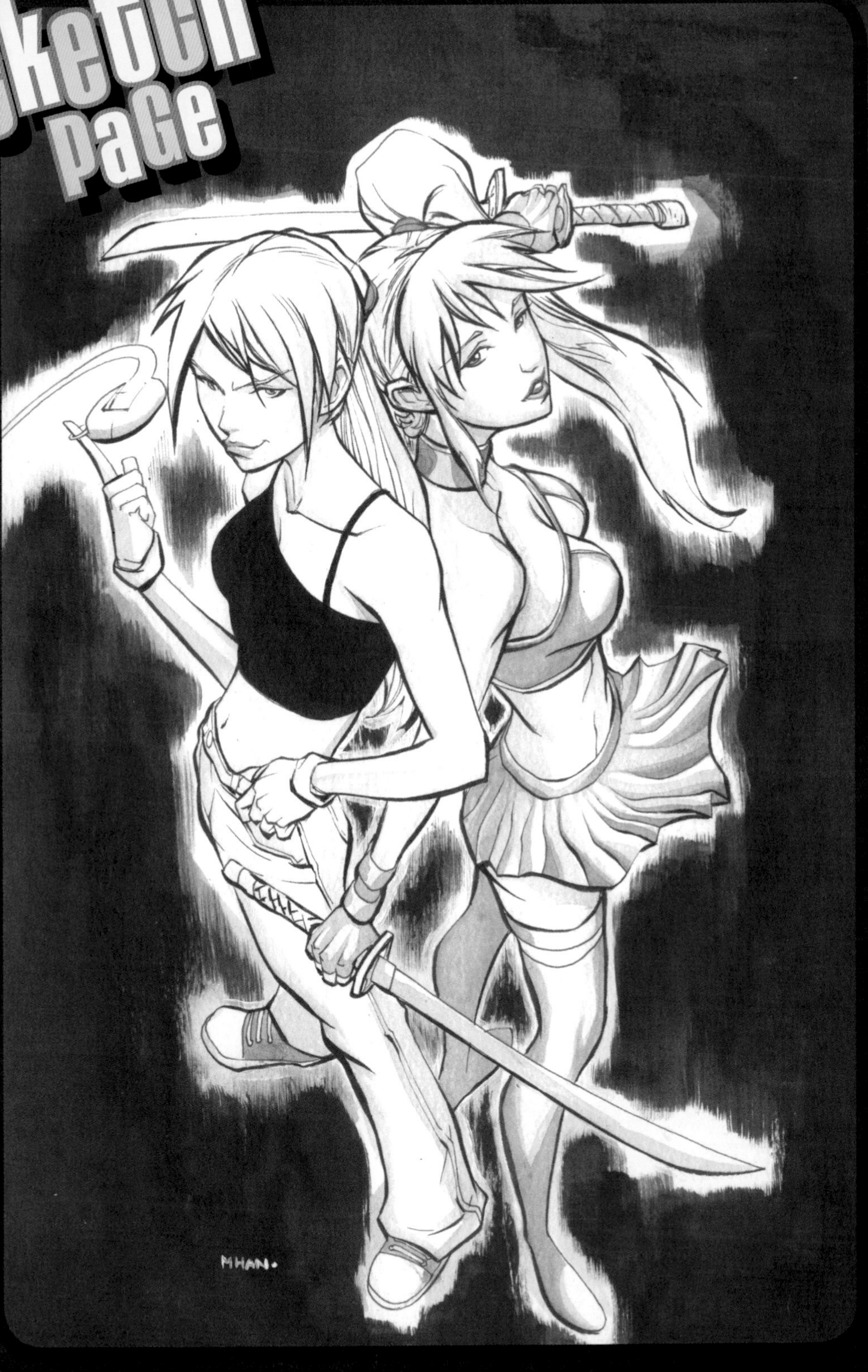
MHAN.

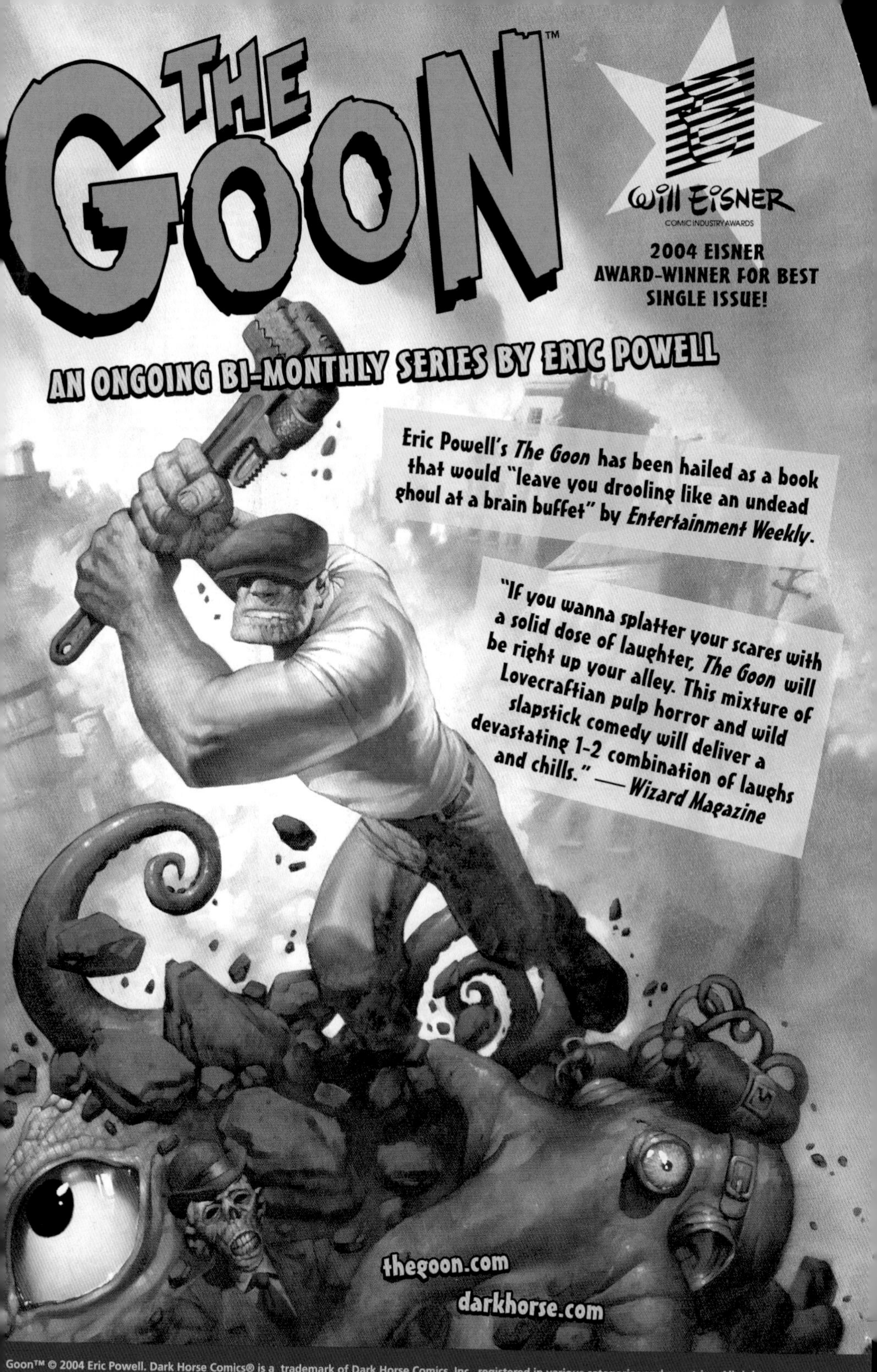
THE GOON™
WILL EISNER
COMIC INDUSTRY AWARDS
2004 EISNER AWARD-WINNER FOR BEST SINGLE ISSUE!
AN ONGOING BI-MONTHLY SERIES BY ERIC POWELL
Eric Powell's *The Goon* has been hailed as a book that would "leave you drooling like an undead ghoul at a brain buffet" by *Entertainment Weekly*.
"If you wanna splatter your scares with a solid dose of laughter, *The Goon* will be right up your alley. This mixture of Lovecraftian pulp horror and wild slapstick comedy will deliver a devastating 1-2 combination of laughs and chills." — *Wizard Magazine*
thegoon.com
darkhorse.com

CHECK OUT THESE SPYBOY COLLECTIONS, FULL OF ACTION ADVENTURE, AND INTRIGUE BY PETER DAVID AND POP MHAN!

SPY BOY
Peter David
Pop Mhan
Norman Lee
The Deadly Gourmet Affair

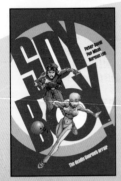

VOLUME 1
THE DEADLY GOURMET AFFAIR
ISBN: 1-56971-463-0 $8.95

SPY BOY
Peter David
Pop Mhan
Norman Lee
Trial and Terror

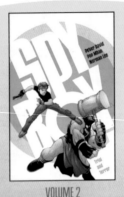

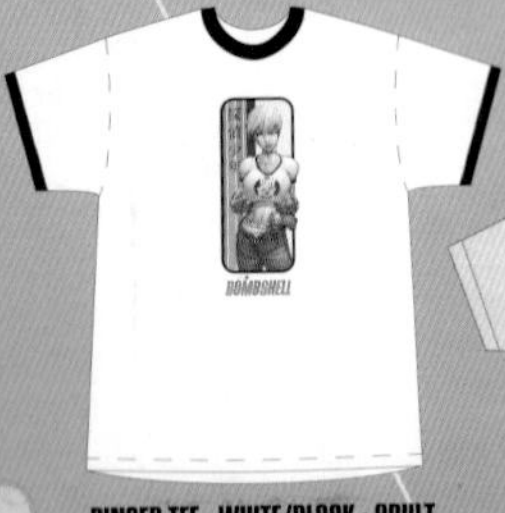

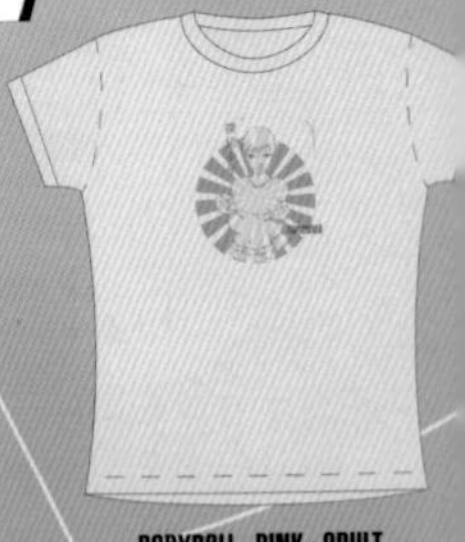

VOLUME 2
TRIAL AND TERROR
ISBN: 1-56971-501-7 $8.95

SPY BOY
Peter David
Pop Mhan
Norman Lee
Carlos Meglia
Bet Your Life

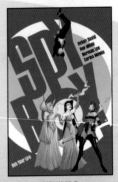

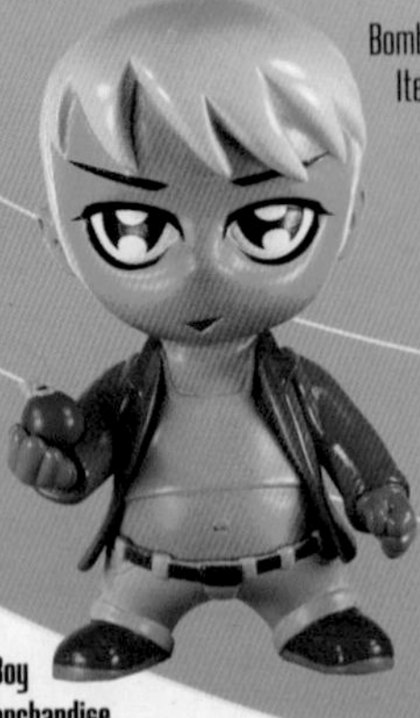

VOLUME 3
BET YOUR LIFE
ISBN: 1-56971-617-X $9.95

SPY BOY
Peter David
Pop Mhan
Norman Lee

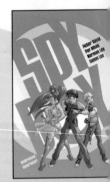

VOLUME 4
UNDERCOVER, UNDERWEA
ISBN: 1-56971-664-1 $9.95

SPY BOY

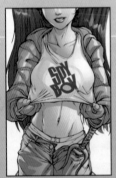

VOLUME 5
SPY-SCHOOL CONFIDENTIAL
ISBN: 1-56971-834-2 $12.95

ALSO AVAILABLE

VINYL STICKERS
$1.99 each

探偵少年
bombshell

Bombshell #1: Shy
Item #11-365

探偵少年
BOMBSHELL

Bombshell #2: Angry
Item #11-367

SPYBOY SPYLIGHT
Look's like a Zippo® acts like a flashlight!
ITEM #19-164 $24.95

BOMBSHELL

RINGER TEE · WHITE/BLACK · ADULT

BABYDOLL · PINK · ADULT

BOMBSHELL T-SHIRTS
Choose from a variety of sizes and styles! Priced from $17.99 – $19.99!

BOMBSHELL PVC FIGURE
Item #11-958
$19.99

SPYBOY SPECIAL (ONE-SHOT)
$4.99

For more information on the complete line of SpyBoy books and related merchandise, visit darkhorse.com or call 1-800-862-0052!

AVAILABLE AT YOUR LOCAL COMICS SHOP, GIFT SHOP, OR BOOKSTORE
To find a comics shop in your area, call 1-888-266-4226

For more information or to order direct: ·On the web: www.darkhorse.com
·E-mail: mailorder@darkhorse.com ·Phone: 1-800-862-0052 or (503) 652-9701
Mon.-Sat. 9 A.M. to 5 P.M. Pacific Time

DARK HORSE COMICS®

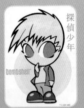

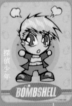

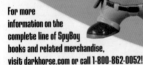

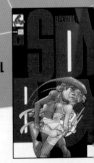